By Word of Mouth

BY WORD
OF MOUTH

'Élite' oral history

ANTHONY SELDON
AND
JOANNA PAPPWORTH

METHUEN
LONDON AND NEW YORK

To our families, old and new

First published in 1983 by
Methuen & Co. Ltd
11 New Fetter Lane, London EC4P 4EE
Published in the USA by
Methuen & Co.
in association with Methuen, Inc.
733 Third Avenue, New York, NY 10017

© 1983 Anthony Seldon and Joanna Pappworth

Printed in Great Britain at the
University Press, Cambridge

British Library Cataloguing in Publication Data
Seldon, Anthony
By word of mouth.
1. Interviewing
I. Title   II. Pappworth, Joanna
158'.3   BF637.15

ISBN 0-416-33020-7
ISBN 0-416-36740-2

Library of Congress Cataloging in Publication Data
Seldon, Anthony.
By word of mouth.
1. Oral history.
I. Pappworth, Joanna. II. Title.
D16.14.S44 1983   907'.2   83-13405

ISBN 0-416-33020-7
ISBN 0-416-36740-2 (pbk.)

Contents

When I turn to memory, I ask it to bring forth what I want: and some things are produced immediately, some take longer as if they had to be brought out from some more secret place of storage; some pour out in a heap, and while we are actually wanting and looking for something quite different, they hurl themselves upon us in masses as though to say 'may it not be we what you want?'

(St Augustine, *Confessions*, Book X, VIII, 12)

Imagination and memory are but one thing, which for divers considerations have divers names.

(Thomas Hobbes, *Leviathan*)

I was chiefly disgusted with modern history. For having strictly examined all the persons of greatest name in the courts of princes for a hundred years past, I found how the world had been misled by prostitute writers, to ascribe the greatest exploits in war to cowards, the wisest counsel to fools, sincerity to flatterers, Roman virtue to betrayers of their country, piety to atheists, chastity to sodomites, truth to informers . . .

(Jonathan Swift, *Gulliver's Travels*)

Preface

This book is concerned with the process and value of asking questions and gathering information from those who forged or witnessed events in history. It is aimed primarily at those new to oral history; and it deals with the theory and practice of interviewing the leaders (be it of a boys' club, a trade union or a nation) rather than the led.

The subject is considered from a number of angles: historical, analytical, descriptive and methodological. It is hoped to make those interested think more deeply about oral evidence. To make the book more practical we have grounded it in the experience of a wide range of practitioners of oral history.

Several sections in the first draft of the book had to be cut in order to keep the book to a manageable length. This material included: a lengthy analysis of the various meanings of oral history; a discussion of the various forms of written evidence available to the researcher writing on the twentieth century; oral history in seminars and groups; oral evidence in journalism, and in radio and television programmes; oral history and education; and oral history abroad. We apologize profoundly to those who provided information for those sections, and regret that we were unable to include them in the book.

In a field developing as rapidly as oral history, it is inevitable that certain people will feel that some work or aspects of oral history have been inadequately described in this book. We have tried at all times to consult those with relevant experience, but if any readers do feel that some subjects have not been dealt with fairly we would be very pleased to hear, so that passages might be amended in any future editions.

Acknowledgements

Two people's names appear on the title page; but the authors wish to express their deep gratitude to the very large number of people without whose help this book would certainly never have been written. Since we tried to draw on all those in this country who have had experience of oral history in the relevant areas, it is impossible to mention everyone by name. Some people do, however, stand out. The following authors replied to our questionnaire, and/or granted interviews: to all these we wish to express our sincerest thanks:

Alan Alexander, Professor T. C. Barker, John Barnes, Professor Quentin Bell, Roger Berthoud, Lord Blake, Brian Bond, Ian Bradley, Lord Briggs, Samuel Brittan, David Butler, Alan Butt-Philip, David Carlton, Sir Norman Chester, Professor Bernard Crick, Professor John Cross, Robin Daniels, Peter Davies, Bernard Donoughue, Charles Douglas-Home, David Edge, Paul Ferris, Martin Gilbert, Victoria Glendinning, David Goldsworthy, Professor Margaret Gowing, Professor J. A. G. Griffith, Nigel Hamilton, Leslie Hannah, Bruce Headey, Michael Holroyd, Anthony Howard, David Irving, Professor George W. Jones, James Kellas, Peter Kellner, Professor Anthony King, Stephen Koss, Professor Nicholas Kurti, Laurie Leavitt-Kahn, Ronald Lewin, Professor David Marquand, Keith Middlemas, H. Montgomery Hyde, Janet Morgan, Kenneth O. Morgan, Sheridan Morley, Margaret Morris, Nigel Nicolson, G. C. Peden, Ben Pimlott, Charles Raab, William J. Reader, Robert Rhodes James, Denis Richards, the late Captain Stephen Roskill, Keith Sainsbury, Professor Robert Skidelsky,

Roger Smith, L. J. Tivey, Count Nikolai Tolstoy, Professor Geoffrey Warner, Charles Webster, Philip M. Williams, Philip Ziegler.

The following people have also been extremely helpful, through conversations and correspondence, and often through reading over sections of the book where they had specialist knowledge, and we wish to express our gratitude:

Peter Abbs, Anthony Alcock, Adrian R. Allan, Lorna Arnold, BBC Copyright Department, Professor François Bédarida, Peter G. Bell, Len Bint, David Blake, Hilary Brash, John Cantwell, Michael Charlton, Général B. A. Christienne, Sir Fife Clark, Christopher Clarke, Derek A. Clarke, W. Coates, Chris Cook, Christopher Cook, Commander P. R. Compton-Hall, Philip Cottrell, Elizabeth Cowan, Nicholas Cox, Ian Curteis, Lord Dacre of Glanton, Joe Davies, William Deedes, Major A. J. Donald, Janet Dudley, John Dundas, Craig Eadie, J. R. Elliott, Sir Harold Evans, David Fletcher, Benis M. Frank, John Gainsborough, Nick Gendle, David Gerard, Peter Glasner, Sir George Godber, Lord Greenhill of Harrow, Kenneth Harris, Barrie Heads, John Hendry, Peter Hennessy, Pamela M. Henson, Robert Heussler, Carol Hinton, the late Lord Hinton of Bankside, Roger Holman, Cathy Holt, Sir Stanley Hooker, Diana Hull, Edmund Ions, Roy Jenkins, Brian Johnson, Geoffrey Jones, Gwyniver Jones, Mark Jones, Anthony King (of BIRS), Anthony Kirk-Greene, Robert Knox, Helen Langley, Brian Lapping, Colin Legum, Peter H. Liddle, William Linnard, Richard Lochead, Iverach McDonald, Squadron Leader J. P. McDonald, Campbell McMurray, John Macnicol, Elizabeth B. Mason, John T. Mason, Michael Mason, Patricia Methven, Anthony Moncrieff, Jonathan Morgan, Robin Moss, William Moss, John Palmer, Sir Peter Parker, Michael Orr Paterson, Roger Peacock, Stephen Peet, Norma Percy, William Plowden, Joan Pring, Graeme Powell, Air Commodore H. A. Probert, Alice Prochaska, Sallie Purkis, Adam Raphael, Angela Raspin, Malcolm Rutherford, Elly Shodell, Anne Sloman, Hon. Henry P. Smith III, Henry Stanhope, Lloyd Stickells, Graham Tayar, Michael Taylor, Ingrid Thomas, Alan Thompson, Boyd Tonkin, John Tosh, David Travis, Brian Walden, John Walford, John Walker, Ian Waller, Joan Warnow, Colin Watson, David Watt, Donald C. Watt, Spencer R. Weart, Vicki Wegg-Prosser, Phillip Whitehead, Eric Wigham, Geoffrey Wigoder, Aaron Wildavsky, Sir Gorden Wolstenholme, Leslie Woodhead, Robert M. Worcester, Hugo Young, Stephanie Zarach, Theodore Zeldin.

It has not been possible to list all the people, including the many archivists, who provided information by letter; so we should like to take this opportunity of thanking all those who responded to our queries or offered their advice.

We feel ourselves to be particularly fortunate in having had the expertise of Margaret Brooks, of the Imperial War Museum, who agreed to write the chapter on the methodology of oral archives. We are also extremely grateful for the appendices supplied by Joe Pengelly and William Isbister, and regret that the necessity of keeping within word limits prevented us from including them.

Boyd Tonkin checked all the references in the book and we have particularly appreciated his help and many suggestions for improvements and additions. We have benefited in particular from the expertise of John Barnes, Brian Harrison, David Lance and Paul Thompson. The encouragement and sound judgement of these academics and leading practitioners of oral history have enabled us, we trust, to keep the book within the bounds of accuracy and good sense.

Finally, we should like to thank Jean Durham and Pauline Oakley for their exceptional and uncomplaining efficiency and good humour in typing the manuscript; Linden Stafford for her thoughtful copyediting; Craig Eadie for suggesting improvements; Anna Fedden and Jane Thompson at Methuen, for their patience and helpfulness; the Nuffield Foundation, for providing a grant for research for the book; and to John Barnes for generating our interest in oral history. Without him this book would never have been written.

*The Scottish Oral History Group issues a twice-yearly newsletter entitled *By Word of Mouth* which contains information, reports and short articles on oral history. The present book has no connexion with this newsletter, and any confusion caused by the similarity of title is regretted.

PART I

The role of oral history

1

Oral history and this book

But has he? *Does* George have a remarkable memory? If so, remarkable
for what? And what is the 'true story' he will tell you? Might it be just
true to George? Or to the person recommending you see him? Why is
the person recommending you talk to George at all? Is George in fact
worth seeing? How would you approach George if you did decide to see
him, and what should you ask him? Should you tape record what he says,
or will that put him off? How could you tell if what George will be
telling you is the truth? How should you use the material, and what will
you do with your interview notes after you have finished with them?
Why bother to see George at all if there are all these questions? Can't
you find out anyway all that George might tell you written down somewhere, and save yourself a lot of trouble?

This book discusses these problems in its attempt to answer the central
question: what have those who have forged or witnessed events to contribute to our understanding after those events are over? Most people,
from junior researchers to senior academics, archivists and civil servants,
presume that such individuals do have something of importance to contribute, but no one seems to be exactly sure how far their observations
are of value to history, and in what way. This question, indeed, we
believe to be one of the greatest complexity: in this book we shall
attempt to provide some answer, focusing on the areas where witnesses
might be expected to make a contribution, how they might, and where

they have – in that order. The book is intended primarily for those new to oral history, but it is also hoped that the more experienced will find some benefit from reading it.

Oral history has been variously defined, and the name has been used to describe a number of different activities. For the purposes of this book it will be defined loosely: information transmitted orally, in a personal exchange, of a kind likely to be of historical or long-term value.[1] The information can then be committed to memory, written down, or put on tape or video. Oral history is thus not a new *kind* of history (although it can be readily employed in sound or vision programmes to convey history in non-literary forms), but rather a type of *source* or *evidence*.

A very broad distinction can be made between two categories of evidence: *documentary evidence*, material produced at the time as part of a policy process, and which itself is instrumental in that process;[2] and *reported evidence*, material abstracted from that continuing policy process, and either remaining inert (as in a private diary kept confidential for a very long period) or communicated to third parties who have no inter-relationship with that process or world. Documentary evidence, being part of a continuing policy process, will itself have an effect on that process (as well as possibly on subsequent writing about those processes and events, i.e. on history); reported evidence, being abstracted from that contemporary process, however, can have an effect, if at all, only on the writing of history. The distinction corresponds to two main meanings that can be given to the word 'history': that which *actually* happens (documentary evidence) and that which is *written about* what happens (reported evidence).

Reported evidence can either be *contemporary*, recorded by the informant at the time, as in a purely private letter or diary entry, or *retrospective*, such as might be recounted in an autobiography written many years after the events it describes. When reported evidence is communicated orally, it can be called oral history (as here defined), and such communication too can be either contemporary, as in the case of a senior politician passing on information to an author writing about a recent political development, or retrospective, when (for example) a Cabinet Minister might be describing a Cabinet meeting years later to a researcher.

Documentary evidence, *where it is available*, we would argue is almost always of more value to the historian than reported evidence. It is the cream of the scholar's sources, consisting in the main of minutes or reports of meetings, background papers and reports, and communications (telegrams, letters, directives, memoranda, etc.), or reports of communications between people. As well as being part of the historical process itself because it is acted upon at the time, it often provides the fullest and most accurate record of events and contemporary thinking and, from the historian's point of view, can provide the most vivid, colourful and profound insight into the subject of research.

This distinction between documentary and reported evidence is not clear-cut, however. Documentary evidence contains much material that *reports* events (e.g. Cabinet minutes), but the fact that the reporting is undertaken for internal record, and often internal action as well, rather than for immediate release to third parties, qualifies it for being considered *documentary* evidence. Some letters written to third parties may be written with the ulterior intention of in some way affecting the policy process; for example, a Cabinet minister writing to a retired statesman (i.e. a third party) might be intending to stir up unrest against the Prime Minister. Communiqués at the end of meetings, or press conferences, on the progress of top-level talks would clearly classify as reported evidence (given to third parties, abstracted from ongoing policy developments, reporting proceedings within the policy process), but the fact that such statements can be consciously intended to redound on the development of policy means that such evidence has some claim to be also considered as documentary evidence. Moreover, the terms must always be related to the subject of the researcher's concern: if one is, for example, writing about government policy in the Suez crisis of 1956, a minister's letters to a third party describing Cabinet meetings would be categorized as reported evidence, but to the biographer of that minister such letters would be considered documentary evidence.

It is not difficult to think of types of evidence that defy the distinction (for example, a media interview with, or a leak from, a politician whose purpose is less to get the record straight than to influence events in the future). Both documentary and reported evidence are prone to distortion through being committed to paper 'for the record'. Memory and conscious editing also play an important role in both. It might be more helpful, therefore, to envisage a sliding scale between the purest form of documentary evidence, such as internal directives and telegrams, to the purest form of reported evidence, that which has no possible effect on contemporary events. The distinction, however imperfect, is nevertheless worth making, because it helps us to understand the identity and status of oral history evidence. Reported evidence is not the *stuff* of history; it is the *commenting upon* those events, whether in writing or by word of mouth. Since written evidence can be (like oral evidence) merely reported evidence, to criticize oral history, but to use reported written evidence in the form of letters and memoirs, is, to say the least, idiosyncratic. Oral evidence, whether reporting facts or concerned purely with interpretation and assessment, is, we would argue, of the same status as an abstracted letter or a diary written on the same day as the events being discussed: it is all history in the sense that it describes, reports or assesses what happens, and it has already progressed along the road of selection and evaluation.

It is a specific kind of oral history that is dealt with in this book. Much that has been written in Britain about oral history concerns the oral history of ordinary people: witnesses to, or receivers of, policy made by others. This book, on the other hand, is concerned with oral history *of* and *about* the 'élites' in society, with those who rose to the top of their chosen occupation, and with whose activities much of modern scholarship, rightly or wrongly, is concerned – Cabinet ministers, trade-union leaders, generals, chief executives, leaders of local government, novelists, and so on, rather than the rank-and-file workers or soldiers. For the purposes of this book, an élite figure is taken to be someone of interest because of the position he or she holds, rather than because he or she is representative or typical of a group. This emphasis on élites does not imply a value judgement on the merits of the oral history of one group as against the others (and still less on the merits of élites as against rank-and-filers). Our intention here is to survey an area of oral history hitherto neglected in Britain,[3] and the one which C. L. Mowat had in mind when he wrote in *Great Britain Since 1914* that it was

> not easy so far to know how [oral history] evidence should be used and assessed. The few historians who have employed it have . . . absorbed it into their general account, and the occasional footnote explaining that the information was obtained in this way does not make considered assessment of the technique possible. We need a proper analytical study of the subject.[4]

It is our hope that this book will go some way to meeting that need.

The history of oral history

Oral history has burgeoned since the Second World War, but it is important for a proper understanding not to see it just as a new device or tool. Oral evidence not only post-dates documentation but also pre-dates it. Before writing became commonplace, and in pre-literate societies today, oral evidence has a unique importance. Even where authors had documentary evidence, they still liked to gather eyewitness accounts – as did Herodotus, and Thucydides in his *History of the Peloponnesian War*. In British history the tradition of talking to eyewitnesses was to continue from, for example, Bede in his eighth-century *History of the English Church and People* and Clarendon in his *History of the Rebellion and Civil Wars in England* (1704) up to the present century.[5] John Morley used oral evidence when writing his *Life of Gladstone* (1903),[6] as did Lewis Namier over forty years later in his *Diplomatic Prelude 1938–39* (1948). Namier wrote: 'the student of contemporary history has the advantage of being able to talk to men who took part in the transactions.'[7] These works cover a broad range: political, ecclesiastical, military and diplomatic history. In the field of labour and social history, pioneering interview work was carried out by Sidney and Beatrice Webb (the latter writing a celebrated appendix on interviewing in her autobiography, *My Apprenticeship* (1926)).

Although the recourse to oral evidence has thus been a constant feature since history began to be written, the tempo has increased dramatically since the war. Certain particular areas of that growth can be identified, the first of these being the use that individual authors have made of oral evidence in books, articles and theses. Before the Second World War, systematic interviewing by individual authors of élite witnesses on a large scale was relatively infrequent, and formal note taking appears to have been the exception rather than the rule. Recollections tended to be gathered at informal meetings or were jotted down on paper at the request of the author. Access to ministers was confined in large part to the most senior or established authors. Thus Montgomery Hyde wrote of his pre-war experiences as a young author: 'I approached people like the late Lord Londonderry and the late Lord Lothian, but it was for permission to see and use their papers.' Having approached these figures, he would talk to them about his subject of writing, but the talks were of a restricted nature and did not involve prolonged questioning.[8] Intrepid indeed would have been the young author who approached Stanley Baldwin, Winston Churchill or Clement Attlee with a request for an interview about some aspect of their political career, and it is unlikely that much of value would have been imparted, if an interview had been agreed to at all. Since the war politicians and civil servants have become more open to critical cross-questioning than they had been hitherto. Initially journalists led the trend, followed a short time later by

academics. Today retired as well as active politicians are frequently
approached for interviews, as are senior civil servants, and most are
happy to oblige. By the 1960s the fact of even junior historians and postgraduate students conducting interviews had become widely accepted.
Historian John Barnes said at an international conference on contemporary history in mid-decade that he believed it 'essential' that
we should be 'interviewing in depth not only the leading personalities of
the day but also many of those in their circle or involved in the political
and policy-making processes'.[9] Oral history evidence is now extensively
used by authors of biographies and monographs on periods and subjects
for which witnesses can still be found.

The fresh impetus to the systematic and formalized use of oral
evidence in the early post-war years can be seen also in politics. The
Nuffield Election Studies illustrate the change. The books on the 1945
and 1950 general elections, by R. B. McCallum and A. Readman, and
H. G. Nicholas respectively, made little or no use of oral history
evidence. David Butler, when researching his book on the 1951 general
election, conducted a few interviews, mainly of party workers, but not
of the most senior party figures. In his *Electoral System in Britain 1918–51*
(published in 1953) Butler wrote: 'this book owes far more to the personal recollections of the surviving protagonists than to any published
lives or histories.'[10] Butler talked to a few of the top politicians for his
volumes on the 1955 and 1959 general elections, but it was not until
1963 that, along with Anthony King, co-author of the 1964 election
study, he began interviewing senior figures on a big scale.[11]

The change is equally dramatic in biographies of figures from the arts.
Authors of biographies are far less often friends or admirers writing
hagiography than was the case fifty and more years ago. Lytton Strachey,
in particular, precipitated the writing of a new style of critical biography.
Subsequently, biographers have tended far more to be relatively detached
observers rather than associates from within the subject's circle, and so
have been particularly anxious to interview people from inside that
circle, to compensate for their lack of personal acquaintance.

Another area of growth is in oral archives, for which in Britain the
sound record is often regarded very much as the main end-product of an
interview, transcripts being considered to be secondary.[12] British oral
archives have been slow to develop, and in 1976 it was suggested that,
from the point of view of oral history, most researchers were 'essentially
collecting information for their own use, rather than performing the role
of a collecting centre for material which will be made generally available

to scholars'.[13] Nevertheless some notable oral archives have been established, although all have been on an *ad hoc* basis, springing up as the result of individual initiatives. There has been little evidence of a conscious policy – of attempts to identify areas where documentation is weak or where there might be an especial advantage in having material recorded in sound in addition to that recorded on paper, and to meet this need by conducting systematic interviews. Accordingly, in some areas of history, documentary and oral evidence are in abundance, and in others the contribution of both is scant. Of the oral archives that have been established, some stand out by virtue of their superior methodology, their foresight in rescuing recorded material that otherwise might have been destroyed, or their conscious attempts to fill gaps in the written documentation. Such archives might be the Department of Sound Records at the Imperial War Museum, set up at the beginning of 1972 under the direction of David Lance;[14] the collection of interviews on the British in India financed by the Social Science Research Council and based at the Department of Indian History at the School of Oriental and African Studies; and the Oral History Society's archive at Essex University, consisting of some 700 interviews. Some oral archives belong to the expanding UK branch of the International Association of Sound Archives. The UK branch, which was founded in 1976, holds annual meetings, produces a twice-yearly newsletter, and promotes the cause of good-quality recordings and professional standards.

A further development in oral history has been brought about by the media. Since the 1930s the BBC has been producing a wealth of sound and film recordings of historical interest, and this material includes a large amount of oral history as here defined (i.e. interviews and recollections).[15] As the BBC is neither constituted nor financed to provide a public access service, until recently it has not tended to encourage outsiders to use its collections, but there is now a more flexible attitude towards access. Independent broadcasting companies have meanwhile shown varying degrees of willingness to provide access to researchers. The BBC itself has for several years allowed selected public archives to hold copies of its material, the British Institute of Recorded Sound (founded in the early 1950s initially as a repository for gramophone records, now the National Sound Archive) being a principal repository.

Since the war oral history has increased in several other areas, which will be only briefly mentioned here because they do not concern the evidence of élites. The growth of non-élite oral history has been more remarkable. Social historians and sociologists have turned to oral history to record information from those groups who hitherto had left little documentation, and whose ideas, experience and culture had been neglected by academic study.[16] George Ewart Evans has done much to illustrate the potential for oral history in social history, as in his pioneering book *Ask The Fellows Who Cut The Hay* (1956), about rural life in East Anglia. The various organizations and individuals primarily interested in social and labour history were brought together in 1973 with the formation of the Oral History Society, which holds regular conferences and issues a twice-yearly journal, *Oral History*.[17] The professed aim of the society is to focus on 'those sections of society who are unlikely to leave behind them any quantity of memoirs, diaries or correspondence from which history can subsequently be written'.[18] The society has done much to stimulate oral history in such areas as women's history, the experience of racial minorities, and education. Under its aegis an authoritative booklet *Oral History in Schools* has been issued, as has an oral history directory, which describes a large number of projects mainly in social and labour history.[19]

Another area of non-élite oral history that has grown rapidly in Britain is centred on the study of dialect, accent and folklore. The Irish Folklore Commission (now the Department of Irish Folklore at University College, Dublin) began collecting oral material on all aspects of the Irish folk tradition on dictating machines as long ago as the 1930s. The School of Scottish Studies at Edinburgh University, the Institute of Dialect and Folk Life Studies at the University of Leeds, and the Welsh Folk Museum all established projects in the 1950s. In addition, since 1945 the use of oral history has grown dramatically among anthropologists and historians of pre-literate societies, in particular of Africa. Because of the need to meet the challenge of writing history with the advent of decolonization, Africanists were the first professional historians consciously to espouse oral history as a technique, with J. D. Fage in the vanguard in Britain.[20] We shall not, however, be discussing 'oral tradition', as it is called, since it does not relate to the main subject of this book.[21]

Are there any factors that can account for the surge in the systematic use of carefully recorded interviews since the early post-war years? Paul Thompson feels an important underlying factor is what he regards as the increasing poverty of documentary evidence in supplying objective and key information.[22] Growing awareness of the incompleteness undoubtedly provides a motive for the change, as does the shift in the subjects of academic concern. As Brian Harrison has argued, the reason why documentary evidence was prized so highly in the nineteenth century was partly related to the type of history predominantly being produced, for which the written document was of central importance: ancient and medieval political and religious history.[23] But in this century, and in particular since the war, the emphasis of academic inquiry has shifted into new areas where oral history evidence has a major part to play: political and social science, contemporary history and politics, and economic and social history.

The new directness and boldness of the questioning, and the range of people available for interview, owed much to a new frank cross-questioning of leading figures by journalists and broadcasters, detectable from at least the late 1940s.[24] A direct link can perhaps be traced in the work of Robert McKenzie, who had gained experience and a taste for interviewing on the radio in Canada, and who employed it to good effect in his *British Political Parties* (1955). Market-research and opinion-poll organizations may also have been responsible for showing to academics the potential for widespread systematic interviewing.

Formalized recording of interviews was an inevitable result of the move away from *ad hoc* conversations to formal question-and-answer sessions. The availability of reasonably inexpensive magnetic-tape reel-to-reel tape recorders from the 1950s, and cassette recorders a decade later, made it possible for oral archives and linguistic recording centres to develop, although it did less to affect the growth of interviewing by individual authors, many of whom still prefer to take notes rather than to tape.

Branches of oral history

This book distinguishes three main oral history activities and seeks to provide guidance on conduct and using oral evidence for each. The methods of assessing oral evidence in each case will be similar, but the objectives and methods of gathering it differ fundamentally.

The individual researcher

Researchers who interview, from post-graduate students to experienced authors, are engaged in the same exercise – personally conducting interviews, in confidence, for the purpose of providing information for a specific book, article or thesis that they are researching and writing themselves. We shall discuss such questions as at what stage in one's research one should conduct interviews, how many informants one should see, what questions to ask, whether to conduct second interviews, and so on, in Chapter 4.

The oral project

This branch of oral history falls roughly halfway between the work of the individual researcher and that of the oral archive, and has been a comparatively neglected aspect. The essence of an oral project is that interviews are instigated by an institution for its own private purposes, the fruits of which interviews may or may not see the light of day in the form of a book or other compilation. The institution may be a sports club, a school, a university faculty or department, a society, a government department or a multinational corporation. An oral project is distinguished from an individual researcher's task because it is instigated by a closed organization for that organization's own (in the first instance, at least) internal consumption, and the material it gathers will often not be of much interest to a wider audience.

Oral archives

Unlike oral projects, oral archives conduct and/or collect interviews not for their own use but for the immediate or eventual benefit of independent researchers. The task of the oral archive differs from the other two branches of oral history in several ways. The interviewer will be asking questions not for his own (or his organization's) benefit, but for third parties, and accordingly will have to *anticipate* the types of question areas in which future listeners to and readers of the interview might be interested. Second, because of the use that might be made of this material in broadcasting, educational cassettes, lectures, and so on, oral archives usually not only tape record all their interviews but ensure that the recordings themselves are of a very high standard. Third, because the interviews are not recorded for the instigators' own benefit, peculiar importance must be attached to ensuring that access and copyright conditions are satisfactorily drawn up.

'Cousins' of oral history

There are a number of activities which have many similarities with oral history, and which can often be used in conjunction with it.

Visiting physical locations

One research activity – allied but separate to collecting oral-history evidence – is to visit the places important to the lives of the person or people about whom one is writing. An author can benefit, in a way similar to meeting people in interview, from visiting a subject's birth-place or favourite haunts, or scenes of particular historical events. A classic early example is that of G. M. Trevelyan, who, for his biography of Garibaldi (in Robert Gittings's words),

> with long, gaunt, raking steps and unquenchable energy, actually walked, often in the heat of the south Italian sun, over every yard of Italian soil that Garibaldi and his armies had covered. . . . The result is a *tour de force* of identification, shared by the reader, which could not have been achieved in any other way.[25]

Roy Jenkins even found that 'Visiting the houses where your subject has lived, and the scenes which played a part in his life, is usually more vividly creative than visiting his friends.'[26]

Biographers are not alone in being able to benefit from this aid in research; so too can writers of monographs. In the United States it has been called visiting 'physical survivals'. The US atomic historians, Hewlett and Anderson, found it a useful technique when researching their book on the development of atomic energy from 1939 to 1946. They describe how they visited 'not only the geographical setting of the wartime project but also the buildings and equipment that have survived'. They even 'rode on the huge bridge crane above the concrete canyons where the plutonium for Trinity and Nagasaki was separated. Finally, we went to Los Alamos. [This helped] the visitor understand the lives of the men who built the bomb.'[27]

Visiting locations in active use too can help one to understand the past; a researcher writing about the Labour governments of 1945–51 might thus benefit from visiting contemporary Labour Party annual con-ferences, or from listening to debates in Parliament. But the approach is more often found to be valuable by social and political scientists, writing about the present rather than the past.

Published memoirs

Many think, like Martin Gilbert, that 'memoirs are a form of oral history'.[28] Memoirs, like oral-history interviews, are dependent upon recollections but are not considered for the purposes of this book as oral evidence because they lack the key ingredient of the interview. Memoirs may indeed be considered the poorest form of written evidence: written often by those very people about whom most has already appeared in print, they contain information often of an uncritical and inaccurate nature – two hazards that could usually be minimized in an oral-history interview. Some memoirs (which one must remember are often written to entertain or inform the general reader rather than the scholar) are, of course, far more informative than others, but taken as a whole they display many of the weaknesses and few of the benefits of oral history evidence.

Acquiring written recollections

Before the formal interview emerged as a common research technique after the war, the practice of asking witnesses to jot down their recollections on paper was more widely adopted. Nowadays such a research method is the exception rather than the rule. Some authors, however, like the naval historian Stephen Roskill, find written recollections more valuable than interviewing: 'I prefer an exchange of letters to interviewing, because I may forget some point if not put on paper, or the interviewee may try to prejudice me by the weight of his knowledge or experience in a tête-à-tête.'[29] Reading written recollections certainly saves the researcher a great deal of time, and can also indicate which of a large list of possible targets might be the most fruitful to interview. (Written recollections too are sometimes sent by witnesses after interviews, to elucidate a point mentioned in interview, or to provide fresh evidence.)

But most authors find that an interview, where feasible, yields far greater dividends. As Brian Harrison has written: 'an interview can often convey types of information which of their very nature can never be communicated in writing. The informant's gesture, intonation and manner will often be as important as the words he utters.'[30] One of the greatest benefits of interviewing people face to face is the ability to cross-question them. Written recollections are certainly worth having, but they can be guarded, bland, and difficult to evaluate.

Interviewing by telephone

Very close to the person-to-person oral history interview is the telephone interview. Like the requesting of written recollections, it can save time, but has the advantage that one can cross-question the informant. There are inevitably several drawbacks. Very few people will talk as frankly on the telephone as in a personal meeting, especially if they do not know their interlocutor. They cannot so easily assess the researcher's reliability or credentials, and the researcher similarly finds it harder to assess such oral evidence. Those who wish to use a tape recorder will find their task made considerably more difficult because of poor sound quality over the telephone. Sometimes there is no alternative, as Ian Bradley found when researching *Breaking the Mould*, his 1981 book on the Social Democrats. Since Roy Jenkins was forced by the pressures of the Warrington by-election to cancel a personal interview, a telephone call had to suffice; it was not as satisfactory as a personal meeting but better than nothing.[31]

In some situations, however, a telephone interview does have advantages. It can be useful as a preliminary warm-up for a personal interview. When Hugo Young and Anne Sloman were compiling their Radio 4 series *No Minister*, they found that a telephone conversation with the interviewees before recording served as a valuable two-way briefing which improved the depth and range of the subsequent interview.[32] A telephone conversation can take the place of an interview when one wishes to gain information from a wide range of witnesses on a small front. Or it can be used most effectively as a follow-up to an interview, to gather more evidence where a second personal meeting might not be thought worthwhile. The personal contact having already been made, the witness is far more likely to be frank and helpful on the telephone than if he had not met the researcher.

A final point: telephone 'interviews' should be noted at the time carefully, and footnoted with the same meticulousness as personal interviews.

2

Criticisms of oral
history

In Britain, despite some scepticism about the value of oral history interviewing, few criticisms or evaluative appraisals have so far appeared in
print. In North America, however, while there is perhaps a broader
general acceptance among academics that a serious contribution can be
made by oral history evidence, a number of articulate criticisms and
reservations have also been published. A respected archivist has said:
'When I was called on in the past to look at proposals for projects in oral
history, one of the things that bothered many was the problem of the
objective validity of the oral history memoir.'[1] From Canada, historian
Peter Oliver has written:

> It seems to me that those who prepare and use the oral record have not
> yet given sufficient weight to the tricks that memory can play, to
> efforts at rationalization and self-justification that all of us make, even
> if only subconsciously, or to the terrible telescoping of time which an
> interview often encourages and which runs counter to the very
> essence of history.[2]

To understand oral history and evaluate it correctly, one needs to develop
some appreciation of how other people's minds work, how one's own
mind works, and how one might be influencing the person one is interviewing. Taking stock of these three areas, we have grouped criticisms
of oral history evidence together under three headings: the shortcomings
of the interviewee, those of the interviewer, and those inherent in the
nature of interviewing itself. Some of these objections overlap; others

could just as comfortably be placed in different categories. Nevertheless such groupings highlight particular problem areas of oral history. The following two chapters draw heavily on evidence given in response to an oral history questionnaire that we sent out to authors of historical, cultural and political science works.[3]

Limitations of the interviewee

It should be borne in mind that many of the following criticisms of oral evidence apply equally to some forms of written evidence, notably diaries and letters.

Unreliability of memory

The unreliability of the interviewee's memory for hard fact and chronological sequence is undoubtedly the major criticism of oral evidence in this group. Bernard Crick, author of *George Orwell: A Life*, was by no means alone among respondents to our oral history questionnaire in being greatly impressed with the unreliability of human memory.[4] Almost all with relevant experience would thus agree with Roy Jenkins that:

> If detailed work on the events of a period a number of decades ago is followed by the opportunity to talk to someone who was there at the time, the only too common result is that his recollections, not only of the dates, but of the sequence of events does not fit the framework of the firmly established written facts.[5]

Keith Middlemas found with his own interviewing that it was 'No good expecting detailed chronology; total recall was often deceptive.'[6] Memory of specific facts is similarly unreliable. David Marquand, who found when researching his biography of Ramsay MacDonald that 'memories are amazingly short and amazingly fallible', advanced one possible reason: 'Of course, this conclusion may reflect the fact that most of the people whom I interviewed were elderly and many were very old indeed; had I interviewed younger people my impression might have been very different.'[7] As Robert Rhodes James has suggested, however, the converse may apply: oral recollections of busy, younger individuals can often be

> clouded by personal impressions and, oddly enough, by the very *recentness* of the episode. It seems to be the case that it is only after a period of time that the mind can put matters in perspective and

differentiate between similar occasions which, in the immediate after-
math, tend to merge into one.[8]

The potential for being misled, noted by Hugh Gaitskell's biographer,
Philip Williams, by 'honest opinions mistakenly held', is all the greater
because there is no conscious effort to mislead. Williams, for example,
found that Roy Jenkins and Peter Shore, because of faulty memories,
initially misinformed him about the duration of Gaitskell's opposition to
British entry into the Common Market.[9] The near-unanimity among
professional authors and historians as to the unreliability of memory to
produce information on sequence and hard fact (dates, names, places,
etc.) would indeed suggest that oral evidence should not be relied upon at
all for the former, and for the latter only where there are gaps in available
written documentation, and where the information can be rigorously
cross-checked with other sources for accuracy. As Lord Blake has judici-
ously written:

> People's memories about facts (as opposed to personal impressions)
> can be fallible. One is probably ill advised to rest any episode of
> importance upon the unsubstantiated testimony of a single individual
> unless he took a written note at the time.[10]

Work by psychologists further does not provide the collector of oral
history with any reason for being complacent about the worth of his
testimony. Recent memory research, as described for example by Alan
Baddeley in *Your Memory: A User's Guide* (1982) suggests that the
evidence of eye-witnesses is even more unreliable than hitherto regarded:
in particular, a suggestion carefully inserted in questioning a witness can
later be reported by the witness as an observed fact. However, memory
research has not as yet come up with any hypotheses which can be
utilised by collectors of oral history as generally-applicable guides in
assessing their evidence. It should also be noted however that research
work on memory as a whole is still in its infancy: in the words of Stuart
Sutherland, it 'consists of many disparate facts in search of a theory'. He
continues: '. . . the relation between short-term and long-term memory
remains obscure. Nor do we know with any certainty what causes
forgetting . . . Above all, we do not understand how memories are
indexed'.[11]

Some researchers do however find oral evidence trustworthy in two
specific instances; for the unique event, which makes a powerful impression upon the interviewee, and the regularly repeated, perhaps even
hum-drum events or routines.

Deliberate falsification

Written evidence, it is widely acknowledged can be designed to serve some 'official' end. If oral evidence is consciously falsified, however, it will far more likely be to serve some *private* end. But the charge of wilful untruthfulness or distortion tends to be made more often by those with little experience of interviewing, who often believe in a homogeneous 'establishment' whose representatives, even after retirement, act in unison or individually to distort or to obfuscate the truth. Nevertheless, the conscious doctoring of oral evidence does pose a real problem, and politicians, current and retired, are frequently singled out as a group peculiarly liable to tell lies or half-truths, or indeed to be prone to self-deception. The less the interviewer knows about the world of the interviewee, the more prone he is to being misled.

The danger of conscious distortion can, however, be exaggerated. Philip Williams has written: 'Deliberate deception was much less of a problem than most people would probably imagine. . . . Unless it was practised much more successfully than I realized, it was neither very common nor very hard to detect.'[12]

Unfairness through vindictiveness

A well-known British diplomatic historian has written: 'The fact is that oral testimony . . . is frequently used as a means of paying off old scores, particularly at the expense of those who cannot answer back.'[13] At first glance, perhaps, oral history might appear to provide a unique forum for witnesses to attack former or current rivals. While historians should be aware that their subjects might be using the exchange for such purposes, hardly any of the sixty respondents in our survey mentioned vindictiveness as a problem when gathering oral evidence. Individual authors can usually discover when people hold strong feelings about others, and so can alert themselves to this tendency. Oral archives, on the other hand, can reduce the risk of vindictive evidence being gathered by imposing time limits on access to interviews with subjects they feel might succumb to the temptation to be less than fair when discussing their contemporaries. If interviewees know that no one can see, or quote from, their record for a period of years, the point of their providing evidence to pay off old scores will be reduced. Most witnesses are, however, found to be honest and fair-minded, and those who are not can usually be brought into line by historians being alert, well informed about their witnesses' predilections, to be and in command of the material discussed.

Excessive discretion

Interviewees are often wary about imparting frank information which they consider confidential, especially if they do not know the researcher or his work. Nigel Nicolson, author of *Alex*, the biography of Lord Alexander of Tunis, noted: 'Soldiers are, on the whole, more reticent than civilians. . . . Some were unwilling to make any criticism of Alex, and others thought any personal revelations about him improper.'[14] However, if the researcher has emphasized the serious nature of his research and has built up a relationship of confidence, the interviewee is less likely to be unduly discreet. He will even find on occasion that the subject will be so relieved that he is able to recall matter of interest to the historian that he will even be anxious to speak frankly and openly to expunge his feelings of guilt at agreeing to be interviewed.

A guarded response may sometimes result from unconfident questioning: the more bold and direct the questions, the more the interviewee will be reassured that the researcher is knowledgable and that he is entitled to be talking on this topic – in particular because at the back of the mind of many who agree to be interviewed will be the nagging doubt about whether it is really 'all right' to be talking to this individual. Frank and accurate information can also be obtained even for very recent events, if interviews are set up correctly and credentials established. Richard Clutterbuck, for example, found when researching his contemporary history *Britain in Agony*: 'Almost without exception [interviewees] were frank and forthcoming and prepared to argue and discuss their views.'[15] Interviews can also penetrate behind people's reserve. When they write their memoirs they are never off their guard.

Superficiality and gossip

Interviewees can give easy, superficial answers for a number of reasons. They might be too busy, or too lazy, to go into the matter in depth; they genuinely might have forgotten all but the haziest of outlines, or they might be reluctant to bring to the surface half-forgotten memories which could be painful. Alan Butt-Philip has found that 'Many interviewees have a "line" about their place in history, their role in society which comes out too "pat". It is sometimes difficult to get behind the "line" to the realities.'[16]

The way to counter the undoubted tendency for oral evidence to be superficial and lacking in subtlety is again for researchers to impress the interviewee with the seriousness of their work, to be persistent in their questioning, and to ensure wherever possible that they can 'capture' the person for a sufficiently long time and in a suitable enough environment to delve beneath surface responses. Only when the interviewer is satisfied (time permitting) that he has exhausted the interviewee's memory on a particular topic should he pass on to the next question.

The argument that oral history is mere gossip is on two planes. One school of thought relates gossip purely to discussion of individuals, and was expressed by one respondent to the questionnaire, who wrote: 'I do not ask "personal" questions, and treated such information when volunteered as gossip.'[17] The retort here is that all depends on the motive of the historian: if he is seeking to muck-rake, or to gather gratuitous personal information, then it is right that he should be obstructed by the interviewee. But any biographer, and indeed many authors of non-biographical histories, will need to gather personal information to form a comprehensive view, and it is this kind of material which interviews are often peculiarly good at supplying. There can be an exaggerated sensitivity on the part of subjects who withhold all information on personalities from a serious researcher on the grounds that they do not discuss 'gossip'.

A more serious objection on this point is that oral evidence is gossipy, or trivial, *in its entirety* – that it is concerned with manufacturing 'an artificial survival of trivia of appalling proportions'.[18] In the United States, Barbara Tuchman has complained that oral evidence is often concerned with trivia that are given new life by recording and passing on to others as 'history' what was best forgotten.[19] Undoubtedly *some* oral evidence *is* trivial, or mere gossip, sometimes of a malicious kind, but this is not the case with oral evidence in *general*, and the same criticism might well be made of some written evidence too. It is up to individual researchers to exercise their judgement about the value of the evidence. In addition, by developing the practice of providing clear footnotes and other attributions, researchers can help to ensure that oral evidence is supplied and used as responsibly as written evidence and thus minimize the risk of gratuitous 'gossip' being recorded.

Over simplification

Interviewees have an undoubted tendency to telescope or condense events, and to rationalize complex emotions into neat packages of verbal testimony. The subject's desire to show that he is articulate and clear about the past can itself be responsible for considerable distortions. A retired Foreign Office diplomat was asked by Anthony Seldon about Churchill's alertness during his last years as Prime Minister. The reply was that he was 'quite ga-ga' and that he should never have resumed office after the war. The same man was asked about Churchill's relations with the Foreign Secretary, Anthony Eden, and the reply was that their relationship was 'very poor'. Those observations are examples of over-simplifications of highly complex matters. Churchill's performance fluctuated widely during 1951–5, and so too did his relationship with Eden; a piece of oral evidence which failed to take note of this complexity was therefore of little value. As a general rule, oral evidence that offers cut-and-dried answers should be treated with particular caution.

Distortion of interviewee's role

People who think themselves responsible for all kinds of achievements, in which they in fact played just a part, are a regular feature of interviewing experience. Sometimes they may deliberately be trying to mislead, but as often as not they will genuinely believe their own role to have been greater than it was. David Irving found that some interviewees 'shame-lessly put themselves in centre stage, or recall an incident as having happened to *them* forty years ago, when in fact they only heard about it third hand from somebody else.'[20] Although it is perhaps inevitable that subjects should consciously (and often subconsciously) exaggerate their own role and importance, this criticism is far more relevant to published memoirs than to interviews, where the researcher can be alert for signs of conceitedness on the part of the interviewee. Interviewees who are particularly modest (and there are a large number of these) – who mis-lead the historian through underplaying their own part or con-tribution – often pose more serious problems than those who are self-important, because the distortion can be harder to detect. How many people, after all, can clearly understand their own role and impor-tance in an organization or project? It is hard enough to have a clear perspective of the part played by contemporaries.

Similarly, interviewees can be boastful not about their own role but about the importance of the organization to which they belonged. Organizations, be they a society, a government department or a political party's headquarters, can miraculously grow in size, scope and impor-tance in their passage from reality to historian's interview. This may be out of a quite natural pride, or because the subject was simply unaware of the importance of other rival bodies in the field (as we shall see below).

Lack of perspective

Interview evidence is prone to overplay the role of individuals en masse, in part because people and their deeds are more easily recalled than the more complex factors underlying events. The witnesses too may well have been unaware at the time of the broader perspective. This problem manifests itself on both an intranational and an international level. For example, civil servants or Treasury ministers, when questioned about the reasons for the success of a Chancellor of the Exchequer, might point to some personal qualities, but such a point of view might well fail to take into account other key factors, such as a highly favourable state of the economy. The setting up of the Beveridge Committee in 1941 provides another illustration. Uncritical reliance on oral evidence could lead the historian into lengthy discussions on the personal differences between Ernest Bevin and William Beveridge, and stories about inter-departmental disputes in Whitehall. The significance of the fact that by the late 1930s many social policy experts were agreed that reform was desirable might well be overlooked – as might the deeper movement of social and economic forces in other industrialized nations, as seen in the publication in Canada of the Marsh Report in 1943 which made very similar recommendations to those of Beveridge.[21]

Oral evidence can take insufficient account not only of the wider perspective but also of the central perspective. Among the figures of interest to the historian of earlier modern periods, many of those who were at the centre of events are likely to have died, and one is thus likely to be interviewing younger people who were either on the touchlines or huddling around the edge of the scrum, rather than those who were actually in the thick of the mêlée. Survivors, such as private secretaries, aides or staff officers were unlikely to have been fully privy to all the considerations that lay behind the determination of policy. A striking example of this is the secrecy surrounding the Ultra intelligence work at Bletchley Park during the Second World War. Only since the publication of the book by F. W. Winterbotham in 1974[22] has the information been made public about how Ultra intercepted and decoded German messages, unbeknown not only to the enemy but also to the vast majority of those on the allied side, bar a few top figures like Churchill and the chiefs of staff. Martin Gilbert has explained the position succinctly: 'None of the surviving members of Churchill's Secretariat knew anything of Ultra at the time. Thus however good a private secretary's memory, he cannot have known what was the decisive factor for hundreds of different decisions.'[23]

Looking forward in time, one can say that today's younger figures, like Bernard Donoughue, senior policy adviser to Harold Wilson and

James Callaghan, or the young personal aides to the Social Democrats'
'Gang of Four', can look forward to a lifetime of periodic requests for
interview by academics, long after the principal actors have died. Close
though these, and others, may have been to those who forged policy,
they were by no means always fully informed of key considerations and
information.

Even senior figures, involved at the very heart of the action, may have
been unaware at the time of a crucial fact. A good example of this has
been provided by the military historian, Ronald Lewin, from his own
experience:

> My division had only just arrived in Africa for the battle of Alam
> Halpha, the final battle before El Alamein and Monty's first battle. As
> the Afrika Corps was withdrawing, a very ineffective British attack
> was made on its flanks. The attack was an unmitigated disaster, and
> my division lost half the number of the Eighth Army's casualties in
> the entire battle of Alam Halfa. Only years later did I discover the
> reason for the miscalculation. A friend, who had been an intelligence
> officer in the division, told me, 'What you have to realize is that that
> night 'X' was drunk.' Once I discovered that, I saw the whole situa-
> tion in a different way.[24]

Distortion due to personal feelings

In his own use of oral evidence, Stephen Roskill found a chief drawback
to be that 'nearly always one had to be on one's guard against highly
subjective views for which documentary evidence is lacking or insubstantial'.[25] A retired Cabinet official told us one of the chief reasons he was
sceptical of oral history was that 'ministers return to their departments
after Cabinet meetings and all debrief their officials very differently about
what they believe to have taken place'.[26] The more personally involved a
person in a particular policy, or the stronger his feelings for or against a
particular course of action or associate, the more coloured and subjective
is likely to be his evidence.

More worryingly, perhaps, the substance of the oral assessment can
vary over time. We have heard of cases where an individual's judgement
on the performance of a colleague has changed diametrically over the
passage of years, often because of the intervention of a new factor, such as
the informant's promotion, or the death of the person under discussion.
Opinions can even change in the course of a single talk! An interviewer
reported hearing a litany of faults being recited by a subject about his
former chief – his failure to consult colleagues, his recklessness, and so

on. After an hour or so the question of the chief's kindness and consideration to his sick wife was being aired. Subsequently, and apparently
without the subject's realizing it, his comments about his former chief
became far more mellow and generous. At least the researcher using
written evidence does not have to contend with that evidence changing
before his very eyes!

Sometimes one can perceive the underlying feeling, and take it into
account when assessing the evidence. A former junior minister at the
Home Office gave an untypically dark picture of a Home Secretary: 'I
didn't like and had little respect for his methods.' It was only later in the
interview that the subject let slip a possible reason for his antipathy: 'he
never once invited me to meet him socially. Most of my friends who
were under-secretaries would go in and see their ''chief'' in the evening
and if there was nothing on they would have a talk together.'[27] But it is
on the occasions when the interviewee's underlying feelings are dis-
guised that the historian must be especially careful.

Self-consciousness

Nathan Reingold has said:

> Most of the documents that pile up in archives and libraries were
> created in the heat of the moment for rather mundane matters of the
> day and were not written consciously to make a record and to be part
> of historical documentation. I think someone considering the validity
> of oral histories will have to think very seriously about the question of
> the self-consciousness of the person being interviewed who knows
> that he is speaking to posterity, who knows that this is his chance to
> make a record or to set the record straight.[28]

Yet this factor need not be considered a major drawback with oral
evidence. Indeed, one of the virtues of oral evidence is that when it *is* consciously put down for the record the evidence is likely to have a greater
integrity than the unrepresentative casual remark or snippet of conversation recorded in a private letter or diary.

Influence of hindsight

George W. Jones, co-author with Bernard Donoughue of the biography of Herbert Morrison, found one of the chief limitations of his
own interviewing to be his subjects' 'projection back of a present
view or emotion'.[29] Philip Williams similarly found that 'politicians

subconsciously adapt their views about the past to fit a stance they have adopted later'.[30]

Interviewees are not equally prone to this particular foible. Again, the more passionate or policy orientated, or self-justificatory, a particular witness, the more likely he is to fall prey to this distortion. Some groups such as politicians, particularly the more ideologically inclined, are likely to exhibit this tendency more than others, such as civil servants. If the interviewer briefs himself on his subject's career and thought subsequent to the period being discussed, he can sensitize himself to his subject's possible points of deviation.

Repetition of published evidence

Some interviewees may thus be unable to differentiate pure recollection of past events as they experienced them from what they have subsequently heard or seen. If the researcher is not aware of this, myth may be heaped upon myth, snowball-like, so that the truth recedes further and further back. For Stephen Koss, the chief drawback of oral evidence was 'An amount of repetition, particularly of familiar accounts gleaned from secondary sources – television programmes, memoirs etc. – and repeated automatically, with general experiences often personalized in the process.'[31] Brian Bond, the military historian, similarly found it difficult in his own interviewing 'to distinguish between genuine recollections and what they had heard, read or imagined since. In one instance a general's recollections in the 1970s of views he had held about air defence measures in the 1930s were the exact opposite of the truth – as I was able to convince him by quoting letters he had written at the time. But suppose I had not seen the letters?[32] A. J. P. Taylor was more dismissive of the contribution of oral evidence on this count. When researching his *Beaverbrook*, Taylor 'talked to practically everyone who knew him or had worked for him. Result: mainly anecdotes which I found on checking they had remembered from other people's books, not actually experienced themselves, though they thought they had.'[33] Martin Gilbert was dismayed when Sylvia Henley told him she had 'read up' a particular episode about which he had been anxious to gain her firsthand recollection as the sole survivor. Instead he heard her give what proved to be a very accurate précis of the incident as described by Lord Beaverbrook.[34]

Limitations of the interviewer

Many of the limitations in oral history evidence which stem from the interviewee can be guarded against but cannot be altered significantly. The problems with oral evidence in this section, however, can to some extent be removed altogether by diligence on the part of the interviewer.

Unrepresentative sampling

The selection of subjects for interviewing can materially affect the findings of any research project. Very few authors in fact appear to seek a representative sample when preparing their interview lists. Many authors also apparently talk only to those with a certain view or who share with them a similar outlook. But selective sampling is, of course, a criticism that can also be levelled against users of written evidence. Sometimes this is unavoidable, when whole series of documents have been destroyed, are missing or are otherwise unavailable. Some historians and biographers, rely heavily on published sources; others restrict themselves to material in the Public Record Office but consult only certain files, principally those from the Cabinet Office and Prime Minister's private office. Not all authors are entirely open about the restricted range of written sources they have employed.

Biased questioning

Questioning often reflects the historian's personal bias. The content of oral history is greatly susceptible to the way that questions are phrased and posed. The same person will tend to respond quite differently to the same general enquiry when it is phrased in two different ways. For example, (1) 'Do you think the loss of Bevan, Bevin, and Cripps from the Labour government *really* made much difference to the party's fortunes at the 1951 general election?' (Likely answer: 'Well, there were of, course, many other factors, such as the economy, to be taken into consideration as well.') (2) 'Surely one can exaggerate the detrimental effect on Labour's electoral fortunes in 1951 of the loss from the government of Bevan, Bevin and Cripps?' (Likely answer: 'Well, their departure had far more significance, you know, than I think was realized at the time.') It is very easy to come away from an interview having learnt just what one expected to hear. Not only personal assessments but also the eliciting of hard fact can be affected by the way a question is phrased. The problem is real one for the individual researchers as well as for the oral archive.

In their interpretations, too, historians may be guilty – albeit unconsciously – of manipulation. Brian Harrison has written:

One serious danger does exist for the oral historian. When he is himself conducting the interview, as opposed to relying on interviews conducted by others for less specific purposes, he may be tempted into moulding the evidence he receives; the barriers against doing this are less formidable with oral than with documentary material. By asking leading questions, by telescoping the transcript (which no other historian will necessarily see), or by approaching only those informants who will give him the answers he wants, he may half-consciously use the interview to distort the truth.[35]

Richard Lochead has also detected the danger of abuse when 'the interviewer's own preconceived ideas might condition the interviewee's responses and thus fall into the trap of the self-fulfilling prophecy.'[36] Many people are alarmed when they read statements like the following in Paul Thompson's major book on oral history *The Voice of the Past*:

> for the historian who wishes to work and write as a socialist, the task must be not simply to celebrate the working class as it is, but to raise its consciousness. . . . A history is required which leads to action: not to confirm, but to change the world.[37]

Clearly interviews conducted by historians motivated by such ideals – as those motivated by any particular political ideology – are going to be very far from what most people mean by 'objective'.

When historians abandon the search for open answers through unbiased questions, the products of such research, however fully conducted, are bound to remain partial. Noël Annan, for example, has criticized those who subscribe to 'a doctrine dear to the hearts of those who conduct social investigations whether they work in higher education or in the media. It is that if a work is "thoroughly researched" its conclusions must be unassailable.'[38]

Deference and bias towards interviewees

Donald C. Watt has written most damningly about the risk of being over-influenced by interviewees:

> It has seduced some of the best-known historians of our day and age, Sir Louis Namier being the outstanding example and John Wheeler Bennett running him a close second. The seduction of being placed on the inside track, being made accessory to the non-written history, is extraordinarily difficult for anybody to resist and I must say most of

all for the young researcher fired as he is with the hope of discovering something sensationally new.[39]

Hugh Dalton's biographer, Ben Pimlott, also found one aspect of his own interviews was that he tended to become involved with the people concerned – 'necessary to get things out of them, but distorting in terms of interpretation'.[40] Brian Bond even found that 'Interviewees expected you to accept their version and publish it'.[41] It is not just British historians who are susceptible to this problem. From the United States, the experienced practitioner of oral history, Ron Grele, has written:

> The excitement of fieldwork, the genuine friendliness of the people we interview, and the involvement we feel in their lives very often leads to distortion. We begin to ask questions which we know our respondents are going to want to answer, and they begin to give us answers which they know we are going to want to hear.[42]

The way around this problem is for historians to be very much on their guard and aware of the need to establish a 'right relationship' with the subject – where they gain the interviewee's trust but where they also establish their position as detached critics. The benefits of actually seeing the person will in any case far outweigh the risks of being over-influenced by one particular witness, and the danger can be circumvented altogether if historians ensure they see a representative sample of witnesses, critics as well as supporters of the topic about which they are writing. One would, after all, hardly avoid using the Public Record Office because one might be over-influenced by a particular file, or by a minister who wrote a great deal (like Harold Macmillan) compared to others (like Clement Attlee) who wrote relatively little. Nor would anyone writing on the Wilson governments of 1964–70 avoid using Richard Crossman's diary because of the risk of being too affected by Crossman who has so far published a fuller personal record than any other minister. The historian's own discrimination and judgement are just as important for written as for oral evidence.

Interviews as a replacement for reading documents

There is a great temptation for the historian to conduct interviews instead of reading the available documentation, because interviews can be less arduous and more enjoyable than working one's way through the written evidence on the topic under study. The broadcasting media too have been guilty of conducting and using interview evidence before the scriptwriters or programme producers have mastered even the most basic secondary literature on the subject. A dread of many who have laboured hard to establish oral archives containing material of real historial value is the researcher who skims through transcripts in the collection and then publishes the most 'juicy' passages, out of context and without cross-checking or balancing the oral evidence – something that has in fact occasionally happened.

Limitations inherent in the nature of interviewing

The third and last category under which the problems of oral evidence are to be discussed concerns difficulties that are almost completely unavoidable (though they may be minimized), since they stem not from limitations of either interviewee or interviewer but from the very medium used in which this type of evidence is collected.

Time expenditure

Several of those who filled in the oral history questionnaire listed as a major drawback the time taken by interviewing. An author might well be better off devoting the limited time at his disposal to written evidence rather than engaging in the lengthy process of interviewing, which many found often to be of uncertain value. Thus Denis Richards, the Air Force historian, thought the 'time taken up' to be the chief snag of interviewing. 'A single interview', he wrote, 'usually took me a full day's work – writing to the person concerned, meeting him or her, writing up or checking notes, writing letters of thanks, etc.'[43] Brian Harrison, a rigorous practitioner but also a stern critic of oral history, goes further:

> We are not gods; our resources are finite; time spent on interviewing is time *not* spent on reading books, processing statistics, thinking about one's data, polishing one's prose, or whatever. Few indeed are the interviews which will justify such prodigal expenditure of time.[44]

It was not just the time taken of which authors complained but the unpredictable results of interviewing: a day spent in a library or the Public Record Office almost invariably led to *some* concrete gain; this was not always the case with a day spent gathering oral evidence. Anthony Howard, for example, author of the forthcoming official biography of Rab Butler, found interviewing 'very time consuming', 'reward often bearing no relation to effort involved'.[45]

Taking short cuts in the writing up of notes or transcribing the tape (short of employing secretarial assistance which is expensive and, as will be shown, creates other problems) is not possible. But there are some ways of lessening the time taken. A visit to an oral archive (though there are few in Britain) or checking with other researchers who may have conducted interviews with the same subjects should reveal who will be the most fruitful interviewees and who will provide no useful information. (However, one should bear in mind that interview response is highly personal, and a subject who may have proved an obstructive bore to one historian can prove a gold-mine of information to another.) Careful planning of interview schedules and studying of maps can save a great deal of time in travel, and it may thus be necessary to see people before one has fully researched the background of their experience.

Financial expenditure

Individual authors, particularly those without special grants for research, may find that the expense of conducting interviews is prohibitive. Even for an established scholar like the economic historian Peter Davies, the main problem with interviewing is 'Cost! Travel or subsistence.'[46] Few indeed are the serious writers, unless they are fortunate enough to stumble on a 'popular' subject, who can hope to make enough profits from the sale of their books to finance a large interview programme.

This financial consideration applies even more to the spending of large-scale funds on oral history projects and archives than to the individual researcher. A strong case can be made by critics of oral archives – particularly in Britain where they have yet to prove their worth to serious academic study – that available financial resources, especially at a time of severe cuts in education and research, are better deployed locating and preserving written documents which might otherwise be lost if not tracked down. To this argument, supporters of oral archives reply that it is not just written records that are in danger of being lost but also oral records through the death of figures of major historical importance. Moreover, they argue, the written documents of many major figures have now been collected, and much money is being spent tracking down written documents of comparatively minor figures, while almost all the major figures of our time die without being orally recorded. Yet the cost of producing one hour of transcript for an oral archive might be (at 1983 prices) between £200 and £500.

Influence of variable factors

Not only are the results of an interview highly dependent upon a number of variables, but those variables are essentially unquantifiable. Factors that can affect the quality of interview material include: the time of day, particularly for old people (many are at their best in the morning); the place of the interview (people are often more relaxed in their own homes); the length of the interview (answers sometimes become more superficial after an hour or so); the state of mind of the interviewee (personal anxieties may cause a different response); and the interaction between interviewee and interviewer. The sex of the interviewer is another variable that may affect the interview: male and female researchers may elicit different responses from interviewees.

The only way of offsetting such variables is for an oral record to list as many details as possible about the interview and the subject (a photograph of the subject at the time of the interview might be helpful), so that a researcher reading the record, perhaps years later, will be able to take into account at least some of these variable factors when assessing the evidence. However, even written evidence, particularly diaries and letters, can be affected by some of these variables.

Some people do not communicate well in interview

In the words of William Moss, archivist of the John F. Kennedy Library in Boston, 'there are some people of an intellectual or analytical type whose whole lives have been spent writing rather than talking who are not happy speaking into a tape recorder.'[47] Such people do not come over well in interview, whether recorded by notes or on tape; they may complain that the interview record does not accurately portray what they intended to say, and that they would express themselves much better on paper.

Such is no doubt the case for some people, but their numbers are small. It tends to be perfectionists rather than the relatively inarticulate who are unhappy or perform badly when being interviewed. Returning the manuscript for their additional comments and corrections goes some way to meeting the problem, and some people have been known to rewrite an entire transcript. Whether it still remains 'oral' evidence is debatable, but at least returning transcripts for comments allows such people to provide a record with which they can be content.

Misrepresentation of what the interviewee has said

This problem shares some common ground with the above but extends far beyond the subject who feels uncomfortable at expressing himself orally. Even the highly articulate can complain of the way they have been represented. This is why a tape recorder can be such a boon, because it establishes beyond doubt the *words* that were said. For that reason, of course, some subjects dislike being tape recorded: it is much easier to deny a statement recorded by notes. Moreover, it is not simply a question of the precise words; it is the emphasis that is given to them and the context in which they are used that can often disquiet the subject. Or it might be that the subject meant what he said two years ago but no longer holds the same views. Many historians must have been dismayed by the experience of asking permission from a subject to use what they thought were verbatim passages from an interview to be told: 'That was not what I meant or said at all.'

Such is the disadvantage (and in some cases the benefit) of using evidence which can 'answer back'.

Oral evidence cannot be verified by others

This point has been forcibly expressed by Enoch Powell:

> With or without the opening of public records, much political history must always depend on the fallible or falsifiable statements of individuals in letters, diaries and (worst of all) memoirs; but these at least are sources which can be compared, contrasted and analysed in the eventual light of day. For all their separate unreliability, work based on them has an integrity which the product of private interviews will lack.[48]

Enoch Powell has made a valid point. But it is not a criticism that need *necessarily* apply to oral evidence. Material garnered from oral archives and properly footnoted, for example, is just as accessible as documents in written archives, and more accessible than many documents which remain in private hands. Moreover, the difference between history based on oral evidence and journalism is precisely that historians do, or should, footnote their oral sources. It is essential for individual historians to retain neat interview notes; and, even if they do not feel it appropriate for reasons of confidentiality for their notes to be placed immediately in a depository where other scholars can see and assess their sources, it is nevertheless highly desirable that they eventually place them there. When all authors do so the undoubted substance of Powell's criticism will be eradicated.

Interview transcripts miss the essence of an interview

'As every journalist, psychiatrist and detective knows, what people say is often less revealing than the manner in which they say it,' wrote Francis

King. 'This is the drawback of interviews. . . . The final product is a
wholly accurate record of what has been on the speaker's tongue but
rarely in his mind or heart.'[49] That criticism touches one of the many
insoluble paradoxes of interview recording. A verbatim transcript is
objective but lacks much of the vital substance of the exchange; conversely an interview record which attempts to give colour and personal
reaction (as, for example, a Terry Coleman or John Mortimer interview
article) runs the risk of compromising the objectivity of the record.

Impossibility of true communication

A literary biographer wrote on the oral history questionnaire that a
major problem encountered in interview was 'finding the right
questions to ask – because you do not always know the nature of the
peculiar things the interviewee may know'.[50] Problems arise when
subject and historian do not use the same language. Thus the political
scientist L. J. Tivey has written: 'many are wary of, and ignorant of,
political-science concepts. So questions have to be in "layman"
language.'[51] Not only may interviewees fail to understand the language
of interviewers and the concepts they use, but often academic and professional historians do not know enough of the background and politics
to make the best of their opportunities. As one experienced historian has
written:

> I have sometimes been present at interviews between statesmen and
> historians at which it became abundantly plain that the historian had
> very little idea of the significance of what was being said and that the
> statesman did not realize how much of the background he needed to
> explain.[52]

Dependence on survivors and those who agree to be interviewed

As has already been noted, historians are often restricted to interviewing
the survivors: people who were in junior positions rather than those who
were centrally involved. A further problem arises when a researcher has
to rely heavily on those subjects who will see him. Although most people
do agree to be interviewed (but distortion can occur if A *and* B agree to a
talk, and only A provides valuable material in interview), there are many
books that have given unbalanced pictures because authors were unable
to interview all the subjects they wished to, and relied heavily on those
who saw them. Charles Raw wrote of Anthony Sampson's *The Money
Lenders* that Tom Clausen 'would almost certainly have taken a more
prominent role in Sampson's book but for one thing: he was the only top

banker who could not find time to see Sampson.'[53] Again there is no way around this problem other than for the author to admit in the text that the account may be incomplete because certain witnesses were not available for interview.

3

Advantages of oral history

The benefits that oral history can provide depend on whether the area of research contains full documentary evidence or whether documentary evidence is poor, non-existent, or simply not available. In the latter case both fact and interpretation are required; in the former often interpretation alone – of events, personalities and documents.

Researchers who have access to most documentation (it would be fool-hardy of a researcher to claim he had examined *all* available documentary evidence pertaining to his subject) will obviously have less to gain from interviews because a large proportion of the primary source material used in their work will come from documents. Nevertheless, authors in this category – be they 'official' historians with privileged access to government papers normally withheld under the thirty-year rule, 'authorized' biographers with privileged access to the full run of the subject's private papers, or modern historians writing about periods for which documentation in the Public Record Office or in private collections has become fully open – still find interviewing to be a useful adjunct to their research.

Many studies could not be written at all without oral history evidence. Biographers frequently find great lacunae in documentary evidence for certain areas of their subjects' lives. Michael Holroyd is one: 'on the life of my subjects I needed information, and often information that was not in written form.'[1] Writers of contemporary or recent history will often find they have few documentary sources to guide them. Without oral evidence their work would consist largely of regurgitation of secondary

evidence, other people's books, newspaper accounts, and so on, which
might well be incomplete.

But even authors of works on modern history (periods for which
Public Record Office material is available after the passage of thirty
years) can find oral evidence valuable in producing specific facts on areas
where documentation is weak. Martin Gilbert writes of his Churchill
biography volume covering the years 1914–16 that by

> conversation and correspondence with those who knew Churchill
> during this period . . . I have been able to include reminiscences of
> Churchill's moods, and of the atmosphere of events not always
> obvious from the documents, and have been able to describe several
> incidents not recorded in any contemporary source.[2]

Some authors writing modern history even find oral evidence more
valuable for fact than for interpretation: Nikolai Tolstoy 'found
descriptions of events infinitely more illuminating than explorations of
actions, decisions, etc., already documented.'[3]

We now look in more detail at some of these benefits to be derived
from interviewing. As in the previous chapter, the information is broken
down into a number of sections. Although the material occasionally
overlaps, the aim has been to pinpoint the various potential areas of
benefit, so that researchers may be able to form a clearer picture of the
particular objectives they are to pursue in their own oral history.

Facts not recorded in documents

Events

Whether information about specific events, times, dates, occurrences,
etc., is required by researchers because there are gaps in documentary
evidence, or because they do not have access to documentation, the
problem is that accounts can often only be checked against other interviews. Nevertheless, it may be all that the researcher has to go on,
although in such cases the researcher would do well to heed Bernard
Crick's advice: 'If one does have to rely on memory alone, one should
make this very clear in one's narrative.'[4] As we have suggested in chapter
2, memory of events is an area where oral evidence is peculiarly weak,
and sequences easily become muddled in the mind.

Oral evidence can, however, provide facts on occasions where the
interviewer can ask such questions as: how often did so-and-so take

place? who took part? how long did it last? how did people concerned react? In addition, documentary evidence is particularly weak on episodes that were considered at the time to be embarrassing or to have been failures: in such instances oral evidence can be invaluable, and it may well be that the failures are more important for the historian to learn about than the successes. Regarding the history of science, Nicholas Kurti has pointed out that 'in scientific research the false starts are very often not recorded in contemporary documentation.' Kurti has also suggested other reasons why key historical information is not recorded: 'When major leap-forwards are taking place in scientific discovery, much work is done in a very short period and only bare details and facts might be recorded.'[5] For reasons of confidentiality, too, contemporary written evidence is sometimes not recorded in whole or in part. Ronald Lewin has thus drawn public attention to the need

> to record for archival purposes the 'oral histories' of the men and women who, at Bletchley Park and elsewhere during the Second World War, were instrumental in breaking the enemy's codes and ciphers, in processing the intelligence derived from this source, and in applying that intelligence directly during operations in the field.[6]

On such occasions oral history is useful not just for the contemporary historian but for historians of any period for which eyewitnesses still survive.

Personalities

This is one of the areas where oral history can make it richest contribution, as one historian has testified:

> In dealing with very recent history, it is often much easier to read between the lines if one has known some of the participants, their mannerisms, habits of thought, and, not the least, the way in which their colleagues are likely to have regarded them.[7]

Facts about people's private lives are particularly valuable for the biographer. Michael Holroyd found his own interviewing essential for 'the personal area rather than the area of published work – about which, after reading other criticisms, I formed my own judgement.'[8] Information about a subject's ideas, likes and dislikes, peculiar traits, pastimes, and so on, might well appear only in fragmentary form in contemporary documentation.

Facts about individuals' working lives appear with much less

frequency in documentary evidence. Interviews can provide rewarding
material about how particular individuals worked – whether they
preferred to do business on paper or by talking; whether they took work
home; what hours they worked; which subjects particularly captivated,
or bored, them; whether they read correspondence, or official papers
and, if not, which individuals or topics they ignored; how they
conducted meetings; whom they relied on most, and for what kinds of
advice, and so on. To provide a practical illustration, an ex-Foreign-
Office civil servant contrasts the working methods of Foreign Secretaries
Ernest Bevin (1945–51) and Anthony Eden (1951–5):

> What made Eden difficult to work with was that he liked to be
> reassured. Bevin never cared. Bevin would say 'All right, Scott, I've
> heard what you say. I don't accept it. We'll do it my way.' Eden
> would never say that. He would say, 'Well, Scott, I don't know.
> You may be right, I don't think you are. I think so and so. Don't you
> agree?' And whenever he said 'Don't you agree?' I always said 'No,
> Sir.' And this got me into a great deal of trouble . . .'[9]

Information about an individual's health might well not be available in documentary evidence, and of course doctors' records are
destroyed. Nevertheless, the state of an individual's physical – or even
mental – health may be of vital significance in understanding why
certain events developed as they did, as Hugh L'Etang, the medical
writer, has clearly demonstrated.[10] Interviews will thus help with
information on, for example, the fitness of Winston Churchill, Anthony
Eden and Harold Macmillan during their last years as Prime Minister.
Even more can it provide information about less public figures, such as
civil servants, whose illness might well explain why no initiatives came
in certain policy fields at different times. By asking witnesses the extent
to which they perceived dimming of powers, and in what areas, and then
by matching and cross-checking accounts (vital in this area in particular,
because witnesses might only have seen 'bad' days), some kind of
consensus view is likely to emerge.

Personal and organizational relationships

Oral evidence can be particularly effective in supplying information
about relationships, because how relationships function in practice is
often very different from how they are officially supposed to work.
J. A. G. Griffith found that, when researching his book on central and
local government relations,[11]

all the published accounts were based on command papers, Hansard, and so on. But we [Griffith and his co-researcher] were engaged upon a highly *political* exercise – trying to find out the nature of the relationship in practice. There was no other way of doing it but to conduct interviews. The information we sought was nowhere written down. It was a matter of personalities and relationships.[12]

As Denis Richards put it, such information on relationships 'does not get into official records'.[13] Yet this information can provide the clue to many key developments, all the harder to understand because such relationships may not only be complex but veiled to contemporaries. In the political world, ministers may not be very intimate with the most senior official, the permanent secretary, but may well be closer to more junior officials in their departments or to the principal private secretary. Prime Ministers might be closer to private secretaries, doctors or friends than to senior Cabinet colleagues, to journalists than to their official press secretaries.

How these relationships worked can be elucidated most effectively by oral evidence, often long after the events. Organisations too can work in the same unpredictable way, and it can often be of crucial importance to know say, what the Treasury's corporate relations were with the Board of Trade or the Bank of England at different periods: it will not be the same as the official view.

Interpretation of personalities and events

Relationships and personal roles

To distinguish objective fact (or what the interviewee believes is objective fact) from personal assessments and views is not always easy, but the latter can be valuable in helping the researcher make balanced judgements. Interviewers may wish to discover their witnesses' opinion of who were the key individuals in a particular project or body, what their influence was, and in what directions their authority manifested itself, as well as their evaluation of a particular individual's role, main priorities and problems – all of which can often be assessed more clearly after the passage of time. It is thus illuminating to learn that Edward Boyle considered that his political master, Selwyn Lloyd, did not take easily to being Chancellor of the Exchequer (1960–2), 'because he was rather a plodder, and he had two limitations. . . . One is that he never was by nature an easy speaker in the House of Commons. . . . The other thing was he wasn't really frightfully good at sustained bouts of work.

He tended to work rather in fits and starts'[14] – a statement all the more interesting because, when Foreign Secretary (1955–60), Selwyn Lloyd had gained a reputation for being a 'workaholic'.[15] Even where the researcher does have access to all the documentary evidence, it is always useful to know how interviewees assess the contribution of their contemporaries.

Where oral evidence has clear superiority over documentary evidence is the ability of an interviewee who has witnessed individuals in action over a long period of time to make comparisons, often stretching over several decades. Civil servants are peculiarly well able to provide the long-term perspective. Many work for up to forty years in the Civil Service, often in the same department. Their comments on changing policies, problems, pressure groups and ministers can be of great importance.[16]

As with all oral evidence, interpretations of (as opposed to specific facts about) relationships have to be carefully weighed and considered but can be of considerable value. Interviewees are often far more honest than might be supposed, particularly when the interview is taking place some years after the events being discussed. For example, Lord Selkirk – First Lord of the Admiralty when Lord Mountbatten was First Sea Lord in the late 1950s – was questioned about their relationship:

> He was always, I would say, extremely nice to me, although we had our difficulties. But his business was to get on with me, and he was quite happy to do that. He reached conclusions – which might be far-sighted – without necessarily following through the steps in too much detail. He decided he wanted to do something and then he'd try to bounce you into doing it. I didn't very much like that because I prefer something to be suggested as an idea, and to say 'What are the reasons for doing it?' He'd say, 'Isn't it splendid, we're going to do this.' I said, 'Are we, are you quite sure you want to?'[17]

Interviewees can be asked whom they thought an associate particularly relied upon, and on what kinds of issue, whose was the more creative role in a partnership, how a particular individual was regarded by his colleagues, and so on. How someone related to his associates, and in what esteem they regarded him, might not be of crucial importance, but it might well help the author understand the role played by a certain key individual in his research.

Organizational developments and policy-making processes

Whether the researcher has sparse or full documentary evidence, it can be hard to trace why events unfolded in the way they did, and witnesses can often help to piece together events. Organizational developments can pose considerable problems, and interviewees may be able to suggest why certain jobs, officers or whole departments were created, what their role was, or why they disappeared. British government has undergone a bewildering series of changes during this century; the reasons supplied for the changes in command papers or in House of Commons debates might well mask the real causes. Some offices – for example, principal private secretary to the Prime Minister and Cabinet Secretary – have grown in stature since 1945; the power of other offices has fallen. Yet such changes are often not apparent where there is no formal change in title. Other jobs derive their importance from the authority of the incumbent rather than from any intrinsic powers attached to the job itself. In all such areas, questions in an oral history interview can produce much clarification. Evidence about the creation of the Department of Economic Affairs (DEA), one of the boldest steps in reallocation of economic functions to have been taken in Whitehall since the war, provides an example. Why did the department, created with such optimistic trumpetings in 1964, cease to exist just five years later? A top-ranking civil servant who served in the department at the time advances his views. 'I think to some extent that is true [that George Brown's departure as Minister in 1966 made the demise inevitable]. There's no doubt that in his first two years, the DEA did live very largely on George Brown's personal enthusiasm.'[18]

Political, business or military historians, as well as political scientists, will also be seeking to understand the policy-making processes. As Brian Harrison has shown, interviews can shed 'light on elusive but important problems such as how decisions are reached, how influence is exerted . . . and how organizations run.'[19] Most organizations do not print information on how they run in practice. Where they do, as on the Whitehall departments in the 'New Whitehall' series,[20] the result is invariably so bland as to make further research by interviewing strongly advisable. Such questions, concerned more with organizational analysis than with policies themselves, may well be answered with greater frankness. As Ben Pimlott reported, his interviews gave him 'a series of free tutorials or seminars in which I could begin to understand a particular area that was puzzling me.'[21]

Relative significance of different issues

A researcher setting out with little or no documentary evidence, and confronted by a mass of secondary written sources – books, newspapers, published reports, and so on – may well require guidance as to the relative significance of the various issues. Secondary sources may be unenlightening, and many, like newspapers, disguise sources: if, for example, researchers do not know on whose evidence a newspaper report is based, they will not know how much weight to attach to it. Interviewing allows one to penetrate behind the surface and to discover for oneself what is important and what is secondary.

The giving of broad perspective, it has been noted, is an advantage peculiar to oral history evidence. In the same way that interviewees can suggest the areas in which an individual made a particular contribution over a number of years, so too can they provide information on what issues were regarded as important over a number of years.

Such oral evidence might well be partial, or one-sided, but it is none the less important to hear the interpretations and assessments of those who witnessed or participated in events, if only as a point of departure.

Interpretation of documents

For historians with access to most documentation, oral history interviewing – apart from providing interpretation of events, personalities and relationships – can assist in the use of the documents themselves. The following sections outline the main areas in which interviews can provide such assistance.

Overall grasp of the documents

To be confronted by a vast mass of documentary evidence can be as bewildering as having to reconstruct the story from secondary sources alone. Oral evidence can give the researcher synoptic accounts of whole areas for which no overall survey exists. The point has been put graphically by American author David J. Mitchell. He refers specifically to biography, but his argument applies equally to other forms of history: 'the oppressive weight of the himalayas of paper found in modern archives can be the greatest obstacle to the biographer interested in encapsulating the experiences and expression of his subject in a single book.'[22] Interviews can provide information about which documents are important. When documents are grouped together indiscriminately in files, it is difficult to know which ones were acted upon, and even which ones were read at the time: 'records have a history of their own', wrote John Barnes. 'Some memoranda are ignored, others widely read and discussed, and the historian without recollections to aid him may not know which is which.'[23]

Particularly if the researcher is coming to a topic fresh, a few interviews early on can save time by giving instruction on how documents were written, which were preserved, and which are likely to be the most fruitful files to examine on different subjects. An interviewee may be able to draw the researcher's attention to documents whose significance might otherwise not have been apparent. As Lewis Namier noted of oral evidence in the preface to his *Diplomatic Prelude 1938–39*: 'Even more important than direct information has been . . . guidance. . . . A great many profound secrets are somewhere in print, but are most easily detected when one knows what to see.'[24] Or assistance may be given in building up a narrative of a difficult episode: 'It may be that in a crisis there is no way that a historian can reconstruct the sequence of events from the mere documents themselves,' Martin Gilbert has said.[25] It is, of course, essential that researchers ensure they have talked the subject over with a fair cross-section of witnesses – otherwise they might find their horizons have not been broadened, and that they are looking through the documents only for that evidence which bears out a particular individual's, or group's, theory of what happened.

Provisional interviews can thus help researchers to gain a good overall grasp of the documentary evidence. Some authors, like Martin Gilbert, find it helps on occasion to go through certain documents in the presence of someone who played a key part in the events being described.[26] Such a technique has also been adopted on a larger scale by the Royal Institute of Public Administration. But the more usual practice is for researchers to conduct the interview with the documents in their mind rather than bringing them physically into the room.

Clarification of factual confusions

David Irving found this to be the most illuminating aspect of his interviewing.[27] Frequently, documents appear to contradict one another, or one cannot trace the whereabouts of a key document. In such cases, interviewing can save time and help clear the blockage. Many indeed are the times that authors on working on periods with no survivors wish that there was *someone* who could help with confusions in documentary evidence. When John Barnes, researching his biography with Keith Middlemas of Stanley Baldwin, had difficulty ascertaining the advice George V received in 1923 about a new Prime Minister, J.C.C. Davidson's oral evidence helped dispel the confusion.[28]

Underlying assumptions and motives

Documentary evidence often fails to provide all the answers that authors need. Minutes of meetings, for example, sometimes do not contain vital facts or offer only half the picture. On occasions, true reasons for decisions might have been suppressed at the time, underlying philosophies and approaches might have been so taken for granted by the participants that they required no contemporary elucidation in written form, or underlying motives might not have been fully understood at the time. Documentary evidence, after all, is written usually for the benefit of contemporaries; for historians, interviews can reveal their unrecorded assumptions – can 'make positive what was latent', as Michael Holroyd put it.[29]

In some cases it is difficult to distinguish the real motives from the professed ones. Oral evidence may or may not help, but it is always worth while asking participants in certain key events or decisions such questions as: 'These were the reasons given at the time for such-and-such, but are they the *real* reasons why you and/or your colleagues took a particular course of action?' Often a 'real reason' lurks below the surface.

Gaps in documentation

A distinguished historian has recorded: 'Interviews may . . . provide a check against the suppression of inconvenient material or the piecemeal survival of documents in a particular archive.'[30] Interviews might well be essential for providing missing facts to complete the picture – as much for researchers with access to the full range of documentary evidence as for those with no primary written material. Even authorized biographers, with access to the subject's papers, find many gaps. Roger Berthoud estimates that between 25 and 30 per cent of the material for his biography of the artist Graham Sutherland came from interviews, including many with the subject himself (who died before the research was completed).[31]

Suppression (or destruction) of particular items or files in the Public Record Office is a problem, if a minor one. The problem is greater with private collections of papers, where a wife or colleague is anxious that certain documentary evidence should not survive. Piecemeal survival is a great cause for concern. If an individual has carefully edited his own papers, 'inconvenient' material may be destroyed. If no editing has taken place, the good may be thrown out with the interesting through carelessness, or more probably ignorance of the historical importance of the written evidence. Documents may also give incomplete pictures because evidence was not recorded about significant events in the first place. Although this is a growing area of concern, on account of the decline in letter writing and the increased use of the telephone, the importance of this factor has yet to be fully ascertained and archivists are by no means unanimous in agreeing that the quality of written documentation has declined in recent years.

Potential benefits of interviewing

Additional personal documents

A common experience of many authors is that interviewees provide them with contemporary documentary evidence. The more one gains interviewees' trust, the more they are prepared to give. Examples abound. Michael Holroyd, commissioned to write the life of Lytton Strachey, visited the latter's brother, James. A somewhat strained 'interview' over lunch was followed by a trip down to a summerhouse at the bottom of the garden, and Holroyd was shown a virtual library of unpublished Strachey material.[32] Philip Williams, when researching his Gaitskell biography, found himself being shown, as an offshoot of his interviews, half a dozen contemporary diaries, as well as notes, memoranda and private letters – particularly important with a subject like Gaitskell who wrote in longhand and hence kept no copies of letters.[33] Martin Gilbert finds that at least one-third of those he interviews produce contemporary documentary material for him to read.[34] When Laurie Kahn, an American postgraduate student, went to interview the widow of philosopher Frank Ramsey (who died in 1930, aged 26, after a brilliant career), she was presented with a suitcase of documents, including an unpublished biography and manuscripts.[35]

Further information after interviews

Once the personal contact has been established at a first interview, the way is open for the researcher to ask for further information: as Lord Briggs described it: 'interviewing to me . . . is part of a sequence, a single technique in a related cluster of techniques.'[36] Interview notes can be returned for further comments (a practice employed more by oral archives than by individual researchers). One can telephone or write, requesting further information, or arrange second meetings, which are rarely refused if the interviewer has established a good relationship.

To send drafts of the thesis, article or book for comments has been found to be profitable. Even very senior figures can be surprisingly willing to read over the draft – indeed, often welcome the opportunity. Seeing what the author has written often prompts further recollections or comments, which may be, some authors have found, as valuable as material gathered in interview.

Atmosphere and colour

Atmosphere – of a particular episode or series of events, or of a whole period – is often what contemporary documents fail to provide, a viewpoint endorsed by Sir Norman Chester: 'the atmosphere of the time often does not appear in the documents.'[37] Martin Gilbert writes:

> for the tightly woven and closely argued narrative of events and decision making, the documents must be paramount; but for atmosphere and mood, for events as seen from outside the inner circle of decision making, and for character and local colour, recollections can be of considerable importance.[38]

Such atmosphere does come over when one is reading a transcript of an interview, in published form or in an oral archive, but it is conveyed most tellingly where the researcher himself conducts the interview. Nigel Nicolson thus found that, when writing his biography of Field Marshal Lord Alexander of Tunis, interviews provided information about 'the atmosphere of a headquarters, what Alex talked about in his mess, how he arrived at decisions, his relations with Monty and Patton, etc.'.[39] Robert Rhodes James reported that foremost among the benefits he gained from interviewing was capturing the *flavour* of a personality or an occasion; to provide the sidelights of characters and occasions that are so vital, yet are so often ignored by biographers or historians'.[40]

One recollection by Lord Hill of Luton, a former minister in charge of government information, provides an example of this type of benefit. He was talking about the autumn of 1956, when the government was being savagely attacked for their policy over Suez.

> he [Eden] had this great dinner at the Guildhall, and Freddie Bishop [the Prime Minister's principal private secretary] and I had to prepare his speech. . . . Freddie and I worked all day long on this bloody speech and we didn't produce it till six o'clock. We were just about done. Eden was in bed; we went and presented this speech to him. And there was a phrase in the speech – it was my phrase – 'to be

criticized is not necessarily to be wrong'. And when he came to this he said, 'I'm not using that sentence. I'm not going to even admit the possibility of being wrong.' Now I'd had it and I said, 'Now, Prime Minister, we've done our best. You may like it or you may not but I don't think that Freddie and I have got anything else to add.' And I went. He used it at the Guildhall and he got a good reception for that sentence. . . . Next morning Eden rang up: 'Sorry, the sentence went admirably.' Now, how many would do that?[41]

The speech itself, the press reaction and papers the Prime Minister worked on during the day will all survive as written evidence. But Lord Hill's anecdote adds something that no contemporary document will reveal – about Eden and his state at the time, about Hill and his relationship with Eden, and about the atmosphere of Eden's parlour.

At times, documentary evidence can be drained of human detail, the results can be dull, limiting the range of audience impact. As noted by David J. Mitchell; 'increasingly large volumes of papers found in archives, official or otherwise, can be colourless and impersonal collections of documents bearing little or no stamp of a person's personality'.[42] Biography which is particularly dependent upon an element of reconstruction, will benefit from the 'colour' that oral history provides; so too will the monograph. Works like the *British Intelligence in the Second World War*[43] have been attacked for reading 'like a university exam paper rather than a work of military history'. This anonymity stems in the eyes of one reviewer from the notion of the chief author, F. H. Hinsley, that 'in order to simulate "perfect" reality he must exclude any mention of individuals' and he thus 'has failed to interview the survivors from among those responsible for British intelligence'.[44]

Discovery of entirely new information

Books based on established written evidence alone depend upon facts already known, which are then reordered and served up periodically in new arrangements according to changing tastes and preoccupations. As Cameron Hazlehurst has written, 'you can compare and collate documents, but you cannot create new ones to answer the questions which the old ones pose for you.' He adds, however: 'With people you can cross-fertilize memories.'[45] A book based in part upon oral evidence has added something new to the record. The interviewer can become, in the words of Brian Harrison 'a sort of midwife', who helps respondents realise not only that their recollections are of interest, but that the process of recording them, which they may have baulked at if it meant writing them down, suddenly becomes much more feasible than they imagined. Interviewing can enable books to be published that would otherwise remain unwritten: one such example is Betty Vernon's biography of Ellen Wilkinson (1982). Through her interviews, Phillip Whitehead writes, the author 'has captured it for us in the last decade before it would have vanished forever'.[46] Critics of oral history might argue that new material of a highly dubious nature is created to confound not only present but also future generations. Researchers must therefore be meticulous in the recording and preservation of oral evidence, so that future generations can see this new material and judge for themselves how much weight to attach to it.

Insight into a subject's personality and thought processes

Even talks held years after the events being discussed give one a feel for how the person thought and conducted himself. Documents seldom convey the way that people thought, but interviews provide the opportunity of assessing an interviewee's character. One might be told that a former Chancellor of the Exchequer found difficulty committing himself, and that his speech bristled with innuendo, but the understanding deepens considerably when one sees this trait still in action. Lord Briggs has pointed to the benefits of oral history in also providing 'information on language patterns, stress and accents'.[47] Denis Richards found interviews especially valuable for this reason in cases where the interviewee had played an important role in events.[48] Roy Jenkins, even regarded talking to friends or associates of the subject of his biography as more important for finding out 'what *they* were like' than for any factual information they could supply.[49] Thought processes, speech patterns and a sense of personal presence all endure into old age. Nigel Nicolson finds that, 'It is not only the subject of the biography who is revealed in these ways but the character of the interviewee, who may have played a great part in war, politics, etc., but never had a book by him or about him.'[50]

Evidence from non-élite witnesses

Documentary evidence is often very sparse for non-élite groups, and thus oral history has a peculiar importance in providing the opportunity to record their evidence. Bernard Crick has written *vis-à-vis* his 1980 biography of George Orwell:

> In writing a biography it is extraordinarily important not to limit oneself to interviewing well-known or élite figures: they tend to have

committed themselves on paper already and to defend what they have written, whereas very often (particularly in the case of Orwell) ordinary, less famous and less literary informants have more genuine and helpful memories and are not involved in defending or promoting their own ideas or publications. So I sought to meet anyone who had met Orwell more than once on any but the most routine business.[51]

As Brian Harrison has argued, these strictures apply equally to the political biographer: 'It is important [for the author] to venture outside the papers of high-ranking politicians, and to see his subject as he was seen from lower down in society. It is often only through interviewing that this can be done.'[52]

Oral history, then, can permit non-élite groups to give their version of events, to confirm or confound that of the élite. Political historians can gather evidence not just from politicians and senior civil servants but from clerks of the House of Commons, political journalists, personal secretaries, chauffeurs, valets, and so on. All will have seen a different side of the key figures in history. Without their oral testimony, the contribution to history of personal evidence will be confined to just those few whose subjective views and thoughts are anyway likely to be well recorded in the written documentation.

Information on éminences grises

Written evidence by or about *éminences grises* seldom gets on to the official record. Foremost among these are wives or husbands, whose influence on their spouses is often profound, yet largely undocumented. Many leading figures have surrounded themselves with *éminences grises*, and interviews can elicit such information as how often they saw each other, what sort of things they talked about, whether they offered views, and whether they were listened to for advice or were considered simply as social companions. Sir John Colville has drawn attention to those people

> who were widely known in their own generation, who sparkled when they talked, who were concerned with the important events of their day but whose names, because they left nothing behind in writing, are destined to be mere footnotes in the memoirs and histories of their times.[53]

Colville mentions Lady Desborough, Sir Philip Sassoon and Brendan Bracken. Bracken's papers were all destroyed on his death, but his contribution (he was, of course, a one-time minister as well as an *éminence grise*) has now been given its due in two biographies.[54] A post-war figure of comparable importance in artistic and political circles, whose influence may well not fully emerge in written evidence, is Lady Hartwell, who died in January 1982. The obituary in *The Times* described her home 'as virtually the last private political and intellectual *salon* in the classical tradition'.[55]

Enrichment of experience and understanding

Theodore Zeldin has written:

> At the moment we reward our best students with scholarships that bury them in obscure provincial archives for several years. I would prefer to offer them instead a trip round the world, and then several jobs in different walks of life. The history book that has the most to offer is written from the basis of rich personal experience.[56]

Michael Holroyd notes how befriending those one interviews 'may enrich one's own life and, I hope, one's work'.[57] Oral history interviewing may not take researchers round the world, but it is may well to them round their own country and provide them with a wide variety of personal encounters with people of very different backgrounds. By doing so, it can prevent academics and authors becoming introverted and closed to those of different mental modes. As one academic described his interviewing: 'It was not so much a research project, more an intellectual, geographical and even emotional adventure . . . an adventure almost romantic in its contrasting experiences and rich revelation of human diversity and resourcefulness.'[58] To see and talk to the people about whom one is writing is often challenging and deeply engaging, always stretching, and it is hoped will result in a more responsible, vivid and truthful account.

So many of our 'social' sciences are anything but social: they are often dogmatic, divisive and based on ignorance of the limits within which people can operate. It is much easier to reinforce one's point of view by selecting just that *written* evidence which bears it out than by going out and meeting the people involved. On one level it is rather presumptuous of academics whose lives revolve around teaching, essay marking and meetings to think they can actually *know* much about the lives of those they write about unless they conduct interviews. Failure to do so is one reason why some academic tracts do not ring true to those who witnessed events from the inside. By talking to those who participated in events, the historian is less likely to make simplistic judgements, and understanding is broadened to accommodate the underlying factors that caused individuals to behave in a certain way. David Irving has put the point well: 'You need to talk to the people at great length, steep yourself in their way of thinking, and learn to see things through their eyes. The documents then take on different meanings.'[59] If researchers remain open-minded, and also interview those who might be unsympathetic to their views, any harsh judgements they may eventually make will be founded on a deeper understanding and less on their own theories, and will be easier to support than if documents alone were consulted.

An extra dimension: sound

Oral history provides a dimension that is missing from written documents: sound. Even if every fact of conceivable historical interest were recorded on paper, there would still be a role for oral history because of its unique advantage of providing historical material that can be reproduced in sound. Oral history interviews can thus be used in a variety of ways – on television, radio, pre-recorded educational cassettes, in museum and exhibition presentations, and so on – deploying the voices of the past to bring history in a vivid form to a wide audience, some of whom might never be introduced to the same material if presented in writing.

PART II

Methodology and evaluation

4

Methodology for individual researchers

There is no one correct way to conduct an oral history interview. While interviewing is, to some extent, an art, nevertheless it is an art that can be acquired through experience and observation; and the awareness of, and practice of, certain procedures can be an advantage. Despite interviews forming an important element in the research of many who write on recent periods, yet very few authors appear to have read any of the size-able literature on the subject,[1] and even fewer conceive of themselves as partaking in an exercise with the generic title of 'oral history'. The tendency to be dismissive of any approach or technique is fairly wide-spread; yet the need for some consideration of the process of interviewing is suggested by the following extract from an author who wrote:

> I am frequently interviewed by complete strangers; they tend to ask for information I have already supplied, and they talk so much that I barely have a chance to answer them. They do not have enough back-ground information to use any material that I do supply. I usually ask interviewers to list information they seek in advance. They then dis-cover either that the information is already available in printed form or that they have no notion of what it is they want to discover. This saves us all from wasting our time.[2]

Quentin Bell's experience is widespread among the interviewed, and points to one reason for supposing that there is more to interviewing than unstructured personal encounters to which little thought is given.

Some researchers will, of course, remain convinced that informal conversations are the best way to gather oral evidence. To find out how individual researchers – for whom this chapter is primarily intended (as opposed to oral archivists, who are directed towards Chapter 5)[3] – conduct interviews in practice, we decided to ask them.[4]

This chapter, which draws in part on that experience, is aimed in particular at the younger researcher starting out interviewing with little or no previous experience, but it is hoped that more experienced interviewers may also gain by reading it. The chapter should also be read in the light of chapters 2 and 3. Because there are no 'rules' in interviewing, the following chapter thus tends to present choices, and the arguments for and against a certain course of action, rather than giving firm instructions.

Much can be learned by being interviewed oneself. If you have never been interviewed, it is worth trying to engineer such a situation, in order to experience for yourself the position of the interviewee. If your interviews are taped, you have the bonus that you can listen to yourself, and you can hear some of the errors you have made. The more self-aware (and self-critical) you can be, the better the interview.

When to interview

The researcher needs to make two early decisions: whether to interview at all; and, if so, at what stage. There may be many occasions when other research methods will be preferable. Ideally, 'interviewing is the preferred tactic of data collection when in fact it appears likely that it will get *better* data, or *more* data or data at *less cost* than other tactics.' The author of those words, the American L. A. Dexter, also pertinently reflects that 'at particular times, in particular disciplines, certain research techniques will be in fashion. They will be used, therefore, unreflectively and sometimes inappropriately.'[5] He points out too that, in political science, research once relied heavily on legal documents, but interviews had superseded them to become regarded as the most natural method.[6] It would seem that, in Britain too, political scientists, historians and biographers sometimes turn too readily to interviews without considering other methods.[7] Apart from fully consulting written sources, parts of which, notably the press, are often under-appreciated, the researcher could consider whether sending questionnaires, or written questions through the post, might not be as advantageous for certain kinds of information. Or, if intent on interview evidence, he should consider carefully the problems of oral evidence listed in Chapter 2, and the fact that a significant number of distinguished authors advise against the practice. In our own survey 11 per cent felt their interview experience had been inherently unsatisfactory, and a further 53 per cent had reservations, although they felt their pursuit of oral evidence had been worth the trouble; only 36 per cent had unqualified praise for the value of interviewing.[8] Interviews are usually best confined to those areas where primary written evidence is either unavailable – as for the contemporary or recent historian – or is nonexistent, as is often the case for the biographer and social historian. Other reasons for interviewing have been discussed in Chapter 3.

Some authors prefer always to conduct interviews at the end of their research. Martin Gilbert finds that on occasion, when interviewing early on, a wrong notion has taken root and become embedded in his thinking on a subject: consequently, he usually interviews after he has written his first draft.[9] A further advantage of interviewing later on is that one will be familiar with the territory, and can thus better absorb and assess what one is hearing. On the other hand, the advantages of interviewing early on are that one can gain useful overviews of the topic under study, and receive guidance on the written evidence – especially valuable if the subject has not previously been written up.

Those are the main issues on either side. The individual researcher will weigh up the arguments before deciding at what stage to interview, but he might well find it helpful to conduct at least some interviews in the early stage of his research to enable him to form an overall view of the territory. In addition, the very elderly, frail, or those known to be seriously ill, if key witnesses, should be seen at the earliest possible moment. 'In my experience,' says Lord Briggs, 'you have to watch age above all: I've lost some notable people through not seeing them in time.'[10] His experience is by no means uncommon, as other interviewers testify. (It would be no surprise if elderly survivors were not struck by how comparatively little interviewers appeared to know about their subject because they were being seen at an early stage in their research on account of their age.) If a large number need to be seen early because of age or ill health (sometimes all potential interviewees are elderly), it is preferable to interview first those who through length of involvement or knowledge will be able to give one a broad view. It may also be worth while approaching at an early stage anyone who may be critical of your subject; Philip Ziegler has found that in his experience 'enemies provide the most interesting material'.[11]

Another consideration – which might even affect the topic selected to

be written about – is the optimal stage of the interviewee's life at which
to conduct interviews. Some authors, like David Irving, have chosen
topics for their writing according to distance from the present day: 'I
select a topic subject about 25 years old; this increases the chance of being
able to use released official documents, while still interviewing surviving
élite figures.'[12] Robert Rhodes James has pointed out[13] that oral
testimony may sometimes be more reliable after a period of time when
the mind is more detached and better able to reconstruct events. Alistair
Horne adds an extra dimension when he quotes with approval in his *A
Savage War of Peace* (1977) the French historian Adolphe Thiers that the
optimal time to write history is when protagonists have reached the end
of their careers – sufficiently removed from events for passions to be
calmed but not so long after that the main actors have died or memories
have waned.

Selecting potential interviewees

Having settled upon one's subject, and decided that interviews would
form a useful part of the research, and bearing in mind that interviews as
a rule should be conducted alongside other research, the next question is:
whom should one see? When planning to interview the eminent, it is
normally simple to locate names of suitable witnesses because their names
often occur in published lists. If one is writing a work of political science
or history, one can go to standard reference annuals like the *Imperial
Calendar and Civil Service List* which lists ministers, parliamentary private
secretaries and non-industrial civil servants; further works that might be
useful are *Dod's Parliamentary Companion*, or the more specialized lists
like the *Foreign Office Lists*. *The Times House of Commons* lists successful
MPs and unsuccessful candidates at each general election. The latest
edition of Butler and Sloman's invaluable *British Political Facts* will
provide a host of information. To discover those involved in particular
episodes, the index to *The Times* can be consulted, or the relevant edition
of the *Annual Register* or *Whitaker's Almanack*. It is always advisable to
have a copy of the latest edition of *Who's Who* by one's side, as one looks
through the lists, to discover who has died and the most up-to-date
addresses. There will always be some uncertainty with most recent
deaths, however, because the *Who's Who* for each year becomes available
only in the following spring (the 1982 *Who's Who* was thus published in
the spring of 1983). A watch on the obituary columns of any of the major
newspapers should keep one abreast of the most recent deaths. Every

effort should be made to avoid the distress to a family that would be caused by one's writing to interview someone who has just died.

Biographers, some historians and political scientists, however, especially when researching abroad, may find it difficult to track down suitable names in standard source books. Reading memoirs, biographies or published diaries as well as documentary evidence can sometimes help, and one will often be surprised by how many people *are* still alive whom one is apt to think dead because they have been out of the public gaze for so long. When all else fails, those one does see might be asked to suggest names – which will often in any case be volunteered.

There are two main approaches for the individual researcher to adopt when drawing up lists of interviewees: that of the social scientist and market researcher, who lay great stress on the need to interview a *representative* sample of witnesses relating to any area under study; and the *ad hoc* approach, where witnesses are interviewed at random and no attempt is made at balance. Our survey showed that some 70 per cent of the authors who responded tried to prepare lists of interviewees before the interviewing began, but very few said they strove to strike a balance or see a sample of people from different areas of interest about which they had been writing; 34 per cent said they found the 'snowball' technique valuable, where one interviewee recommends another, the danger with this approach being that informants tend to suggest those of similar outlook. Lists given by the subjects of a biography can also be slanted, as Roger Berthoud found when writing the life of Graham Sutherland.[14]

The best approach is to compile a list of potential interviewees, grouped according to which area of one's research they have experience of, and to see a similar percentage of people in each area. It is then easier to secure a balance between written and oral evidence for each area, and hence to evaluate that oral evidence. But there will always be cases where this systematic approach is not possible.

Assuming one cannot see everyone on one's list – and rarely do authors exceed 200 interviews per book, the norm being around 25–100 – one has to make *some* selection. The relevant questions are: how long was the person acquainted with the subject under study, and was this firsthand experience or not? How successful was he in that organization (bearing in mind that 'failures' can be better witnesses than the highly successful)? If he has published memoirs or other writing, this could indicate that he is historically minded and therefore potentially a good witness; on the other hand, often interviewees find authors of autobiographies repeat in conversation almost exactly what they have written.

One can also ask fellow academics or authors which witnesses they found particularly helpful, although one should guard against seeing people 'known to be good interviewees', since one will often find they have a particular line to follow. People known to be 'good raconteurs' may also be far more suitable for a broadcasting producer than for a researcher, to whom accuracy is essential. One may frequently find someone else's 'five-star' (or 'dead loss') informant to be exactly the opposite.

This 'grading' of potential informants is a difficult task and includes a large element of arbitrariness, of trial and error. It can be helpful to place potential interviewees in one of three categories: 'essential', 'probable' and 'possible'. A further practical point is geography: someone with an 'essential' grading might have to be forsaken for a 'probable', or even a 'possible', on the grounds of distance.

A further point is whether it is better to see 'top people' than 'subordinates'. L. A. Dexter has written:

> There is a tendency, particularly by journalists . . . but also by social scientists, to assume that the head of an organization is *ipso facto* a good informant. . . . There may be some much better informant in a less prominent post. As a matter of fact, a good many senatorial assistants are better informants than their senators.[15]

Beatrice Webb came to the same general conclusion: 'It is', she wrote, 'almost axiomatic with the experienced investigator that the mind of the subordinate in any organization will yield richer deposits of fact than the mind of the principal.'[16] Why might subordinates be better witnesses, as several interviewers have found? Often those who are currently in office do not have enough time to devote much care or attention to an interview; the subordinates, for whom the interview might be more of a novelty, will often put more thought into it. Their views are also likely to be less personally biased, and they may be in a better position to see and understand organizational and personal relationships than those fully caught up in the action. On the other hand, subordinates may sometimes feel less confident about what they can say, and, the more junior they are, the more reserved they are likely to be.

It is arguable that some categories of interviewees make better witnesses than others. Some researchers say they have found civil servants (current or retired) evasive and unhelpful; others, however, take the opposite view. Philip Williams found that, when writing his biography of Hugh Gaitskell, 'as a category they stood out' as especially rewarding witnesses, having the benefit that they were 'professional politician-watchers'.[17] Others found principal private secretaries to be the most valuable single group of witnesses.[18] Politicians were generally thought to be far less useful witnesses by respondents in our survey; typical was John Cross, who wrote: 'In general, the civil servants were far better value than the politicians, with a greater ability for reasonably accurate and relevant recall.'[19] A political scientist with wide experience of interviewing wrote: 'leading politicians are very difficult. They distrust each other as well as the interviewer, and tend to change their "testimony" according to circumstances.' The same respondent also found that 'The more "academic" the interviewee, the more co-operative and informative.'[20] Military men some find open and helpful, good at giving straight answers and assessments. Nikolai Tolstoy concludes: 'The soldiers are very good interviewees' and, interestingly, 'the lower their rank and more modest their role the more accurate and precise were their memories'.[21] H. Montgomery Hyde found that in his long experience of interviewing 'Lawyers were the most reliable [witnesses] because their memories of facts and cases are so good'.[22] Philip Williams was not alone in finding trade unionists difficult to contact and subsequently to extract much information of value from: more than many groups, in this case it can help to have introductions, to be able to show some affinity or connection. Trade-union leaders are often not greatly impressed by authors of academic studies wishing to see them.

Family will usually be seen by biographers, and can often provide historians too with useful information. One also might wish to talk to them in connection with papers. Particular sensitivity is required in dealing with family, and interviewers should make more than the usual allowance for bias. Some, like Anthony Howard, even considered family to be 'the most candid' witnesses 'and usually (dates apart) the most reliable'.[23] Stephen Koss, however, summed up the experience of many on interviewing family when he wrote: 'I have had sons and daughters whose recollections were vivid and easily corroborated, others whose testimony I knew to be untrustworthy.'[24]

This brief outline indicates that some groups may have distinctive characteristics and may require different handling. But no group should be condemned out of hand. The art rather is to be aware of these characteristics, and thus to maximize the yield from each interview.

Approach and acceptance

Once one has drawn up a list of potential interviewees (say, 200), one should decide how many interviews one can afford the time and money to conduct (perhaps between 25 and 100) and break these down into manageable units of not more than 20 to send out in 'lots'. The decision will have to be taken on whether one is to focus on one area of research at a time (e.g. a specific period) – in which case all one's letters in the early batch(es) will relate to that area; or whether one wishes to advance on all fronts at once – in which case the composition of one's batches of letters can be determined by the three considerations of age (first), location of interviewees (grouped according to whereabouts) or those able to give overviews of the subject (first or early batches).

A final consideration before writing letters might be to reflect on one's own status. The researcher's status will affect not only the percentage of people who will agree to see him but what those who do see him will say. The least experienced researchers conducting oral history interviews for the purposes of original research will probably be postgraduate students writing masters' or doctoral theses, and, although they are likely to receive positive responses from many of those they contact, they will have to work harder to convince their informant that they really are engaged on serious research, and that they can be entrusted with confidential information. Established academics and authors will find the going easier: often the informant will have heard of them and be interested to meet them, and will know whether they can be trusted. Several respondents in the survey noted that the better the witness knew them the more fruitful the talk. Those writing with some 'official' blessing are unlikely to encounter difficulty gaining access to informants, but they may find interviewees unwilling to volunteer heterodox opinion. These authors might be commissioned by an organization (e.g. a company), by a family or trustees (in the case of a biography) – in which case they will be receiving a fee; or they may be 'authorized' – in which case they are given the blessing of some body or person in a position of authority but are not usually paid. Janet Morgan spoke of the benefits of being an 'authorized biographer' when writing her biography of Agatha Christie:

> There had been a number of unauthorized lives, and the fact that I was *the* authorized biographer put me at an advantage: having the family behind me, for example, meant that they could help me gain access to those with whom she had 'private' relationships, as with her agent and her doctor.[25]

Philip Williams thought, with regard to his book on Gaitskell, that his official status was of real importance only in the main with personal and family friends.[26]

Letters are almost always the best way to make the first approach. If one is a senior or recognized figure oneself, it might be possible to phone direct (as journalists do), but often researchers have found this approach has received a dusty response: a telephone call invades privacy and may catch your conversant off guard. Appeals in the press for information, which most newspapers and weeklies are generally willing to publish (except *The Times*, which insists the letters it publishes do not appear elsewhere), are a possibility, though they are not generally found to be very fruitful.[27]

Letters to potential interviewees should generally contain the following information: the scope and aim of one's research, and the subjects (in general terms) one hopes to talk about. One should provide a brief outline of one's own background and relevant experience of the subject, and emphasize that all material will be treated in accordance with the informant's wishes. Dexter stresses the inadvisability of laying out in too much detail the nature of one's inquiry: 'One way to discourage many interviewees or to get shunted off to a specialist is to *explain* in detail what the project is or is supposed to be about.'[28] Generally it is unnecessary to mention the name of someone who recommended their name, and this can lead to embarrassment if the informant does not feel very happy about being interviewed. But it may be an advantage for junior researchers to mention the figure they are working under, especially if well known. It is important that letters should sound enthusiastic about seeing that particular individual. As Paul Ferris has written: 'Flattery is at the root of most successful interviews.'[29]

People who are still in office will also be far more willing to agree to be interviewed if there is something 'in it' for them (as we examine below). MPs receive a large number of requests for interviews, and some even refuse to see any researchers who do not live in their constituency, but if one can point to an end-product – a book – in which their views might be recorded, they are likely to be more agreeable. It is worth mentioning the publisher, if one has already been agreed.

Although it is preferable to allow the prospective interviewee to suggest a time and place, it should be stressed that *you* would like to travel to see *him*. If one is available only at certain times during the week, that should be made clear in the initial letter. Since some informants may prefer to telephone, one's telephone number as well as address should be

provided; and a stamped addressed envelope should always be enclosed.
Copies of all correspondence should, of course, be retained. If you are
uncertain about forms of address for people in certain professions, ranks,
etc., a useful book is *Titles and Forms of Address* in the most recent
edition.

   Most respondents send a favourable reply: in our survey (admittedly
mostly of established authors) only five (out of fifty-five) admitted to
having less than a 90 per cent success rate. If respondents refuse it is likely
to be for one of the following reasons: they (1) are too busy to see
researchers in general, (2) are too busy to see you in particular, (3)
genuinely do not believe they have anything to contribute, (4) are unsure
about how much they are able to say and apprehensive about what you
might do with the information they give, (5) are too old or unwell to be
able to make the effort, (6) feel some embarrassment about their part in
what you are researching, perhaps believing they performed badly in an
office, or had a bad or a private relationship with your subject if you are a
biographer, (7) are those who never, or practically never, give interviews – in this final category are the Royal Family (including the
monarch's private secretaries) and (very few) individuals, such as Harold
Macmillan. Only in cases five to seven is it usually best to give up. In the
first and second instance it might be as well to leave it for a year or so, or
longer if possible, and then to write back, referring to your previous
letter, and saying that you are now completing your study, outlining
how much research you have done, and why you feel it particularly
important to see them at a final stage in your research. In the third and
fourth instances a letter might with advantage be sent back almost at
once. As Paul Thompson has said, 'Many people will protest that they
have nothing useful to tell you, and need reassurance that their own
experience is worth while'.[30] Therefore, in the third case, if you think
the person sufficiently important, it is best to write back reassuring them
that it is not a recollection of precise fact and detail but more the broad
picture you are after, and that you really would find a general chat most
helpful. In the fourth case you might reassure them in particular of the
serious nature of your research, and say that you will not use any
information they give you in your writing without gaining their prior
approval. As one respondent to our survey wrote: 'It is a long-term
thing: you have to win people over. You can't necessarily do it in one.'[31]
If there is no reply after six weeks, and the address has been checked
where possible, a reminder note should be sent (to a different address, of
course, if the individual has more than one known address).

Under no circumstances should researchers offer to pay the interviewee. If an interviewee does ask for a fee, or refuses to be interviewed
without payment, it should be explained that it is not the custom in
serious research interviewing for witnesses to be paid. If the practice of
payment were to spread, it would make life very hard for impecunious
researchers and introduce a climate where interviewees come to expect to
be paid for information. It is, however, quite acceptable to pay for people
to travel to see you, if they are making a special trip, and to pay for a
drink or a meal if one is entertaining them.

Location of interview

If the informant suggests meeting at a certain place, it is best to accept
that suggestion, particularly if one has had no previous contact with that
person. If the choice is left to you, it is generally best to arrange an interview in his home: over two-thirds of authors in our survey found the
home to be the most satisfactory venue, because the informant tends to
feel more relaxed and less vulnerable in his own environment, there are
fewer distractions, there is longer time generally available to talk, and
home is often the place where personal papers are kept and where one is
most likely to be shown them. Paul Ferris thus voices a common finding
when he writes that the best location is 'The subject's home, without
doubt; second best, place of work . . . the sense of advantage and
security that the subject derives from being on *his* home ground is
paramount.'[32] Homes also provide the most satisfactory location from
the point of view of recording the interviews, whether by notes, or, as
explained in Chapter 5, by tape recorder.

If one is writing a work of political science, or where one is interviewing working people, one may have little choice in the matter and will
usually be invited to the office, since the interview is likely to be regarded
as work rather than pleasure, and not to be intruded into weekends or
evenings at home. Many people do not like inviting strangers to their
home and will probably invite one to an office. The only rules about
offices are that it is desirable to say that one would like a 'private' session,
without the presence of secretaries or assistants; otherwise, as one
respondent noted, 'the target then, implicitly, talked more to them than
to us'.[33] If you are asked, 'Shall I have phone calls diverted?', some feel
one should say 'No', so that one can hear the informant in action. On the
other hand one might lose valuable time while he talks on the telephone.
So it is probably better, if one has the chance, to stress the need to avoid
all interruptions. A small minority, like Alan Butt-Philip, even found

offices to be the most satisfactory venue: 'this is psychologically important', but this was in part because it 'permits unpublished written material to be looked up and consulted by the interviewer',[34] and another respondent found the more formal atmosphere of offices more conducive to establishing the correct atmosphere for his questioning. Bernard Crick found similarly that interviewees were 'much more discursive and difficult to keep to the point' in their homes – but still found their homes the most satisfactory venue, where they are 'much more relaxed'.[35]

The third possible venue is a neutral meeting area: MPs and peers frequently like to give interviews at Parliament, often in the airless audience rooms, and some peers favour the House of Lords, perhaps because some like being seen with interested young researchers. The main disadvantage with Parliament is the interruptions from telephones and division bells. Clubs and hotels are generally unsatisfactory unless one can book small private rooms. An invitation to lunch or tea in a crowded dining room is usually to be accepted only as a last resort, or if you make it clear that you would also like an hour or so's quiet talk in a private spot before or after the meal. However, it is also true that the more you can chat informally to people connected with your subject, the more you learn. It might suit some interviewees to come to your own place of work (or even your home); for a postgraduate student a quiet room can normally be booked on the campus or in college.

Interviewees' motives for accepting

It is worth considering the interviewees' motives for accepting, since these will affect the subsequent response during interview. Researchers should be alert to the possibility that interviewees may wish to see that events are 'correctly' written up (i.e. in accord with their understanding of it), or even that they want to pay off old scores. However, they may be quite disinterestedly concerned to help. They may regard it as a duty to the dead friend, or friends, about whom you wish to question them, or an obligation to an organization or cause. If they are retired, they might enjoy the opportunity of being again the focus of interest (albeit very briefly), and to have what must be a fairly rare opportunity to discourse in detail to a willing audience about the past, and perhaps a past when they held a position of importance. Some informants will have a genuine desire to teach, which might mean, as Dexter suggests, that younger people (looking more in need of guidance) get more out of interviews than older interviewers.[36] Some may hear of your interviewing, and respond affirmatively out of curiosity, or a desire not to be left out. In addition, interviews can give people the opportunity at least to put on record information or thoughts that they may have mulled over in their minds for many years.

One respondent to our questionnaire, political scientist James Kellas, wrote: 'When dealing with current politics (unlike history of at least ten years back), the interviewee always assessed what is in it for him.' He continued, 'Academics are distrusted because they expose weaknesses and are more prestigious than journalists – who can be useful in advancing a career.'[37]

Before the interview

Before the interview takes place, a number of final questions need to be considered, first of these being the need for preliminary research. Beatrice Webb states the point with admirable clarity: 'The first condition of the successful use of the interview as an instrument of research is preparedness of the mind of the operator.' She stresses the importance of interviewers' familiarizing themselves with all facts readily available in printed sources, and emphasizes that 'Especially important is a familiarity with technical terms and a correct use of them'.[38] One obviously does not want to intimidate interviewees with one's vast knowledge of the subject (which they might regard as academic, and slightly bogus), nor to be set in one's thinking with one's conclusions already formed. But as Paul Thompson writes, 'It is nevertheless generally true that the more one knows, the more likely one is to elicit significant historical information from an interview.'[39]

Above all, it is essential to have mastered all their relevant writing; informants quickly become irritated if you have not taken the trouble to do so, and are correspondingly pleased when you can cite their published works. Relevant bibliographies or *Who's Who* should be consulted for their publications. If you have previously interviewed the person, the record you made should be reread, and it is worth seeking access to an archive interview with the informant (if one exists), so as not to waste time asking for material he has already put on record, and to help you get to know his mind.

Oral history manuals tend to regard a preliminary meeting with the interviewee as a necessary stage in interviewing.[40] This may in some cases be beneficial, in particular for oral archives, permitting the opportunity to meet informants and reassure them about any anxieties they may have about the interview and the value of their own contribution, and in some cases to decide whether or not they are suitable to be interviewed. A preliminary meeting may also give an opportunity to ascertain the areas and subjects to be covered in the main session (or sessions) and provide reassurance that the information given will be used only in accordance with the informant's wishes.

A main disadvantage with holding a preliminary meeting is, as Margaret Brooks explains, 'that it might remove some of the spontaneity from the actual recording if the informant has become bored with the exercise or if he has to try to recount particular stories'.[41] In addition, it is doubtful whether the preliminary meeting achieves much more than can be done by a telephone call or letter. Even brief meetings take up valuable travelling time which might be spent interviewing someone else.

We conclude, therefore, that the individual researcher stands little to gain by arranging a preliminary meeting. Even an oral project or oral archive should consider carefully whether it is worth the effort. When administering the British Oral Archive of Political and Administrative History, Anthony Seldon had only two preliminary meetings, at the informants' suggestion, and neither in fact proved to be preliminary to anything: no formal interview took place. Since many of those one seeks to interview will be very busy, they may not readily agree to giving their time to preliminary meetings unless they can see tangible results. In some cases, however, an informant might request an initial informal meeting; where the impulse comes from the interviewee, one should always concur with his wishes, taking care to note his particular concerns.

The number of interviews to be arranged for one day depends upon the overall time-plan of one's research. An author of an 'instant' history clearly has to interview at a different rate from a doctoral student. It is best not to cram too many into one day, in order to avoid having to curtail a valuable interview to hurry off to another; and (especially if you are still new to interviewing) it is best to allow a short break between talks to reread questions, tidy up notes, and so on. Accordingly, it is probably unwise to arrange more than two, or at most three, interviews in one day.

Some researchers send questions in advance. The advantage of this is that informants delve back into their memories or notes before the interview and so (notionally, at least) are better prepared. A question list can also help reassure those who have doubts about being able to make a real contribution. The disadvantage is that they will give prepared answers and may be unwilling to answer follow-up questions. They are also more likely to give guarded and self-censored (and perhaps self-justificatory) remarks than if the questions come at them out of the blue. An additional disadvantage for oral archives and broadcasters in particular is that answers will lack spontaneity and freshness. Probably the best practice, then, is to indicate in a letter the types of area you would like to talk about, without specifying precise questions. Experience suggests that the most rewarding information comes when informants are presenting their minds afresh to the subjects they are being questioned about, even when they occurred twenty-five or more years earlier.

Method of recording the interview

The most hotly disputed question among those who collect oral history is without doubt the method of recording interviews, and what one subsequently does with those records. There are four basic ways of recording interviews: (1) memory, with notes written up subsequently; (2) notes written during the talk; (3) tape recorder, from which a transcript is made; (4) video. Since the last is effectively out of the question for individual researchers, the choice falls back to the remaining three. Throughout the discussion it should be borne in mind that this chapter is directed at the individual researcher, not an oral archive. Brian Harrison has commented: 'The historian's priority will not be completeness of transcription or quality of tape recording, but the quantity of authentic and spontaneous information conveyed.'[42]

Memory

Among some older researchers and journalists it is a point of pride to be able to memorize even lengthy conversations, and from memory to be able to produce a full, accurate and cogent record after the interview. Beatrice Webb states one of the main reasons for relying on memory:

> You may easily inhibit free communication, or the rise to consciousness of significant facts, by arousing suspicion. For instance, whilst a careful plan of examination should be prepared, no paper of questions should be apparent: and no attempt should be made to take notes during the interview.[43]

Some people today still find that memory yields the most satisfactory results: 'I am sure that the presence of a tape recorder or my own taking of notes would in most cases have led to a much more stiff and formal atmosphere which would have inhibited the interviewee from talking freely,' one political biographer wrote.[44] A military historian has said: 'I find a tape very inhibiting and harmful to the intimate relationship vital for a successful interview.'[45] He does not take notes, finding that these too can be a distraction.

There may be some cases where one *has* to rely on one's memory, if the interview had to be arranged over a meal, or at a bar. In such instances one can always jot down odd points on the back of an envelope (if necessary saying 'That's very interesting: would you mind if I just made a note of that?') or adopt the tack utilized by one respondent who takes periodic lavatory breaks to write down key words and facts. If one has had to rely on memory, it is advisable to write down a full record, or speak it into a tape recorder at the earliest possible moment after the talk. 'Never trust your memory a moment longer than is necessary is an all-important maxim', as Beatrice Webb has written.[46] A good way of proceeding is to sketch immediately all the areas covered in the talk and any key dates or facts, and once one has this framework one can flesh it out afterwards. If it is not possible to make a full record immediately, experience suggests the memory can usually retain a fairly clear picture of the interview for twenty-four hours or so – but not if you have more than one interview within that period. If you have for any reason to rely on memory, the best way of recalling the talk as a whole is not to try during the exchange to remember particular passages but rather to attend carefully to the interviewee's words and mannerisms.

The practice of taking notes is now so widely accepted that it does not normally deter or inhibit conversation. L. A. Dexter has found that most United States élite interviewees *expect* notes to be taken and has not observed any who appeared to object (except in unsuitable environments, like restaurants or at social occasions).[47] Some interviewees might even resent it if some form of notes were not taken, feeling that they might be misrepresented, or that their words are not esteemed sufficiently highly. Unless one has the type of mind that can recall conversation almost verbatim, and because of the danger of losing both accuracy and content through incorrect memory of what was said, where one has the choice, it is better to make at the time some permanent record of what is being said.

Notes and tape recording

The advantages of notes over tape are often negative. First of all, the tape recorder certainly does put off *some* witnesses (but only a small percentage in our judgement). Some witnesses are found to 'perform' or to become verbose in front of a tape recorder. Transcribing tapes is a lengthy process (to transcribe an hour's interview might take up to six hours' work), and no one can do it as satisfactorily as the researcher himself. Locating relevant material among lengthy pages of transcript can be laborious, whereas records from notes can be grouped under relevant headings and are much more manageable for subsequent use. Note taking can be used to guide the conversation. If one is writing frantically, the interviewee can *see* how valuable you are finding his information; if you only write the odd word (and he *will* notice whether or not you are taking notes), he can see that you are not much impressed by his testimony and hopefully will return to the subject at hand.[48] Finally, some respondents feel the tape is unreliable, since it can break down without the failure to record being detected at the time.

Approximately 60 per cent of respondents in the survey preferred to take notes, but a significant 18 per cent preferred tape recording (the remaining 22 per cent relied on memory and subsequently wrote up notes). Some senior academic authors find it helpful to take a research assistant along with them to make notes, but the problem with this arrangement is that it can inhibit the informant from talking freely on sensitive subjects if a junior is present, of whose reliability he is not sure. For the individual researcher, the main arguments in favour of taping are as follows. Nothing is missed and one has a comprehensive record of the talk – which is important because most people miss far more in a conversation than they realize. A tape is undeniably more objective than one's own notes, and will help ensure that one correctly appreciates what the interviewee is saying. One can also point out to the interviewee that having a tape recorder playing guarantees an accurate record of the talk and reduces the risk of his being misrepresented. A tape is also far more likely to be of value to historians in the future than one's interview notes. One is not always in a position to judge at the time what *is* important, whereas a microphone is not selective and will record what at the time one might have rejected as irrelevant but subsequently came to see as significant. Tapes record accurately not only what is said but the *way* the informant says it, the emphasis, uncertainty and manner. They allow one to maintain eye contact throughout the interview. Writing notes is certainly distracting and can break the rhythm of the informant's dialogue and your questioning as you battle to scribble down what is being said. If a tape recorder is used, one will have a verbatim record, and it will be easier to quote in your work the actual words the informant said. Shorthand can be of use in some cases, although it has limitations where specialized vocabulary or unfamiliar proper names are much-used, or when the interview goes on for a long time.

For every interview one will have to judge which method would be most appropriate. Rather than arranging the method in advance with the interviewee, which as well as being time consuming may cause anxieties among those not used to being interviewed, you can take along a tape recorder, if you decide to use one, and ask the interviewee as you settle down for the interview whether he minds being taped. Paul Thompson finds that 'most people . . . will accept a tape recorder with very little anxiety . . . and quickly lose any immediate awareness of it.'[49] The more of a fuss you make about asking if you may use it, the more likely they are to object. Nikolai Tolstoy, who always takes a tape recorder and is in most cases allowed to use it, finds that 'Those who declined were influenced by inexperience of the technique rather than from any fear of committing themselves.'[50]

If one decides to (or has to) take notes, one should not attempt to write down every word but rather to select key words, expressions, and all names, dates and places. As with memory, as soon as possible after the talk is over, everything else you can recall about what was said should be recorded.

One's decision to tape or take notes will again depend on how much time one has available for transcribing. Our general guideline, time and interviewees permitting, is always to tape those you judge to be the most important figures in your research, and, even when you consider notes to be the more suitable method, a tape recording can still be made in tandem. The notes then become your working copy, the tape a back-up when you want to check exactly what was said.

A large variety of modestly priced cassette recorders are available at about £30–£40 (at 1983 prices), and a lapel microphone (which clips on easily), the most convenient type to use, costs around £15–20 (1983). The internal microphone should never be used. Good-quality cassette tapes should always be used. (Further details of recorders and tapes can be found in Chapter 5.)

Before the interview you should ensure that you are fully proficient in the use of the tape recorder and that the heads have been cleaned if necessary, in accordance with the manufacturer's handbook. Batteries (long life or high power) should be used in preference to mains supply, for three reasons: it can be time consuming and disturbing hunting around for a mains socket within reach; many homes still have old round pin sockets, and adaptors may be required; and mains electricity supply causes noise interference on the tape.

Preparing questions and background information

Questions should always be thought about and prepared carefully in advance of the meeting. One of three main approaches can be adopted: the questionnaire approach; question and answers tailored to each individual informant; and informal, looser questions, as advocated here by George Ewart Evans: 'Let the interview run. I never attempt to dominate it. The least one can do is to guide it and I try to ask as few questions as I can. . . . Plenty of time and plenty of tape and few questions.'[51]

The questionnaire approach

This method (standard questions for informants in the same area of research, but not questions requiring 'yes' or 'no' answers), is often adopted by conductors of opinion polls and market researchers and may be suitable for social scientists making a study of practices or attitudes (for example, the reading and viewing habits of higher civil servants) or a comparative analysis (such as the degree of autonomy of county chief education officers throughout England and Wales, or the attention given to particular foreign affairs issues by elected national representatives throughout the European Economic Community). Once one has settled on the questions one wishes to ask, subsequent preparation prior to each interview is much reduced, and further detailed research will not be required. But, even where the questionnaire method is used, the researcher should maintain some flexibility, and insert new questions or ask follow-up questions if appropriate.

The tailored question-and-answer approach

This is the most suitable method for historians or biographers, or political scientists engaged in collecting information about a heterogeneous array of topics within their subject of research, for which they will want to ask very different questions to very different people. Detailed research is always necessary in preparing these questions: if insufficient work is put into this it will quickly become apparent to your interviewee that you are not in command of your subject, and you will also run the risk of failing to ask key questions which you may not have a second chance to put to the same interviewee. Thorough research can also mean one maximizes the effectiveness of the talk. Since perhaps as few as fifteen questions might be suitable in an hour's interview, it is essential to optimize their value. The questions should be well edited, and, where possible, should be in a logical or chronological order. If the outline questions are learned before the interview, one can avoid having continually to look at the list of questions during the talk.

Although the precise questions will vary from person to person, the following might be a help in indicating the general *areas* that you might want to cover in an interview:

1 How did the interviewee come to be involved with an individual or organization? How close and how frequent were/are his contacts with him/it?
2 What were/are the main stages in the development of the individual/policy/organization?
3 What were/are the main influences on him/it, both personal and organizational? How have they changed over time?
4 How did/does the organization/individual organize itself and run from day to day? What were/are the distinctive working methods, working relationships and themes?
5 What was/is the influence of certain key individuals, offices, organizations? How has that influence changed over time? Where does/did power/influence lie in practice?
6 What were/are the objectives of the individual/policy/organization? How have they changed over time?
7 What does the interviewee judge to have been/to be the main strengths and weaknesses of the individual/policy/organization? What does he think accounts for its success/failure, overall and at various stages, including his own personal success/failure, where relevant?
8 Are there any significant incidents which he feels were incorrectly reported at the time in written records, or have since been portrayed incorrectly (in his judgement) in published works?
9 What were/are the constraints under which the individual/policy/organization operated/operates?
10 What effect did/does the individual/organization/policy have?

The actual phrasing of questions is a matter to which some thought should be given before the interview. Suggested guidelines are that they should be straightforward and in readily understandable language; neutral; single questions at a time; so framed as to avoid a 'yes' or 'no', or a 'pat', answer.

An informal approach

Informality is found more appropriate by biographers and historians, but some authors of political science and contemporary politics also prefer an informal approach. Peter Kellner, for example, found this method most effective, 'but I usually prepared six or so questions in advance to cover at some point in the interview'.[52] David Marquand believes

> that for political biography interviewing a highly structured interview would have been disastrous. . . . I had a general idea of the things I wanted to talk about before I started the interview, but it very often happened that my original inclinations turned out to be wrong and that the person I was interviewing led me into quite different areas, to my immense profit.'[53]

Others found that, where they adopted a fixed interview structure, there was a danger of imposing their own outlook on the material given, and still others that interviewees were repelled by too rigid and mechanical questioning which gave them insufficient opportunity to develop their own thoughts.

In the absence of a better method, it is advisable to adopt a formula that combines the comprehensiveness and comparability of set questions with the flexibility of the open-ended informal approach. This can be achieved by letting informants talk at the beginning of the interview – the *sequence* in which they say things can itself be significant – and by allowing them to develop themes that arise from your questions. Time is obviously paramount, and one will have to stop interviewees if they spend too long talking, however interestingly, about one particular issue. Yet every interview is unique: some informants will expect and need constant questions; others will not allow you to get questions in, or, if you do, will give a peremptory nod and carry on with their own train. Bernard Crick's comment is particularly apposite: 'One simply has to be very clear oneself beforehand what questions one wants to put, but completely opportunistic and patient about when and how one puts them.' Crick himself, when writing *George Orwell: A Life* (1980), initially tried to adopt a fixed-question approach

> but found, in the nature of biography, it was quite impossible without bullying people and thus causing them to dry up, to keep them to what one wanted, their own authentic memories of the person, and away from what they wanted to do, to talk about him at large.[54]

Background information

It is essential to know about the informant's official life – his jobs and performance. An outline can be found in *Who's Who*, which among others lists all those who have ever been MPs, senior civil servants and senior officers of the armed forces, plus leading cultural figures. The skeleton outline of career (positions held, with dates) should be supplemented with information from other written sources and from other interviews. Even if one is interviewing someone about only a small segment of his life, it is an advantage to know in outline about the rest of his career. In particular you will need to find out if there are any matters that might colour his oral evidence, which might well not appear in printed works: was he perhaps dismissed from a certain post, or did he feel that his efforts had ever been unrecognized or undervalued; does he hold particularly strong views about any people, politics, policies or organizations?

The informants' non-official life is of relevance only if there has recently been a major hiatus. Has the interviewee recently lost a spouse? Has he recently had a serious illness? These things should, if possible, be ascertained in advance. If one is being entertained informally, such as to a meal in their home, it will be an advantage to find out about your host's interests, which can sometimes be discovered from *Who's Who*. In addition it is useful to find out whom you are likely to meet at the home. This cannot always be inferred correctly as recently discovered: a lady was in attendance during the interview with an elderly male informant, and at a subsequent meal. Throughout the meeting (and on the telephone beforehand) she addressed him as 'daddy', and was thus talked to as if the daughter. Only at the end of the visit when he addressed her as 'mummy' was the error realised.

When preparing one's questions, it is essential to consider what the informant might have witnessed, what kind of relationship they have had with the subject of the research, and so on. Spouses, for instance, often 'absorb' a great deal of the cares and thoughts of their partners, but, while some have a very close grasp of their official life, others know very little. It is therefore always worth talking first to colleagues and ascertaining the nature of the relationship. Personal secretaries, on the other hand, see correspondence and personal meetings that take place in the office but will often not know what takes place at the meetings. Through talks with colleagues they may have a good idea of how others in the organization regard the subject, and they will also know a great deal about their boss's working methods, main objectives and anxieties.

Private secretaries, however, may well have been present throughout much of the subject's official business. Even when they were not present, such as at a top policy-making discussion, and thus cannot discuss their boss's performance, they may often know what was discussed.

Those with whom the subject has had a professional relationship outside his main work environment, whether doctors, solicitors, accountants or writer's agents, may well have developed a personal friendship with the subject but will not usually have seen him in action in his own milieu and can talk with authority only about the specific relationship they had with him. Cabinet ministers can tell you about how your subject acted in Cabinet, or Cabinet committees and in Parliament, about his relationship with the Prime Minister and colleagues, and about where he stood on certain issues; but they will know little or nothing about his relations with his department, pressure groups or constituency.

The interviewer's responsibilities

A problem of great delicacy and difficulty is the status and preservation of the material obtained in an interview. The custom has built up among oral archives and oral history associations that those who are interviewed should sign forms governing the use and copyright ownership of the oral evidence given in interview.[55] When one turns to what authors do in practice, however, one finds that none of the fifty-five who responded in the survey had made copyright arrangements, and only a small percentage made definite arrangements with the informant about using the material.

Academic interviewers generally do not see themselves engaged in an 'oral history exercise' (a typical choice of words) but in a private contract with the informant or conversation partner (academics often do not like using the word 'interviewee'). But if these *are* purely private conversations, rather than formal interviews, why do over 75 per cent of the respondents of the survey admit to having preserved their notes? The fact is that the question is simply not one to which most academic interviewers have given much thought, and only a handful had made arrangements for depositing interview notes. The status of their interview notes becomes an issue for most interviewers only when letters begin arriving from other researchers saying 'I read in your Acknowledgements that you have interviewed X: is there any possibility of reading your records?' If authors do not sort out the status of this material during their own lifetime, it can create difficulties for executors after their death. Several authors who had accumulated considerable quantities of interview material told us that to their *chagrin* they had no idea what to do with their notes.

So continuation of the *ad hoc* attitude is not advisable, and some guidelines are necessary. If oral evidence, moreover, is to gain scholarly respect and to secure its rightful place as serious source material alongside written evidence, collectors of oral evidence must be encouraged to preserve the unique evidence they have gathered, and preservation entails the adoption of a code of practice. (The legal status of oral evidence incidentally is complex, and those who want to read more about it should turn to Appendix A.)

Such a code is suggested below. It is straightforward and practical, and, if adopted by researchers (with some flexibility according to what they find practical or relevant to their own work), it should result in more satisfactory interviews being recorded because interviewees are more aware of the basis on which they are talking, and it should ensure that after interviews researchers are clear about what use they can make of the material, and what they can do with their notes and recordings in the long term.

First of all, interviewers should explain absolutely clearly, in outline in their initial letter, and more fully at the outset of the interview, what is the subject, aim and end-product of their research. Before the interview, interviewers should draw up a form, have it typed and duplicated, and make a photocopy for the interviewee to be sent after the interview. The form should contain the following information:

1 The names of the researcher and the interviewee.
2 The fact that this form relates to a record of a talk that took place between both on a certain (specified) day.
3 The fact that the interviewee agrees to talk on the following terms, of which he is to select one: (a) the researcher has *carte blanche* in the use of the material; (b) the researcher may cite or quote from the interview during the interviewee's lifetime only with his prior written permission; (c) the talk may not be quoted from or cited during the interviewee's lifetime.
4 The fact that the interviewee agrees to the record of the interview becoming available to others should they be interested, on the following terms, of which he is to select one: (a) it should be immediately available with no conditions; (b) it should become freely available to other serious researchers only after the passage of a certain number of

years (which he must specify, and which would normally be in the region of five to thirty years) or on his death, whichever comes earlier; (c) it should become available to the media and others for possible use in print or broadcasting only after the passage of a certain (specified) number of years, or on his death, whichever comes earlier; (d) it should never be consulted by others, and the interview record should be destroyed by the researcher after he has finished with it.

5 The fact that the interviewee transfers the copyright in the talk to the researcher. The interviewee should be asked to sign this, and he should be informed (if he asks) that this does not sign away his right to reproduce elsewhere the recollections he is giving you, but that it refers only to the physical record produced from the talk.

6 The form should be signed by both interviewer and interviewee, and dated.

At the beginning of the interview, interviewers should explain – whether relying on memory, taking notes or using a tape recorder – that they intend to preserve a record of the interview for their own use and that in due course others may wish to read their interview notes or (where relevant) listen to the tape recording. It should be pointed out that it will be in the interviewee's own interest to sign the form, since it will guarantee that his wishes for the interview will be respected. If he says 'I don't care what you do with it', he should be asked to sign the *carte blanche* passage. If he says he wants time to think it over, the form should be left with him. If he says 'I don't want you to keep any record', he should be asked to sign the passage stating that the notes will be destroyed when you have finished with them. After the interview, a photocopy of the form should be posted to the interviewee and the researcher should ensure that it is acted on to the letter.

This procedure will no doubt seem irksome, or irrelevant, to many experienced interviewers, and some may feel that it will impair the frankness of the interview. In fact it is likely to do quite the opposite, for it will impress on the interviewee the seriousness of the exchange and his responsibility to give of his best, and will help him to realize that he is not embarking on an under-the-counter or journalistic interview but one that will make a serious contribution to the record. The procedure will also help make researchers realize their responsibility to the documentation of history and culture. If they know that their records may be consulted in the future by others, they will be encouraged to take greater pains to ensure that a full and faithful record is produced.

To those who have interview notes extant without any prior

agreement about their long-term usage, and in the absence of any better formula, we would recommend depositing the notes in a suitable archive with access to researchers forbidden for a thirty-year period. A small percentage of authors and academics feel that interview notes should not be kept at all and should never be seen by other researchers. Yet interviews are given to researchers on the understanding that they will in some form make a contribution to the record. Of course, it is much better to clarify the status of this material at the time, in the manner we have suggested, but where this has not been done we would argue that to maintain that these records should be destroyed is to have a misplaced sense of propriety. If they contain material of genuine interest, unrecorded elsewhere, it would be an act of irresponsibility to destroy them unless specifically requested by the interviewee.

The interview

On arrival, if it has not been ascertained beforehand, it will be helpful to ask how long you have to talk, so you can pace your questions accordingly: as a rough guide, interviews in places of work will normally last between half an hour and one hour. In many instances you will have little choice about where to sit and will be directed to a particular chair. If you have the choice, the most important factors are a quiet room (particularly if taping), and a seat that is not only close enough for you to hear the person clearly but that enables you to sit in a position face-on or as near as possible face-on to the informant so that you can maintain eye contact in a natural way. You should then explain the subject, aim and end-product of the interview, discuss the form and present it to him to be signed, and ask him if he objects to a tape recorder (if you want to use one). If you or he decides against a tape, you should ask him if he minds your taking notes.

If a tape recorder is being used, you should check that the tape is already loaded inside, and that the microphone can be swiftly put in place, whether on a lapel, or on a table. The tape recorder should be placed conveniently near to you where you can see the tape (or dial) moving and the sound meter (or light) flashing, and where you can easily check it every ten minutes or so, and a note of the time the interview starts should be made, so you will know when to turn over the tape. With practice, the tape recorder and microphone can be put in place in a few seconds. Spare tapes and batteries should be taken with you, but it is not feasible to take a second tape recorder. If the machine stops, as it has done at some point with most interviewers, and neither new batteries nor a new tape can cure the problem, there is no choice but to switch to taking notes.

It is best to reveal that you know enough about the subject to make the informant feel he is talking to someone competent and interesting, without appearing to be showing off. Similarly, at this stage (if you have not already been asked) you can mention that you have had talks with several people, giving as examples three or four figures he will respect (and not feel threatened by). Hugh Heclo and Aaron Wildavsky, when researching their *The Private Government of Public Money* (1974), found that

> The moment the interviewer shows unfamiliarity with the subject (though why else would they be there?), he will begin to feel himself on the smooth slipway to the outer office. Ministers and officials need to be reassured that they are talking to fellow insiders who will understand what is being said. They will also want a return on their investment of time in the form of an exchange of information.[56]

The need to know (and to show that you know) the subject well is put by another respondent who wrote: 'Élite people get quickly and rightly bored with interviewers who waste their time, ask silly or tendentious questions, or cannot follow up in discussion.'[57] The display of inside knowledge and understanding may also be necessary to combat the tendency noted by some interviewers for informants to adopt a hostile or sneering attitude towards them – the 'what does an *academic* know?' attitude. On the other hand, some informants will neither want to hear, nor benefit from hearing, how much inside knowledge you have, and how many key people you have seen.

In any interview, you must remain in command, but that still leaves a wide degree of flexibility, particularly with regard to how much you dispute with an interviewee. Beatrice Webb, on the one hand, has written: 'It is disastrous to "show-off", or to argue: the client must be permitted to pour out his fictitious tales, to develop his preposterous theories, to use the silliest arguments, without demur or expression of dissent or ridicule.'[58] Herbert Butterfield, in contrast, has written:

> A Foreign Secretary once complained that, though he tried only to be helpful, Professor Temperley persisted in treating him as though he were a hostile power. It is possible to be unnecessarily militant, but one thing is fundamental: the historian who is collecting evidence must pursue that work as a remorseless detective.[59]

Some general guidance can be given, however, as suggested by L. A. Dexter, who writes that a high percentage of businessmen and politicians in the USA feel more comfortable when stimulated with a moderate amount of aggression than they do when faced with a very polite interviewer.[60] Heclo and Wildavsky also found their interviews worked best when the informants were 'aggressive, eager to exchange opinions, savouring a good argument with fellow *aficionados* of their craft'.[61] The sharp and even aggressive style is more suitable for those still in office or only recently retired, and where one is engaged in an investigative form of inquiry. Yet the danger of appearing too belligerent has been put, interestingly enough, by an author of historical investigatory studies, Nikolai Tolstoy (author of *Victims of Yalta* (1978) and *Stalin's Secret War* (1981)), who writes: 'I did not argue with, oppose, or try to guide my interviewees, being anxious to discover their real opinions and memories uninfluenced by hindsight or other considerations.'[62] The danger of over-assertive interviewing, such as one often hears on the radio and television, or reads in the interviews of the celebrated interviewer Oriana Fallaci, is that the informant can become defensive and unforthcoming, reacting, rather than openly recalling.

Informants will often be anxious about their contribution, and it is important that your first two or three questions give them something to bite on: questions like 'When did you first meet X?' or 'Why were you appointed to, or why did you join, Y?' are to be preferred to such gambits as 'At the meeting on 19 February 1942 what exactly did Z say?'

If they have written anything bearing on the subject, you might say that you enjoyed reading their book, and that in the talk you will be asking questions stemming from it. (If they have written on the subject, the fact should certainly not go unacknowledged, but you might prefer to mention their book(s) in your initial letter.) They may wish to begin the interview with a monologue outlining their thoughts on the subject, or break into such a monologue in the middle of questions. If you can both afford the time, it is best not to cut them short: apart from not antagonizing them, you might learn things not covered in your questions, and they will feel that they have had a satisfactory exchange, and said what *they* believe to be important. You might also find that in such a monologue an informant will cover some, if not all, of the questions you had intended to ask.

When the informant is speaking, it is preferable to communicate with your eyes, face or hands, rather than using your voice to say 'That's interesting', 'I'm sorry to hear that', and so on. This is particularly important if a tape recorder is in action, on which 'Rights', 'Yeahs' and 'Reallys?' are a distraction. When he has finished answering a question, he will doubtless expect some kind of response, if only something like 'That's very interesting'; not to make any acknowledgment at all can seem distinctly odd. If you are using a tape recorder, it is important to keep an eye on it (checking every ten minutes or so that it is still going), remembering to turn in good time at a suitable break, in preference to breaking off the informant in mid-answer. You should also keep track of the time, to ensure that you will be able to cover all your questions. If you are running short of time, you will have to interrupt the informant politely when he wanders too far off the point. And, even if the interview is being taped, it is best to jot down any items you want to follow up.

Provided you can prove its genuine relevance to your work, no interviewee should mind answering any question, even about sensitive or difficult matters – including personal relationships, death and personal belief. These sensitive questions may be phrased in such a form as 'I've read that, or heard it said that, X was never the same after Y moved jobs/died/married his best friend: I wondered what you felt about that.' It might be necessary to point out that you will use the evidence he gives you in a responsible fashion and only in accordance with his wishes.

The main questions will have been prepared in advance, but follow-up questions cannot be anticipated. Bearing in mind what it is you want to learn from the talk, you might ask further questions if you feel the interviewee has not given you the type of information you are after, but which you feel he knows. Some interviewers feel that these second questions, like 'supplementaries' in parliamentary Question Time, are far more valuable than the first. Ronald Lewin finds that there are two distinct kinds of answers: the easy or 'pat' answer, and the profound answer that is often only extracted by supplementary questions and arises when the interviewee's mind is actually directed towards a specific point.[63] Peter Oliver, writing specifically of politicians, but offering advice that is applicable to all groups, remarks that 'few will resent being pushed to re-examine their initial responses if it is done with some tact and skill, and often it is only by doing so that the interviewer will uncover truly significant material'.[64] One reason for being especially alert to asking supplementary questions was made by a political scientist who complained that officials, among others, meekly answered his questions with brush-off answers: 'It was only comparatively late in the day that one civil servant said "You've been asking me about *a*, *b* and *c*, but what you really want to be asking about is *x*, *y* and *z*." [65]

Follow-up questions should, in particular, be asked in the following circumstances: (1) when you have not fully grasped or heard what the informant has said; (2) when he 'smudges' or glosses over a point without making it explicit; (3) when he makes unsupported assertions or judgements, you should ask for instances; (4) when he describes a scene without making clear whether he was present, you should ask him if he *was* present; (5) when you judge he has not told you the whole truth; (6) when you think he has told a lie; (7) when you think there is something he would like to, or would be prepared to, talk about but needs some encouragement.

The informant may have allotted you a certain time – which will generally be too short for your purposes – and may be prepared to go only a few minutes beyond this. When the duration of the interview has been left to you, you will probably find that the value begins to diminish after ninety minutes or two hours, and if you are to continue a break would be advisable. The minimum satisfactory time, unless you just seek clarification of a few odd points, is probably forty-five minutes, and most would agree with Keith Middlemas, who writes that 'few sessions of less than an hour are worth much'.[66] The older the people, and the more sensitive or personal the subject-matter, or painful the memories, the longer time you will need. Margaret Morris even found when interviewing for *The General Strike* (1976) that 'I usually spent at least half a day and frequently a whole day with the subjects. I do not think this could have been shortened. The whole process of achieving a relaxed friendly atmosphere and of sparking off reminiscences among elderly people cannot be rushed.'[67] *Very* elderly people may sometimes require a few minutes to warm up, and some may be able to give of their best for only half an hour, even though they may never mention that you are tiring them.

If you have not established a precise time for ending the talk, when you are ready to bring the interview to a close, you might ask if the informant objects to talking for, say, another ten minutes. This will encourage him to give his attention fully to you. You will have to begin to decide (if you have not already done so) whether you have covered all the ground you wanted to, and whether a second interview might be necessary (second interviews are discussed below). Sufficient time should be allowed to ask him if he has anything else he would like to say about the subject: he may tell you something you had not thought of asking;

and he is given a final chance to speak his mind. It is a good idea to have a couple of questions in reserve, or matters you would like to re-examine, in case he does have nothing to add, and you still have a few minutes left.

Everyone, to varying degrees, will require some reassurance that he has been of help to you, so once you have brought the interview to an end you should stress how valuable his contribution has been. Unless he has another appointment or work to return to, there is no need to rush away. In Paul Thompson's words: 'You need to stay, to give a little of yourself, and show warmth and appreciation in return for what has been given to you.'[68]

After the interview

On leaving the interview room, at the first possible opportunity, and certainly within twenty-four hours, the following steps should be carried out. The tape and its container should be labelled with the name of the interviewee, your name, the date, place and length of the talk, and the number of the tape in your own series of tapes. A letter of thanks (enclosing a photocopy of the interview form, if completed) should be sent, mentioning any areas of the talk that you found particularly rewarding. If you have made arrangements for a second interview, you should restate the date, time and place in the letter. If any further questions or points in need of clarification occur to you in between the end of the talk and writing the letter, these can be put in the letter (enclosing a stamped addressed envelope). Regardless of the medium employed for recording the interview, you should write down or talk into a tape your impressions of the interview, anything of relevance the interviewee might have said but which you did not record at the time, names he may have mentioned of others you should see, any immediate opinion of the reliability and accuracy of his evidence, in whole or in part, and any words he may have spoken about his willingness to see you again 'if there is anything else I can do'. If memory was relied upon, you should write down all you can remember of the talk; if notes, you should go back over them immediately and write clearly above any illegible or semi-legible words, and fill in all gaps.

There are also two questions which should have been thought about beforehand. One of these is whether a second interview should be sought. These are seldom refused, but there are a number of disadvantages to be considered. The chief drawback is time; a second interview with the same person might not give you more than the same time and effort spent seeing a new person. Some informants, particularly if being questioned about a narrow period – perhaps a relationship, or a specific event in the past – will have only a limited amount to say, and you may find them repeating exactly what they told you before. The advantage of a second (and third or more interviews) is that, the better one gets to know the person, the more they will feel able to divulge. Particularly if the person was interviewed early on in your research, you may well discover that some of the questions asked were fairly naïve, and that some key questions were not broached. Some experienced authors, such as Martin Gilbert and Michael Holroyd, stress the benefit of getting to know the informant, and even making a friend of him – something that necessitates several meetings.

It is best to keep in mind the balance that had been sought when drawing up the list of prospective interviewees. Should you decide that the interviews are going so well that you wish to devote more time to them, however, numbers in every category can be increased, providing the opportunity for more second interviews. Experience will soon show whether further interviews are worthwhile or not, and there will always be a small number of people of major interest to your research whom you will wish to see more than once, perhaps first early on, with a second interview towards the end of your interview programme.

Another question is whether to return a record of the interview. This is another option which you will have had to think about in advance, and which you might want to broach in the talk itself. The interviewee may even ask to see the record himself, in which case he should be sent it as soon as it can be prepared. The disadvantage of sending back a record (either typed transcripts or typed notes) is that the informant might become alarmed at what he has said and want to make major changes (although, if by doing this he provides new information as well, it can be an advantage). He may simply be too busy, and regard the notes as an intrusion on his privacy, or as a bore. The advantages of sending him a record are that it will be a further spur to ensure an accurate and neat record (particularly useful where difficult and unfamiliar names were spoken) and, more important, if he reads and thus approves the record, its status as evidence is enhanced. As we have seen, it might also act as a catalyst for producing new recollections. It is a procedure that oral projects or archives which regard the transcript as the prime record should adopt, and it is also one which, time permitting, can be profitably adopted by individual researchers. Less than 10 per cent of the authors in the survey in fact returned records voluntarily, although a larger percentage did so when asked by interviewees.

Related to returning records for comments are three further practices. You may find yourself entering into correspondence with informants, often at their instigation, around the subject. Informants subsequently may be sent early drafts to read, a tactic found by many to be very valuable, and, finally, they may be sent a copy of the eventual book, if they have been of exceptional help.

Preparing interview records

If you relied on memory or on written notes for recording the talk, you will need to produce as soon as possible a typed record, which includes at the top the interviewee's name, your name, the date, place and length of the talk, and the method employed to record the talk. There are a number of different methods of actually recounting the interview, each of which has benefits: you can reconstruct the questions asked (you will probably not be able to recall the follow-up questions) and type the interviewee's reply after each question, using his own words as much as possible; you can group all the evidence given under various headings, regardless of where in the talk the words were spoken, and probably switch to the third person ('The interviewee Mr Smith said . . .'); you can type the record in continuous prose using your own words. The advantage of the first method is that you can preserve the informant's own words as far as possible, and more can be understood about the context and the sequence in which the informant said various things. However, the second method has the great advantage of convenience when writing up: at a glance you can see all that the interviewee has said of relevance on a certain subject without having to look at a number of different places in the record. The final method, the form adopted by most professions when writing up notes of meetings, has the advantage of fluency, providing structure to the record and enabling you to include your own observations and evaluations whenever desired.

If a tape was used, it will almost certainly be advisable to transcribe it. It is best if you do so personally because only you will be able to recall precisely what was said when words are unclear (as on occasions they will be) and you will be more familiar with proper names and technical words. Unfortunately, transcribing interviews is a long and arduous task. You should allow up to six hours of typing to one hour of interview (an interview for an oral archive will take longer). (If you had not done so before, you will quickly come to appreciate the advantages of good-quality sound reproduction.) Ideally, you should then listen to the tape again against your transcript, and you will also want to prepare an index or contents list. If you have not the time, or lack the ability to type, you will need to find a typist prepared to undertake audio work. Typists must be made aware of the need for discretion if the material is sensitive, and will need a list of all proper names and technical words. Secondhand transcribing machines (in effect a standard tape recorder with foot-pedal control and a back-space facility) can be purchased (for yourself or lent to your typist) reasonably cheaply, and will quickly pay dividends in time and effort saved (see Chapter 5 for details). Tapes transcribed by a third party should always be checked against the tape, and transcripts headed with the same interview details as listed above for records typed from notes or memory.

Carbon (or top) copies or photocopies can then be made for returning to the interviewee, if you have decided to do this. If the informant asked you not to keep any records after you have finished with them, or stipulated that a certain remark was 'for your ears only' (or words to that effect), obviously you should destroy all relevant records.

The comments you made about the interviewee can be filed with the interview record on a separate piece of paper. Any notes you made about what the informant said of relevance outside the interview might best be recorded in a private notebook, which may also be used to jot down your purely personal observations about each subject. This you will find helpful if you come to interview the same subject again after the passage of some years.

5

Methodology for oral archives

MARGARET BROOKS

Oral evidence, as has been shown, has been used by historians for hundreds of years. What is new, however, is the existence of collections of recordings – of oral history archives – facilitated by the increasing availability since the war of convenient and modestly priced tape recorders. There are two types of sound archive: those that acquire and care for extant recordings through purchase or deposit – in the manner that libraries acquire books and traditional documents; and those that create their own documents (i.e. recordings), conducting or commissioning their own interviews.

Many oral archives have not fully exploited the potential for recording good-quality interview material, and have met with criticism as a result; the observation of certain practices can immeasurably improve the yield and thus the long-term benefit of oral archival work. This chapter will set out the main guidelines and signposts for individuals or organizations who wish either to establish an oral archive or to improve an existing one. It is also aimed at historians carrying out their own research, in the hope that more researchers, in whatever field, will deposit their oral history recordings (or, if recordings have not been made or preserved, transcripts or interview notes) in suitable archives. Historians who erase their oral history recordings are equivalent to those who might find some unique written documentary sources only to destroy them after taking notes exclusively for themselves.

Questions of personnel, techniques, equipment, and so on, should be subsidiary to, and stem naturally from, the archive's priorities, principles and intentions. This rule should be borne in mind, if financial resources are to be utilized to best effect.

Establishment of oral history archives

Aims

The purpose of an oral history archive is to use oral history as a means of documenting and preserving the past. The initial task is to design a framework for the programme of collecting recordings. This is simple enough if the archive exists solely to look after recordings produced for another purpose and deposited for safekeeping – as, say, a university library's collection. A more structured approach is required of archives that actively seek oral history material or which commission or conduct their own interviews. Archivists need to analyse existing sources and evidence in the disciplines relevant to their archives and to define both the gaps that oral history may fill and the areas in which oral evidence may be complementary. Some archives will be primarily interested in a particular subject area, while others might focus on individuals. For the archivist organizing an 'élite' oral history programme, the memoirs, speeches, diaries, letters, paintings, essays, etc., produced by potential informants must be taken into account when defining the archive's and inter-viewer's general and specific objectives. An archivist actively collecting for an archive will also need to consider carefully the projected and potential use of that collection.

Selection of interviewees

For the purposes both of interviewing and cataloguing, the most effi-cient oral archives tend to group informants into coherent, discrete projects, defined chronologically and by subject area. Potential infor-mants, where not known already to the archive, or where names are not available in contemporary published lists (see page 58), can be located through letters to the press or by direct contact with appropriate organizations. In selecting the projects as well as the individual infor-mants, the archivist obviously needs to make policy decisions about pri-orities and the balancing of aspirations with resources. Further, since oral evidence, unlike written or material evidence, is irretrievably lost with the death of its owner, particular attention should be given to oral history programmes concerning elderly eminent people. An archive with an interest in the history and culture of the first quarter of the twentieth century, for example, would do well to engage additional staff or freelance interviewers for what soon must be something of a salvage operation. One of the advantages an archive has over individual collectors of oral history is institutional continuity. This advantage can be put to good use by recording (or acquiring recordings of) eminent figures at more than one point in their lives – say, at the ages of 45 and 65, depending always on personal career patterns. By this practice we may investigate their changing environment, ideas, emphases and candour. Similarly, an archive can make a concerted effort to interview and record elected officials when out of office and other prominent people when out of favour. And eminent failures can inform the future as much as eminent successes.

Selection of topics for discussion

An archive needs to co-ordinate the work of its interviewers and, even if there is only one, historical analysis benefits if the interviews are comparable. A formal questionnaire, however, tends to intrude between the interviewer and the informant, can take the initiative from the interviewer by imposing too rigid a structure, and can adversely affect the informant's responses by making him over-conscious that there is a next question waiting. Co-ordination is best achieved by producing detailed research papers which briefly outline the topic areas to be investigated but not the precise questions, whether the recording project concerns an individual or an era. The interview is then an improvisation from this base, within this structure. The project papers should be reviewed continuously and, if there is more than one interviewer, they will need to discuss the papers and the progress of the recording projects regularly, both among themselves and with the archive's director. Whether the interviews are the work of an individual or a team, and whether they are conducted for the archive or initially for private research, an outline of this type is valuable for reference while the work is under way and as documentation of the range of the programme after it is completed. The project paper, along with notes of significant changes, should thus be preserved and made available to future users of the collection. This is particularly desirable where the organization of the interviews was not instigated by, or in the control of, the archive.

Staffing

The staffing of an oral history archive depends on its programme and purposes. Although there can be no single formula, an appropriate ratio might be one cataloguer and one part-time typist to one or two interviewers. Just a part-time technician is probably sufficient, unless the archive has particularly labour-intensive work – for example, copying several different tape formats (sizes and speeds) or inadequate equipment. A further person may be required to assist and supervise the archive's visitors; or the job could be undertaken by an otherwise part-time typist or technician, making a full-time position. The number of public assistants required is related to the nature of the archive, not to the number of interviewers. A full-time interviewer can carry out about 100 visits in a year (as well as the related preparation and administration); the number of interviews that represents depends of course, on how many visits are required for each interview.

Recording equipment

As we have seen, some individual collectors of oral evidence do not tape record; for an oral archive, however, a sound recording of an interview, rather than just notes or typescript, is essential. The significance of an informant's answers can be better understood if the researcher knows not just the questions, but the manner and context in which they were asked, including the intonations, the pauses, the informant's emotional state – in other words, the kind of communication that was taking place between the interviewer and the informant. Sound recordings – or, even better, sound film or video – will bring future historians more benefit than their typewritten shadows.

To be worth preserving, it is crucial for the recordings to be of reasonable quality. A term sometimes used is 'broadcast quality', which merely means a clearly audible voice, faithful to the speaker's natural timbre, with no extraneous electrical or mechanical noises caused by the equipment or the recording environment. There exist strange and fascinating early recordings of luminaries such as Edison (1888), Tennyson (1890) and Franz Josef (1900). Sadly they are so squeaky and indistinct as to be humorous rather than evocative or informative. But with modern equipment we *can* make and preserve recordings that are true not only to what a person says but to the *manner* in which he says it. While it may be better that almost anything be preserved than nothing at all, the difference in expense and effort between a poor recording and a good one is no longer a major hurdle.

Because of the competition in the field of recording equipment and ancillary supplies, archivists and individual historians who know precisely what they require may be able to take advantage of bargains. Those who need advice and service would do better at specialist shops and should be wary of discount warehouses. Archivists may be able to purchase equipment or tapes in bulk from the manufacturers, with a trade discount for their institutions.

Archives that produce their own oral history will naturally wish to adhere to the highest current standards, and to stay abreast of new developments. But what of individual researchers? There are, in fact, no reasons other than financial ones why scholars or writers carrying out their own research need aim or settle for any less. Unlike notes (for which everyone is entitled to their own private illegible scribble), taped interviews are documents in their own right – whether the interviews are recorded specially for oral archives or deposited in archives after their use in individual research. When the informant is an eminent individual, and no one else's views and reminiscences will suffice equally, thoughtfully produced evidence is ill-served by technical helplessness. A tape recorder may be more difficult to operate than a telephone, but certainly it is less difficult than driving a car. Fortunately we shall probably be the last generations to feel helpless in the face of technical equipment, as tape recorders and other machines become more widely available and familiar, both in schools and at home. On the other hand, it must be borne in mind that carefully considered practices are as important as the equipment itself.

If some of the following sounds complicated to those who are not technically minded, it is well to remember that organizations such as IASA (the International Association of Sound Archives), the Imperial War Museum and BIRS (the British Institute of Recorded Sound, now the National Sound Archive) are generally eager to encourage oral history, and are pleased to give advice on equipment, materials and techniques to interested fellow practitioners.

Tape recorders

Until recently cassette tape recorders were markedly inferior to open-reel machines because of the poor quality of the recording: unnatural, distorted, muffled, noisy. Their alleged merits were lower price, more compact size and greater ease of use. Technological advances have resulted in significant improvement in quality, but at the expense of cost and portability. If semi-professional equipment is to be used, with either a cassette or reel-to-reel machine costing about £500 in 1983/4, open-reel tape recorders are still generally more suitable for individual researchers, and certainly for archives. The following guidelines help the oral archivist in the selection of machines. Techniques and equipment for archive studio replay, monitoring and correction are beyond the scope of this chapter.

The recording of conversation, however animated, does not require the same frequency range as music recording. For speech the frequency response should be approximately 10,000 cycles (as opposed to at least 15,000 cycles for music). The specifications of particular brands of tape recorder are available from the manufacturer or dealer. The best frequency response for speech is usually given at a speed of $7\frac{1}{2}$ ips (inches per second), which causes less noise and distortion than $3\frac{3}{4}$ ips or lower speeds.

Cassette machines are likely to be less robust and reliable than open reel. If the tape recorder is going to be used for frequent interviews at different venues and/or for cataloguing and indexing the interviews, a sturdy machine will be needed. As cassette machines have smaller, more delicate components, they are more susceptible to tape jamming or tangling, and require more frequent cleaning and checking. Ironically, less technically minded collectors of oral history, who might be particularly tempted by cassettes, are more in need of reliable equipment than those who can service their own. Not only are open-reel recorders more likely to prove reliable, but if the tape should become twisted or break the problem can be seen and rectified easily on site – which is not possible with cassettes. A sturdy work-horse of an open-reel recorder will probably be quite heavy and may not be comfortable on long walks, but it will be readily manageable on and off trains, and up and down steps.

The collector of oral history requires a tape recorder with external-microphone sockets, recording-level indicators and recording-level control. Automatic volume control is not an asset, because it results in a false dynamic range, and the background noise level varies; the level is thus best controlled manually. Some cassette machines have a limiter, which is preferable to automatic levelling. The machine should have a facility to record either using rechargeable batteries or off the mains. As was pointed out in Chapter 4, battery power allows freer positioning, carries less risk of extra hum, and avoids the problem of incompatible plugs. Open-reel machines tend to run longer on a charge than cassettes. Cheap rechargeable batteries with a low ampere-hour (Ah) rating indicated on the batteries themselves are a false economy, since they will run at full power for only a couple of hours – not enough of a reserve for oral history recording.

The recorder should have a transparent window through which the tape may be seen easily. An interviewer using an open-reel recorder can see at a glance that the tape is moving properly and how much remains before the end of the reel, particularly if transparent spools have been chosen; it is thus easier to be confident – and to convey that confidence to the interviewee. Cassette recorders, on the other hand, do not have easily visible tape movement. Their main advantage is that their tapes need no lacing up but are ready as soon as they are slotted in position; but rapid, trouble-free lacing of open-reel tapes comes quickly with practice.

Both types of tape recorder are available in stereo and mono versions. Stereophonic sound is of no benefit or relevance to the two stationary voices in an interview, but stereo machines have the advantage of providing two microphone inputs. This allows not only more flexibile seating arrangements but separate control of recording levels. Some mono recorders also have this facility. For those that do not, an adaptor plug can be used to feed two microphones into one socket, but both share the same recording-level control.

Open-reel machines are designed to record full, half or quarter track. A full-track recording puts the signal on to the entire width of the tape, so that when the whole reel has been recorded from beginning to end no further recording can be made without erasure. The half-track method records on the top half of the tape along its length, and the tape may then be turned over and an equal amount recorded on the other track. Full track is most appropriate for archival master tapes, with the best prognosis for long-term durability and stability. Half track is suitable for interviews that will be copied for preservation, though particular care must be taken to avoid confusion of the tracks and hence accidental erasure. Coloured leaders are helpful: green for the beginning of tape or of track 1, red for the end. Stereo half-track machines produce a full-track recording with two microphone inputs, one on each half of the tape. This is referred to as 'twin track', and the tape cannot be turned over to continue the recording. These machines can also be used for mono half track. Quarter-track recorders should not be used because it is possible to confuse two different tracks on each 'side', and the tape is more susceptible to physical damage and hiss on the narrow tracks. Cassette tape is always half track, even for stereo models.

The portable tape recorders which are used most widely in Britain for archival-quality oral history and for broadcast recordings are the open-reel Uher 4000 (mono) and 4200 (stereo) series, recently superseded by the Uher 4200 Monitor which has three heads, allowing the interviewer to monitor the recording in progress (approximately £500 in 1983/4). The Uhers have been found to be reliable over several years. Nagras are more sophisticated and expensive, and of greater interest to people recording music. Good quality cassette recorders are the Maranz Superscope CD320 and CD330 (approximately £150 at 1983/4 prices), the latter with three heads, for monitoring. The Sony TCD5 is very suitable, but rather more expensive (approximately £475 in 1983/4). Good portable open-reel recorders may be expected to last more than ten years and are sometimes available secondhand. One might be more likely to see them advertised in a professional publication or *Exchange and Mart* than in popular domestic hi-fi magazines. Cassette recorders cannot be expected to last as long as open-reel recorders.

In the span of less than a century the field of sound recording has utilized various media: tinfoil and wax cylinders, flat discs at different speeds, wire, optical film and magnetic tape. Cassette machines are currently enjoying a boom, with extensive advertising and promotion and frequent model changes. For the archivist, however, there is considerably less possibility of confusion and obsolescence if open-reel tape recorders are used. None the less it must be noted that significant developments are in progress in digital recording. Within a very few years there will be new systems, with a trend towards smaller size with greater capacity and fidelity – and at a lower price. Therefore, even if money is available, it would not be wise to invest a very great amount in recording equipment.

Microphones

Recorders of the quality required for oral history are not sold with microphones, as are some cheaper machines. The microphone should be of comparable quality and performance to the tape recorder, since together they will only be as good as the inferior of the two. Desirable technical qualities in a microphone are sensivity to voice frequencies, lack of distortion and lack of propensity to handling noise from friction against the user's body or clothing. Electret capacitor clip microphones are the most appropriate for oral history interviewing and are not expensive. These small clip or neck microphones are preferable to table or hand-held microphones because they are less obtrusive, give a less formal or journalistic atmosphere, pick up less background noise and allow the informant freedom of movement without affecting the quality or level of the sound. The interviewer must ensure that neither he nor the informant twiddles absentmindedly with the microphone lead, because that produces a crackling sound on the tape that is inaudible at the time of recording; the tempting portion of the lead can be tucked into a corner of the chair. The microphone should be attached to a stable portion of clothing about 8 inches from the speaker's mouth. Suitable brands are Ross (also sold as RS 249–463) (around £12 in 1982), Sony ECM150 (about £33 in 1982), Eagle PRO M60 (around £18 in 1982).

Some cassette machines have built-in microphones. As has been advised in Chapter 4, these should never be used for oral history recording, since internal microphones inevitably pick up an unacceptable level of machine noise.

Transcribing machines

A machine appropriate for recording will be cumbersome for transcribing because it will lack facilities for the frequent starting and stopping that is necessary. The most important facility for a transcribing machine is a foot control, which enables typists to start, stop and back-track while leaving their hands free. An earphone socket is useful, because most typists find it easier to concentrate when wearing headphones – which should be the very light stethoscope type if they are to be worn for long periods. A tone-control knob can be useful in making less distinct voices easier to understand. Suitable transcribing machines are the Uher 5000 for open-reel recordings (around £400 in 1983/4) and the Sony BM46 for cassettes (around approx £220 in 1983/4).

Preservation and storage of recordings

Technical-description records

Whether the processing and preservation of tapes is the job of a trained and experienced technician or a jack-of-all-trades archivist, a permanent, descriptive technical record should be kept for each interview. Although no standard system exists for oral history, forms have been developed by the Imperial War Museum and the technical committee of the International Association of Sound Archives (IASA) which include the following information: accession number, informant's name, duration of recording, dates of recording and of all copying, tape used for original recording and all copies (with manufacturer and batch number for archival master tapes), track configuration (e.g. full track, monophonic) and speed for original recording and all copies, tape recorder and microphones used in original recording, playback equipment used in producing copies, details of noise-reduction process used for cassettes, and a space for any relevant comments. Any oral archive can, and should, note down the preceding items. Archives with technical staff will want to add further details: technical advice is always available on how to make a note of additional features for the benefit of future technicians who may be involved in the preservation or reproduction of the recordings when the archive expands, or when a much-needed national oral archive is established. Such additional notes would include levels of reference signals or test tones (for assessing deterioration), details of peak flux (the maximum level a recording reaches, determined by the manufacturer of the recorder, for setting replay equipment), equalization (the process used to overcome shrillness caused by the reduction of lower frequencies, international standards differing between Europe and the USA) and filtering (cutting certain frequencies of extraneous noise). All oral archives, of whatever degree of professionalism, should compile such a technical-description note, which can consist simply of a form with boxes to tick, to make it simple and speedy to complete.

Tape selection

An archive will require at least one duplicate of each recording; the master tapes should be carefully preserved and kept separate from the working copies. If resources will permit, it is desirable to hold each recording in quadruplicate: the archival master; the working copy which is for staff use, such as cataloguing and producing copies for public sale; a reference copy for researchers who visit the archive; and a transcription copy for the typist (which may be erased and re-used when the transcript is finished). The archive may have various sources of material, even if it does conduct most of its own interviews. Whether the recordings it acquires are on cassette or open-reel tape, or even on old discs, they should ideally be copied to a uniform format – full-track, professional, quarter-inch, standard-play tape, 1.5 mil thick, with a polyester base and in uniform unit lengths. It is particularly important that any acquisitions on acetate-based tape be copied, since this material has been found to deteriorate seriously, curling, cracking, shrinking and warping. Acetate tapes are no longer used but may be identified by the fact that they snap rather than stretch when pulled slightly and are shiny with (usually) a reddish-brown colour. Tapes from the USA – where acetate was used more extensively – may be suspect.

The polyester-based standard-play tape is most appropriate for long-term storage of archival master tapes because, compared with thinner and more flexible tapes, it has higher signal-handling capacity, greater physical strength and lower 'print-through' characteristics (the tendency of the signal recorded on one section of tape to imprint on adjacent layers as it lies wound on the spool, resulting in extraneous sounds). Iron oxide tape is considered to be more stable than chromium dioxide. Matt backing is preferable to shiny for evenness of winding, particularly at high speed. Archive tapes should be splice-free because the joints may open or stick to the next layer. There are a number of good tapes available, and equipment manufacturers can advise on tapes best suited to their recorders. The following brands of standard play tapes are all appropriate for archive purposes: Agfa PEM 468, Ampex 406, BASF SPR 50 LH, Zonal 675, Maxell UDXL 50 (very approximately £5 per tape in 1983/4, but if the archive is able to buy in bulk there will be a dramatic reduction in cost).

If a portable machine is used for the original recording, standard-play tape will probably not give the best results. The motors, which are small and relatively weak, cannot give the best head-to-tape contact with stiff standard-play tape; the more flexible long-play (1 mil thick) and double-play (0.5 mil) tapes are therefore more appropriate. Triple-play tape should be avoided, because it is so thin that it is susceptible to damage and its print-through characteristics are poor. Even though the original recordings will be copied on to high-quality standard-play tape for the archival masters, it is important to use the best-quality tape the archive can afford, since distortions due to the shortcomings of the original recording medium cannot be corrected merely by copying on to better tapes. The main features to look for in long-play or double-play tape are low distortion and noise with good print-through characteristics. Good double-play tape can be re-used twenty times or more. The following brands are appropriate: long-play, Agfa PEM 369, TDK Audua, BASF LP 35, Maxell UDXL 35; double-play, Agfa PEM 269, BASF DPR 26 (approximately the same prices as the standard-play tapes listed above).

Extended-play tapes also have the advantage of providing longer recording and playing time. A 5-inch reel of standard-play tape lasts 15 minutes at $7\frac{1}{2}$ ips, of long-play tape 22 minutes, and of double-play tape 30 minutes. A 7-inch reel at $7\frac{1}{2}$ ips lasts 30 minutes using standard-play tape, 45 minutes using long-play, and one hour using double-play. The half-hour reels produced with double-play tape on the common size of portable recorders using 5-inch spools or standard-play tape on bigger studio machines are a convenient unit length for subdividing the interviews for preservation, cataloguing and reference use. Cassette tapes are not recommended for serious archival purposes because of their thinness, fragility and susceptibility to print-through. So, even where the initial recording has had to be on cassette, it is best to transfer the recording to open-reel tape for storage. The long-term stability of cassettes is not known; cassette tape is made of a different substance from that of open-reel tapes. Where preservation is not of primary importance, as in duplicate copies of interviews for public reference, the cheapness, smaller storage requirement and ease of use of cassette tapes have much to recommend them, and the two lugs or tabs (located on the opposite side of the open face) can be removed to prevent their being erased. C 60 cassettes (30 minutes each side) are the most convenient and suitable duration; C 90s and C 120s should be avoided, since they are prone to breaking and jamming. Ferrous-type cassettes are preferable to chrome: the latter are likely to wear out machine heads more frequently and to have more unsatisfactory print-through and distortion characteristics. Metal cassette tapes have not lived up to their promise and should be avoided. In the absence of other guidance, the following brands of cassette are generally reliable: Agfa, Maxell, Sony, TDK (all approximately £1.50 per C 60 in 1983/4).

With cassettes, even more than with open-reel tape, it is important to refer to the suggestions of the machine manufacturers, since tape recorders are aligned for particular tapes. Hi-fi and specialist magazines (e.g. *Studio Sound*) carry cassette and open-reel tape reviews from time to time; changes and advances are very rapid.

Tape care and storage

Magnetic tape is a relatively new medium invented during the 1930s and in use since the Second World War. No one knows how long it will last, but sufficient expertise has been gained in the last few decades to establish good principles for tape storage. For individual researchers collecting oral evidence, or the many archivists with very limited resources, there are still points to bear in mind for ensuring the safe survival of a tape collection. Each archive will have to weigh its aspirations against its capacities and resources, but there is no doubt that there is little point in conducting or acquiring interesting, well-planned interviews with sensitive equipment if one does not take care of the recordings. The priorities for archival storage are good-quality, well-wound tapes and a stable environment.

The recommended storage temperature for magnetic tape is 45°F to 55 °F (7°C to 13°C), and the recommended relative humidity is 40 to 60 per cent. Stability of temperature and humidity is particularly important; it has been suggested as a general guide that, in the absence of an air-conditioned storage room, tapes be kept in dry areas with comfortable working temperatures not subject to variations of more than 10°F (6°C). A warmer room requires drier air, to avoid the danger of condensation and fungal growth. Changes in temperature cause stress patterns in the tape, and higher temperatures increase distortion and print-through. Direct sunlight on the tapes or their containers is obviously to be avoided.

As signal loss can be caused by physical contaminants such as grease from the hands and electrostatic attraction of dust, archival master tapes should be stored in plastic bags within their containers. Polyethylene bags, 5 mil (0.12 mm) thick, and either sealed or folded over, are suitable. Public reference copies must, of course, be handled with care, but rigorous protection is impracticable. Signal loss can also be caused by magnetic fields – which are all the more dangerous for being invisible. All tapes should be kept in a magnetic environment not exceeding 10 oersteds. Normal power supplies have a negligible magnetic field, but the vicinity of high power lines or electrical distribution points should be avoided. Print-through, erasure and extraneous noise can be caused by placing tapes close to loudspeakers, microphones, transformers, bulk tape erasers, test meters, signal-level meters and fluorescent lamps. A distance of a foot between tapes and ordinary equipment is likely to be safe.

Archive master tapes should be stored on rigid spools not less than 7 inches in diameter. Smaller spools have such narrow hubs at the centre that the tape is very tightly curved and can become deformed. Spools without slots in the sides, or flanges, offer the best physical support and protection for archive masters. Tapes which will be used by interviewers, cataloguers, transcribers or the public are more convenient to handle and to view if the spools are transparent plastic with slots or windows.

Steel storage boxes for individual tapes have the advantage of durability, strength and ability to deflect stray magnetic fields. Sturdy plastic or cardboard containers are also suitable and are cheaper, but, for durability, cardboard should have a low acid content. In areas of high humidity cardboard is subject to fungal attack. Tape cartons should always be stored vertically (with the tapes on edge). The container for every copy of every reel of every interview should be labelled indelibly with the accession number and the informant's name. The most convenient way to order archive masters and copies is by accession number.

Tape should be shelved on secure racking. Wood has the merit of having no adverse effect on tapes, but steel shelving can protect by deflecting stray magnetic fields. Although high-carbon steel can retain a magnetic force, most steel shelves will not hold the charge they deflect. Only ferrous metal has these characteristics, of course; aluminium shelving offers no advantage.

Before storage, and after every use, tapes should be wound smoothly and evenly so that the tape is under even tension and no sections of it rise above the rest, making it susceptible to damage along the edges. Uneven tension can cause wrinkling and slippage. Playing a tape with repeated stopping and starting and changing of speeds results in a ridged and uneven wind, but all that is required to rectify the unevenness is to spool through the whole tape before returning it to the shelf. Most machines wind smoothly at normal recording and playback speeds and some do at high speeds; especially if matt-backed tape is used. Open-reel tape should be stored tail out – that is, it should have been spooled through from the beginning of the reel to the end – so that when it is to be used it is placed on the right-hand spool carrier of the playback machine and rewound to the left side before commencing play. Rewinding the tape before use reverses curvature and minimizes the chance of irritating pre-echo print-through.

Original recordings and archival masters (which may, of course be the same) should have been recorded at $7\frac{1}{2}$ inches (19 cm) per second. About 60 seconds (10 yards (9.5 metres) at $7\frac{1}{2}$ ips) of blank tape should be left at the beginning and end of each reel of the masters to safeguard against damage. Test tones or reference signals may be recorded as interviews are being copied on to archival master tapes – or at the beginning of standard-play originals. This can be done by recording a 1 kHz sine wave signal of 10 seconds' duration at 10 dB (3 VU) below actual peak level, followed by a few seconds' blank tape and then a 10 kHz signal at the same level. The great advantage is that the level of the test tones may be measured in future years to ensure that the original recording quality is being maintained. Deterioration can thus be measured and remedied before the tape sounds wrong to the casual listener, by which time it will be too late to rectify.

Routine inspection of the collection should take place at regular intervals – say, every other year. If the collection is too large for inspection of every item, samples may be selected. In addition to the reference signals, tapes should be checked visually for signs of brittleness, fungus, warping, adhesion of layers, or loss of the oxide coating. Some bodies have recommended annual rewinding of all tapes. This is not only impracticable for an archive with a large collection but may actually be more dangerous than leaving the tapes on the shelf. Even with care the tapes would be exposed to the possibility of ridging or uneven wind, breaking, or damage of the oxide coating.

If archival master tapes need to be transported, it is important to examine them briefly before and after the journey and to pack them in large batches for stability, standing on edge and well protected from vibration and stray magnetic fields. They should not be exposed to direct sunlight or extremes of temperature or left in exposed areas either en route or on arrival. It is generally safe to send individual tapes not intended for preservation purposes through the post, providing they are packaged securely. A padded mailing bag enclosing the tape's own container should give adequate physical protection. Archivists must, however, always be aware that tapes have been spoilt by magnetic fields – for example, in electric trains. Tapes being transported by train should not be placed on the floor of a train running on electrified track (this includes underground trains) or beside sliding electric doors. There have been no reports of damage from airport security checks.

Archivists should also be aware of fire risks. Polyester tape is not prone to spontaneous combustion but will burn if in contact with flames. The gases emitted are toxic. Carbon dioxide fire extinguishers are recommended by IASA: powder extinguishers will ruin the tapes, and water will cause nearly insurmountable drying problems.

Conduct of the interview

Some guidelines for conducting interviews have been discussed in Chapter 4, but there are some further considerations that apply more specifically to archives. Since the need for a degree of professionalism is even greater for an oral archive than for an individual interview, and interviewing facility and ability are acquired through experience, it makes sense for an archive to have its own permanent staff interviewers and/or to engage freelances on a fairly long-term basis, at least for a couple of years or for a series of interviews in a particular field.

A preliminary interview is on balance advisable for an oral archive, and, although this may be conducted over the telephone, a face-to-face meeting is more effective and provides the interviewer with the opportunity to assess the recording environment. Interviewers should give informants the option of being recorded on or away from their own territory but, whatever venue is agreed, it should be reasonably comfortable and free from frequent interruption and persistent background noise. Noises such as traffic, aircraft, clocks, voices, appliances or machinery and animals are obtrusive if they are regular or continuous. Interviewers should listen carefully and consider what steps can be taken – whether a window should be closed, a fluorescent lamp turned off or another room investigated. Adjustments will generally take only a few minutes and will result in a considerably improved recording. Since little effort is involved, it behoves individual oral historians to consider future archives and ensure that the recording environment is the best under the circumstances.

The most suitable rooms for recording are those with carpet, curtains and soft upholstery, because hard surfaces reflect sound and give a noticeable echoing effect on the tape. If the informant's office/workshop/laboratory is not a good recording environment, their home or a colleague's office or a room at a club may be more suitable. Interviewers need to have a very quiet room of their own to offer, and some informants may, in fact, prefer to come to the interviewer. There are, of course, subtle influences in the ownership or significance of the venue. Only one of these is that a recording studio proper (although it certainly establishes that the interviewer is serious) cannot help but give a more formal ambience and is likely to increase the tendency in an eminent informant, used to speaking or writing for public consumption, to address the interviewer as a journalist or a public meeting.

A further warning: beware of life's simple pleasures. Interviews should never be conducted outdoors: even if there are no birds, wasps, cars or neighbours, a gentle breeze blowing across an unshielded microphone is not merely obtrusive but can make speech unintelligible. Smoking makes some noise and may possibly cause slight damage to the tapes or equipment, but it may be the only way the informant can relax; there is no excuse for the interviewer. Eating and drinking, which similarly make noise and present risks, should be confined to the time before or after recording – or between tapes.

If the interviewer appears relaxed, confident and competent with the tape recorder, and shows no concern whatsoever once it is set up, it will tend to disappear into the furniture of the room. Since the interviewer has to keep an eye on the tape recorder – which can be done with rapid, unconcerned glances, particularly while the informant is looking elsewhere – the best position for the recorder is by the interviewer's side, on the side towards the informant, so that the interviewer does not have to turn sharply and noticeably to see it. The tape recorder is less obtrusive if it is on a low table, but should not be placed so low that the recording levels are difficult to see or to reach if necessary.

The recording-volume levels should be set before the interview formally begins and will need to be touched only very slightly, if at all. The level depends upon the individual speaker's voice but should be set rather low so that the needle is barely flickering, in order to minimize environmental noise or room acoustic and to avoid incurable voice distortions due to over-recording when the informant suddenly becomes excited or makes an emphatic point.

The only overt attention the interviewer need give to the equipment is a verbal identification at the beginning of each reel of tape within the interview. As each completed reel is removed from the machine, the interviewer should also label and number the box in which it is then placed.

Copyright and access

The copyright in the information in an oral history recording – that is, the informant's actual words – is the informant's own, even though the physical tape belongs to the interviewer or the archive and the copyright in the recording as a work is the property of the interviewer or archive. Therefore the interviewer/historian technically may not publish extracts from the interviews without the informant's permission, and archives may not make available any oral history recordings without copyright clearance. The informant's willingness to be interviewed gives no legal entitlement to access to the tapes; it is thus the responsibility of the individual researcher or the oral archive to make explicit arrangements.

All that is required is a clear, written statement, signed and dated by the informant. The precise wording will be determined by the situation, but the following is an example appropriate for archives, as used by the Imperial War Museum in London. The subject is discussed with each

informant, who has a chance to ask any questions. After the interviewer's last visit the informant is sent an individual letter of thanks
which also includes the following questions:

> In order that we may administer the tapes in accordance with your
> wishes would you please let me have your answers to the questions
> below:
>
> 1 May the Museum's users be granted access to the recordings and
>   any typescripts of them?
> 2 May the recordings and typescripts be used in the internal and
>   external educational programmes of the Museum?
> 3 May the Museum provide copies of the recordings and the
>   typescripts for its users?
> 4 Would you be prepared to assign your copyright in the
>   information in the recordings to the Trustees of the Imperial War
>   Museum? This would enable us to deal with such matters as
>   publication and broadcasting, should they arise, without having to
>   make prior reference to you. If you agree to this assignment it does
>   not, of course, preclude any use you might want to make of the
>   information in the recordings yourself.

It is best to include mention of both typescripts and recordings, even if
the interview is not to be transcribed at once, to avoid having to make a
separate agreement at a later date.

Some informants may wish to restrict access to the recording for a
certain number of years, or even to retain the copyright. In the latter case
the Imperial War Museum asks informants to confirm that copyright
will pass to the museum on their death and/or to name their executors. It
is frequently more difficult to settle conditions of deposit and access with
heirs or executors than with informants. In any event it is useful to make
the arrangements as straightforward as possible. One informant assigned
copyright to the Imperial War Museum with the stipulation that the
material be available only to friends of Republican Spain. As this was not
necessarily easy to ascertain, it was suggested that the informant retain
copyright himself so that he could ensure that his tape was used only by
people he thought were suitable. After consideration, the informant
decided to assign copyright unconditionally, thereby leaving administration to the museum.

One of the differences between the contributors to 'élite' oral history
and the rest of humanity is their – and other people's – concept of their
significance as individuals. Eminent informants are much more likely to

hesitate, to make ambiguous arrangements or to try to insist on closing even rather mundane and non-controversial records for thirty years. To the extent that they are in the public eye and are held responsible, they feel (and are) much more vulnerable and need reassurance and protection.

In addition to the imperative arrangements with contributors, archives may wish to include a statement on an order form used by visitors making explicit terms of sale or loan as a safeguard against abuse. For example, from the Imperial War Museum:

> The Department's recordings and transcripts are sold on the understanding that they are for the private use of the purchaser only. No public or commercial use of the material is permitted, neither may it be copied or otherwise reproduced in any form whatsoever, without the prior written permission of the Keeper of the Department of Sound Records.

In addition, the museum reserves the right to limit the quantity of recordings and transcripts that any single customer may purchase. Special agreements are drawn up with other archives or collecting centres giving them the right to hold Imperial War Museum oral history material (subject, of course, to the informants' wishes) on condition that it is available for reference purposes only and limited to the archive's premises, with any requests for copies to be referred to the original Imperial War Museum archive.

Museum visitors who wish to obtain copies of recordings or transcripts are asked to complete a very brief form stating their purposes. (This form also yields statistics on patterns of use of the oral history collection and so helps to improve the collection and the public service.) Permission is nearly always granted for use of the material. In cases of commercial, as opposed to scholarly, applications, a copyright or reproduction fee is charged. Where oral history material will be quoted or cited, authors are requested to use the footnote convention 'Ardizzone, Edward: oral history interview 004525/05; Imperial War Museum, London, 1979.'

Documentation and cataloguing

Despite the paperwork involved, it is essential that oral history archives keep methodical records both of their own interviewing procedure and of the contents of their collections. The purpose of the archive in acquiring, commissioning or conducting the interviews may be different from

that of the historian, teacher, broadcaster or biographer who eventually
seeks access to the collection. Future users will best be able to assess the
nature and relevance of the oral history material if they are able to study
the framework of the appropriate part of the collection – such features as
the criteria for selecting informants, and the topical project papers used
by the interviewers. Since it is obviously helpful if archives that merely
act as repositories for other people's oral history also can obtain this sort
of background information, individual collectors of oral history should
ideally adopt archivists' procedures in this respect.

Oral archives must also establish some form of catalogue describing
each item and directing users to informants and topics relevant to their
needs. A special problem of oral history tapes is that, unlike visual documentary evidence, their contents are not immediately available to
cataloguers or users. No book – or manuscript – classification system
will really be appropriate, and there is no satisfactory extant oral history
cataloguing system, although the Imperial War Museum and the
Museum Documentation Association are developing models. Whatever
approach an archive borrows, adapts or devises, it is important to operate
within the context of available resources and likely future trends. A
limited but methodical system encompassing the whole collection is both
more practical and more useful than an over-ambitious system covering
only a part of the collection. Prospects of using a computer-based system
may not be immediately likely, but as the appropriate technology
becomes more widespread – and less expensive – it is not only possible
but probable that oral history archives will wish or need to use
computerized information-retrieval systems. Therefore a computer-
compatible manual cataloguing system should be used, to avoid the need
for future recataloguing; and its rules should be unambiguous, fairly
detailed and applied with rigorous consistency.

For a specialist cataloguer working steadily for several hours every
day, it is easier and more efficient to catalogue directly from the tape,
perhaps wearing headphones for concentration, rather than from a
transcript.

The first stage of cataloguing is identification of the items in the collection. It is the interviewer's job to put a verbal label on to the beginning
of each tape, naming the informant and numbering each reel of the
interview. Each interview, regardless of duration, should be regarded as
a separate item and allocated a unique accession number from a single
consecutive series. (One interview may, of course, take place over several
days.) The accessions register provides an immediate inventory of the

collection as a whole, and the individual numbers identify and cross-refer the contents of the collection. Oral history interviews should be accessioned immediately upon acquisition – before technical processing, more detailed cataloguing and possible transcription. The only information required is the date, the informant's name, a very brief description or the title of the recording project, and the form or method of acquisition – assuming all material does not come from the same source. The accession number can be used to indicate the size of the acquisition; for example, in 004525/05 the first part of the number designates the individual interview and 05 indicates that it consists of five reels or tracks of tape. All copies of an interview, regardless of format (including transcripts), should have the same number.

The second stage of cataloguing is an individual card or form for each interview which identifies the informant and the circumstances of the interview. Relevant information includes: accession number; interviewee's full name and title or style, other or former names, decorations and qualifications, date of birth and (in due course) death, nationality; title of the series or project; interviewer's name; dates covered by interview; language; recording date and location; duration of recording, original medium and speed, recording quality; sponsoring organization; existence of copies and transcript; copyright, contractual restrictions; associated material (e.g. diaries, publications, photographs, relevant interviews in other collections); explanatory notes, subjective comments of interviewer (optional); date catalogued. The cataloguing should be carried out consistently and (with the exception of the optional, subjective section) impartially. Detailed guidelines and conventions will clarify points such as whether the date on which the recording was begun or completed is required, how accurate the timing of duration need be, whether the name and rank should describe the informant as he or she was when the interview was recorded or during the period covered in the interview – the last point applying particularly to women whose professional and social names may differ, to writers with pseudonyms and to eminent people who have acquired titles or honours late in life. Cross-references should, of course, be made for all names.

The archive will also wish to produce and maintain a personal file on each informant, amplifying the sketchy information in the catalogue entry – for example: place of birth, information about parents and siblings, education, marriage, career outline, publications. The informant's file will also contain correspondence relating to the interview and to copyright and access agreements, and interviewers' notes.

The informant's address should be confidential, as may other information in the file. This file will have the same accession number as the
informant's interview; where two or more separate and distinct interviews have taken place, all the numbers should be listed. Interviewees'
files are best arranged alphabetically rather than numerically.

The third stage of cataloguing is producing a summary of the subject
content of each interview to provide users with an objective, clear and
brief guide to the significant subjects discussed and the overall nature and
pattern of the interview. A synopsis of fifty to seventy-five words per
thirty minutes of recording is appropriate. The contents of each reel of
tape in an interview should be summarized, even if the same subject is
covered more than once. Individual reels may be further broken down by
timings made by means of a tape-driven cumulative stopwatch-type
timer (such as Reel-Time). The type of information to be included is:

> Description of events, conditions, objects and activities, with their
> locations and dates when possible
> Opinions and attitudes expressed by the informant; opinions he heard
> expressed about himself or others
> Personal recollections about other people
> Brief indication of the subject-matter of illustrative stories and
> anecdotes.

When preparing the interview synopsis, it must be borne in mind that
the information given rather than the questions asked is to be catalogued.

The fourth stage is to index the records – important because an index
allows users to appreciate the relevance and interrelationships of the
collection as a whole. Decisions will need to be made – based on the
archive's intentions, the nature of its users and its staff resources – about
the type of information to index. The simplest system is to list (with
reference to informant and accession and reel number) purely positively
identifiable and concrete names and terms – for example: places, people,
specific events, organizations, publications, equipment. The only
problems likely to arise here are in establishing conventions for identifying and cross-referencing variables such as personal and place names.
Conceptual indexing creates much more complicated problems for both
cataloguer and user but is likely to increase the value of the collection and
broaden the range of potential users. In this case it is the cataloguer's job
to create or assimilate, and work consistently within, a controlled
vocabulary of key words or preferred terminology. The cataloguer will
need detailed schedules and the user a chart or guide to the classification

hierarchies. The nature of the archive will dictate the appropriate level of detail for indexes. The caveat about computer compatibility is particularly important with regard to conceptual indexing, and advice from a librarian or archivist with suitable training and experience is desirable.

A fifth stage is dissemination of information. The archive will probably wish to circulate information about its oral history collection, both to potential users and to other archives or institutions. Depending on the size of the collection, such listings could cover all holdings or could be divided into appropriate chronological periods or subject fields. A computer-based system can quickly and easily generate lists, and manual compilation is straightforward if cataloguing has been consistent. The type of information appropriate would be: informant's name, accession number, identifying occupation, organization or rank, dates covered by recording, duration of recording, existence of transcript, access and copyright restrictions, and either the reel-by-reel catalogue summary or a brief descriptive paragraph.

The compilation of technical-description records has already been discussed. In a computer-based system this would be stored with the other documentation.

Transcription

Although orally delivered material can be reproduced fully and precisely only in an aural form, it is most expedient for oral history archives to maintain their collections both in tape and transcript form. (The term transcript is used here in its common meaning, a written rendition of the recording. The BBC uses the term to refer to tape copies of tapes, such as those sent to other radio stations.)

The significance of the transcript is both as a finding aid to the tape itself and as the only way that a verbal document may be reproduced in print. The average rate of conversational speech is less than 200 words per minute, which is therefore the average rate of listening. A trained ear can comprehend speech at two or more times that speed, but even this is slower than average reading speed: printed material can thus be skimmed considerably more quickly. Further, the contents of a tape are not physically accessible without playback equipment and processes. A transcript is of such convenience that it is a luxury bordering on necessity. A historian may wish to use a quotation in a book; a broadcaster may need a text on which to make editing marks, even though the final product will not be written.

Transcribing is an extremely slow (and expensive) procedure. An accurate transcript of standard speech will take an experienced transcription typist approximately nine hours per recorded hour, and additional time will be taken checking the typescript. If the speaker is indistinct, or uses a large proportion of foreign place names or scientific terms, or has a regional accent to which the typist is not accustomed, the ratio of typing time to tape can be significantly increased.

When an archive is not able, or does not wish, to transcribe all interviews, some criteria must be established for the selection of interviews to be so favoured. To transcribe half of the interviews accurately is more useful than to transcribe all in such a haphazard manner as to necessitate more work in the future. The selection criteria will be based on the archive's particular requirements and interests, and on analysis of the anticipated needs of its users.

The form of transcript that is most useful is an accurate verbatim account of the interview with the informant's (and interviewer's) own words and grammar retained. The typist should do no editing but produce as literate (rather than literary) a document as possible through appropriate use of punctuation, sentences and paragraphs. Oral history transcribing is a somewhat specialized skill, and training as an audio-typist is not likely to be an advantage. Because of the concentration involved, this job is particularly suited to part-timers. The typist will need a set of conventions and guidelines appropriate to the particular archive, covering such points as structure and layout, punctuation, abbreviations, capitalization and use of figures. A wide left-hand margin is useful, to leave space for a binding process and to accommodate timing or indexing numbers. In addition, it makes sense to provide the typist with lists of technical terms and unusual names specific to each interview. The most suitable person to work with the transcriber on any difficult passages is the interviewer, who knows the material best. The interviewer is also likely to be the best person to check the transcript, though it may be more expedient for a cataloguer to perform this task. Each archive will find its own best balance – and, of course, in small archives these three roles may, in fact, be performed by the same person.

Whether the transcript should be sent to the informant for correction or comment is a point that has been discussed in Chapter 4. Some eminent informants, particularly those who are accustomed to seeing their own work in print, may react with dismay or even indignation. Few people speak in private in the style in which they write for the public, and over-zealous correction will make the transcript less useful as a finding aid to the tape, and may even change the meaning of what was actually said. Additions or amendments – other than grammatical – are best added to the transcript, if the informant wishes, as appendices, with a note at the beginning calling attention to their existence and origin. Factual slips of the tongue, such as an incorrect date, may be corrected in the text using square brackets.

While the transcript is being checked against the tape for accuracy, an indication of timing may be made in the margin and later transferred to the master copy. Alternatively, the typist may enter these figures. It is more convenient to use standard intervals (e.g. two minutes) than to try to time each question or change of topic individually. A tape-driven, cumulative stopwatch-type timer (such as Reel-Time) is required, since digital counters are idiosyncratic to each machine.

The archive should hold two copies of the transcript, the master for preservation and a carbon or photocopy for public use. To keep these presentable, notes for corrections should be made on another carbon or photocopy, or at least on a separate sheet of paper. The master transcripts should be typed on good-quality paper and kept as loose sheets in a separate file for each informant; copies for public access will need some form of binding. Photographs of the informant at the time of the interview and at the time of the events under discussion may be dry-mounted and bound with the public transcript. Various commercial processes are suitable for binding in hard covers or in soft covers with a rigid spine and are available from photocopying shops as well as printers and bookbinders. Ring or clip binders sold at stationers are not suitable if they are easy for users to open and perhaps remove pages. Though the expense is greater, it is more useful for each transcript to be bound separately. They are best shelved in alphabetical order, with accession number also indicated.

Transcripts will always have a role in oral history but if the tapes are well recorded and convenient they will be increasingly used. At the Imperial War Museum the ratio of users' requests for tapes to transcripts to tape and transcript consulted together is 5:2:1. (This applies, of course, to tapes that are available in transcript form.) For purchases the ratio is 15:6:1.

6

Oral projects:
methodology and
practice

Methodology

The first chapter delineated three main types of oral history exercise: the individual researcher, conducting his own interviews for a study on which he is working; the oral project, whereby an institution initiates its own interview programme focusing on its own history for its own internal purposes; and the oral archive, where an institution committed to research either conducts its own interviews or collects those conducted by others (or both) into subjects of recent history (other than its own) for immediate or eventual use by researchers and other interested parties.

It is a common experience for employees – often those who have put in long service or support – to wish to interview those concerned with an earlier period of the history of the institution concerned. The desire to do so is often prompted by the feeling that if steps are not taken, part of the collective history of the organization will be irrevocably lost with the death of important early figures.

The methodology for establishing an oral project has much in common with that of an individual researcher, as described in Chapter 4. In addition to adopting individual researchers' methods, those wishing to establish an oral project should consider the following issues which, if properly thought through, can make all the difference between a failure and a successful project.

Reasons for the project

If a clear conception of why the project is being conducted is not borne in mind throughout the research, much of it is likely to be fruitless, and the fund of goodwill on the part of interviewees (which an internal oral project usually finds at its inception among those willing to talk) will become quickly exhausted. The vague idea that it would be interesting or fun to build up an oral project is insufficient. One must be clear what the objectives are, and constantly relate the procedure to those objectives. For example, if an eventual book is the prime aim of establishing the project, one should gather only material that is likely to be of use in the book and consult the relevant written and documentary material to discover what is already in existence. If the project is to produce material for an exhibition on the institution's history, the material should be appropriate to the needs of the likely audience. The purpose of the work also affects the choice of recording medium.

Time and money available

If it can be decided at the outset how much time and money are available, then the interview schedule can be properly planned. This will ensure that a *balance* of relevant people is interviewed (one cannot, of course, usually see everyone who remembers relevant information), and that there is sufficient money to produce transcriptions from the tapes and handle the necessary correspondence. If transcripts are to be produced (as most prefer because of their accessibility), adequate provision of time must be made. A one-hour interview can take up to ten hours to type and check, and perhaps a further five hours to re-check if the transcription is to be sent to the interviewee for his comments. (Time can be saved here if a word-processor is employed, but that costs more money.) It would be unwise, therefore, to budget for a secretary (who would have to be adept at audio typing) to type and edit more than three to five hours of interviews a week.

Confidentiality

In order that confidentiality can be maintained, the problem of access to, and use of, interview material should be dealt with at the outset. The following is one of many possible formulas that one could adopt. Each project should appoint an officer (perhaps the legal adviser, if there is one) as trustee of the material. Before the interview begins, the interviewee should be told about and shown a form that stipulates the conditions governing access to and use of the material supplied. The form, which may be completed either at the time of the interview or after a transcript has been submitted, might offer three choices, from which the interviewee has to select one.

1 The interview is to be confidential between the interviewer (and transcribing secretary) and the interviewee. No one else is to see or hear it during his lifetime – or for a period of, say, 10–30 years without his prior written permission, to be presented to the trustee.
2 Senior officers of the institution may also, should they wish, see or hear his record without his permission, but, should others wish to see or hear it during his lifetime, his written permission is required.
3 No restrictions are to govern access to his record.

Some institutions prefer not to allow interviewees to have any say in the use to be made of their interview (whether in a book, article, film or exhibition); others prefer to offer interviewees the chance of vetting before use any passages they regard as particularly sensitive. Still others feel that interviewees' confidence will be gained if the policy is adopted that, before any direct or indirect quotation be made from their records during their lifetime, their prior approval be sought; this procedure is seldom found to lead to interviewees restricting use. Whichever approach regarding use is adopted, the rules governing quotation of the material should again be made absolutely clear to the interviewee *before he begins to talk.* It might well be desirable to ask interviewees to sign a separate clause transferring the copyright to the institution.

Contemporary oral projects

Oral projects can in addition have an important contemporary and historical purpose. Many leaders say after their retirement that they were so swept up by the day-to-day action during their period in office that they were unable to see themselves and events objectively. Oral history techniques can help to allow individuals to view themselves when in office more clearly. We have drawn up a ten-point questionnaire, which a sympathetic interviewer could put to the leaders of an institution at regular intervals – say, every twelve months. Interviews would be taped and transcribed, and the transcript(s) of previous sessions would be shown to the individuals after each session to help them assess their progress and view their work with more objectivity. The records would then also serve as a valuable resource for future historians, their contemporary nature helping to ensure a high degree of factual accuracy in recording the unfolding of policy and thinking. Indeed, because of their doubts about the distortions of longer-term memory, some critics would regard such contemporary and regular recording of information as the *only* valid role of oral history. Suitable questions might be as follows:

1 What have been your major endogenous problems (i.e. those originating from within your own area or responsibility) in the last year? How have you faced up to them? How have you sought to ameliorate them?

2 What have been your major exogenous problems (i.e. those originating from outside your own area or responsibility) in the last year? How have they been met?

3 What have been your personal and your area's successes in the last year? What or who was responsible for them? How will you ensure continued openness to the same or different stimuli in the future?

4 What new directions has your area embarked upon in the last year? Why were these departures taken? If practices or policies remain unchanged, have they been considered afresh?

5 How and how well have you maintained contact with subordinates in your area in the last year? Do you feel that the vertical communication has been satisfactory? How might it be improved?

6 How and how well have you maintained contact with peers throughout the whole organization in the last year? Do you feel the horizontal communication has been satisfactory? How might it be improved?

7 How and how well have you maintained contact and obtained information about comparable external organizations/your competitors in the last year?

8 How well informed, generally, do you feel about local/national/world-wide developments and new ideas related to your own area of responsibility? What relevant journals, newspapers and books have you read? Have you had sufficient time for reading and thinking?

9 Has the pressure and volume of work increased or decreased in the last year? Do you feel that you have been working too hard? To what extent do you delegate? Could you delegate more? Have you allowed yourself sufficient time for relaxation, for reflection?

10 How would you describe the nature of your job? Has that perception changed over the last year? Are you able to maintain a balance of interest over your range of responsibilities, or have you focused

too much upon one area? Do you decide how you spend your time, or do external events dictate? How could you strike a better balance?

Oral projects in practice

This section will discuss a small number of projects that highlight the potential, and some of the problems, of historical oral projects.

Academic institutions have shown a peculiar readiness to interview their own teaching staff, both current and retired.[1] The University of Reading has for some time been recording retired academic staff,[2] as has the University of Liverpool. The archivist responsible at Liverpool, Adrian Allan, has established an oral history programme to cover former and current members of staff, both academic and technical, who have served the university for a long period.[3] Academics interviewed include former professors of physics, education, French, geography, botany, social science and medicine. Good use has already been made of relevant transcripts by Emeritus Professor Thomas Kelly in his centenary history of the university, *For Advancement of Learning* (1981). In advance of the interviews, Adrian Allan supplies the person concerned with the topics and questions he wishes to explore; sometimes this has meant sending them an *aide-mémoire*. This includes questions such as: why did you join the university staff? what did you earn? what work did you do? what were your students like? how was your department organized? how did it function during the last war?

The Polytechnic of Central London more modestly has been recording individuals who played a prominent part in building up the organization. 'A gentle programme of two luminaries a year' is planned.[4]

The potential for oral projects of businesses has been recognized for a long time. J. H. Clapham in 1906, for example, called for the training of interviewers to collect 'the memories of businessmen' which were, he considered, 'the best original authorities' for recent economic history: with their death is lost 'some of the most valuable records of nineteenth century history'.[5] Little progress was in fact made in Britain by firms recording their employees. Seventy-five years after Clapham, Sir Peter Parker has restated the case:

> On the importance of interviewing, I have always felt that British industry has been miserably unimaginative in not setting up archives of recorded experience in industry. It should be a national objective to tape-record experience: there is experience, unwritten, abundantly available to skilled interviewers.[6]

A number of companies have had their histories written (as described in Chapter 8), but very few have instigated and conducted interview programmes for the benefit of future books or projects. ICI were probably the pioneers in Britain in establishing such an oral project.[7] The former company secretary, J. D. Cousin, recalled:

> ICI had commissioned two volumes of history, by Dr W. J. Reader, taking the story up to 1952. During the course of researching the volumes it became clear that talks with serving and retired staff were valuable in adding flesh to the dry bones of the written records. Some of the retired staff being interviewed were quite elderly, and it seemed to us that we ought for the future to establish a procedure for interviewing people as they retired so that their oral comments would be available alongside the written material. We believed that all events were reasonably documented, but thought that it would be helpful to give people who had been involved in some of the key decisions the chance to record what they felt about the issues.

Arrangements were accordingly made for each retiring director to be interviewed by W.J. Reader; as the writer of the two volumes of the ICI history, it was felt he would know how to structure the interview so that it would be readily usable by anyone working on further volumes of the history. As a general rule interviews have been with those associated with the ICI main board, rather than with those who had been responsible for running some part of the group, because it was the former who had been involved with the major group issues which would be the concern of future historians. In order that people might comment freely, the record of each interview is confidential and is kept by the Company Secretary. W. J. Reader explained the differences between his approach in interviews for the ICI oral project and those he conducts for his own writing of company history as an individual researcher.

> The questions were similar, but for a book interview I would take more for granted: it was necessary to be more selective. But for an oral project interview, I tried to take everything down that they said, and cover a wider area – asking about personalities, policies, assessments.

All interviews were taped and transcribed; the first took place in 1966, and over forty have subsequently been recorded.

To assist any company considering embarking upon an interview project, we set out a list of questions. The model we have chosen is for a multinational mining house for the period 1945–75, but the questions can be readily adapted for different types of corporation. The questions – which would serve as a basic aide-memoire and would be adopted for different interviewees – are divided into those appropriate for headquarters personnel and for those who work in the field. First the headquarters personnel.

1 The subject's entry into and departure from the Company, and his intervening work.
2 The development of projects – the stages, key figures and main problems in that development.
3 Personal contributions of leading figures with whom the interviewee worked, and assessment of those contributions.
4 Relations between subsidiary associated companies and the parent company, and the change over time.
5 How projects were financed, deals put together, and mergers effected. Background to unsuccessful mergers and deals.
6 The background behind all other major decisions (e.g. vertical integrations, expansions into new mineral/metal areas).
7 How the body in which the individual worked (main company, subsidiary, department) was organized: the role of the boards throughout all stages in the post-war story, key figures on it, and other key company bodies, e.g. executive committees.
8 The development of the commercial, financial, exploration, technical etc., departments at headquarters.
9 Relations with national and state governments in the relevant countries: how often the company met them, where, why and with what result.
10 Relations with companies in similar fields, but not within the group.
11 Key figures, philosophies and strategies in, and other factors behind, company expansion 1945–75.
12 When and why the various companies became aware of the non-commercial considerations, e.g. environmental and social.
13 The peculiar characteristics of the metals/minerals market with which the individual was concerned at different stages: how and why decisions were taken.
14 Financial questions: decisions to go public, change shareholdings etc.
15 Employment policy. Strategies and philosophies towards employees; innovators in the personnel management area; attitudes to trade unions; causes of labour unrest and solutions to the problem.

These question areas list fifteen areas of relevance more to headquarters employees. Below are listed questions to be directed more to those who worked at or saw developments in the various group mines and plants around the world.

1 *Exploration/initial purchase*

Who initially found the mine; how and when was it found, or why was it decided to purchase it; what equipment or techniques were used if found by the group; how were the exploration rights arrived at or how was the mine purchased; how did the geologists and technicians interact with headquarters; how did headquarters react to the news of the discovery?

2 *Evaluation and planning*

Who was responsible for evaluating the content of the mine (or worth of new project); what techniques were employed; who was responsible for organising the pilot project; what were the peculiar characteristics encountered at each mine e.g. adverse climate, low grade orebody; to what extent were employees from elsewhere in the group taken on; to what extent were lessons applied from other mines both inside and outside the group; was there a difficult local political position; who managed and how fared discussions with the national (and regional) government? Why were the considerations behind the degree of vertical and horizontal integration taken?

3 *Finance*

Who arranged the financing; what methods were employed; were any unusual features employed; how was the ratio of equity to loan capital arrived at; which banks and financial markets were utilized, and for what reasons?

4 *Construction*

Who took the major decisions on the shape of the plant (shovels, conveyors, crushers, concentrator, filters etc.) and infrastructure (town, roads, power stations, ports, railways); which engineers and contractors were employed, and for what reasons were they selected; how did they fare; how were they supervised?

5 *Environmental*

How prominently did environmental considerations feature; what steps were taken to minimize land and air pollution; did environmental initiatives occur as a result of internal (i.e. at the mine) initiative, headquarters pressure or as a reaction to outside pressure groups/government requirements?

6 *Labour/social*

What were the peculiar labour problems; what were the peculiar township problems; how was the labour recruited, how were they

trained, and were there any problems; how well did the labour perform at the construction stages; how well after operation began;
who in particular was responsible for managing the labour?

7 *Commercial*

Who decided at what output the mine should produce; what were
the reasons and what methods were employed in arriving at the conclusion; who managed the marketing of the produce; what negotia-
tions took place and what special methods were employed?

8 *Organizational*

How was the management structure organised at the mine; how was
the Board organized; which decisions were taken on location, which
were referred to the local company and which to London; if two or
more companies were major shareholders, how did they relate to
each other and to operations at the mine; if a major partner was
sought, what were the reasons, and if decided to make it a group
enterprise solely, again, what were the reasons?

9 *Operation*

What were the main problems encountered after production began;
how was the initial concept modified; what commercial, financial
and organizational changes were found to be necessary; how well did
the equipment perform technically?

10 *Conclusions*

What were the major problems/lessons learned in the development
of the mine; what were the reasons for the mine's success/failure?

The future of oral projects

Oral projects are likely to be the largest growth area of oral history, in
part because comparatively little such recording has so far taken place,
and in part because there are many organizations that would like to
record their former employees or members, but have yet to get round to
it. The problems with this work need, however, to be clearly spelt
out. (1) Some organizations embark on projects without considering
whether the money could be better spent on putting their written record
in order: many pearls lie hidden on shelves and in boxes, and money in
almost every case could be better deployed weeding and cataloguing this
material, if not already done, than on conducting a programme of interviews. (2) Once word spreads that the organization is conducting interviews, people will start to notice who is being interviewed, and the
possibilities for causing offence are large if a man or woman not selected

for interview interprets this as a comment upon their contribution to the institution. Yet if one leans over too far to assuage wounded pride, the interview needs to be thought out at the outset, and, if necessary, a notice could appear in an appropriate place explaining that a programme of interviews is being conducted, but that only a very limited number can be interviewed. (3) Institutions, unless very large, find it hard to absorb into their organization an oral history exercise. Although senior figures might give the project at first their blessing and encouragement, their minds are soon taken over by more pressing concerns, and the work may find itself sinking to a low priority pastime. It might, therefore, be better to conduct the oral project in a short burst, rather than to allow it to spread out over a number of years. (4) Finally, as noted at the beginning of the chapter, an oral project needs to have established for itself clearly defined objectives, and to relate all questions to those aims. Good intentions are not enough.

But if such considerations are borne in mind, the potential for satisfying and satisfactory projects is considerable. For school or college history, pupils or undergraduates can perhaps be selected to record some interviews, and they will learn much by the process. Or an institution might prefer its own employees, senior or junior, to conduct the interviews. Alternatively they might prefer to ask or employ an outsider to conduct the interviews, who could bring a more professional, and a more detached, attitude to the work.

7

The evaluation and use
of oral evidence

To extract oral evidence is only part of the story. Two key questions remain: how is its worth to be assessed, and how is it to be actually employed in writing? These are related but distinct questions and will be examined separately.

Evaluation

The central distinction that we have made between categories of evidence is not between oral and written evidence, but between documentary and reported evidence (as explained in Chapter 1). Documentary evidence is not, of course, immune from the need for careful assessment. As Charles Wilson remarks:

> Documents by themselves can be as misleading as human memory – and even the most clear and honest memory is often at fault: interpretation becomes a task without end or certainty. It is a sobering and gruelling discipline but one which has its moral for the day when the apprentice turns back to those centuries whose witnesses have long since ceased to be available for cross-examination.[1]

But when evaluating oral evidence we find many tests apply equally to all forms of reported evidence; some are of direct relevance just to oral history.

Assessing reported evidence in general

If the evidence purports to be reporting fact, it may be an eyewitness account, or it may be second-hand evidence (i.e. 'reported' reported evidence). Some witnesses will imply (perhaps to show they are 'in the know') that they were present when in fact they were not: cross-questioning will establish the facts of the matter. Even if the informant *was* present, and has perfect recall, his recollection may still not be accurate, because he might not be in possession of certain facts without which he cannot properly understand what is taking place, or he might not *physically* be in a position to observe all that is taking place and may have missed a crucial occurrence. Not even a camera or tape recorder can comprehensively record the events of Parliament. And even with perfect recall, and possessing *all* the relevant facts and 100 per cent observation, an informant still cannot give an objective picture because subconscious selection processes will always affect the recollection of events. Moreover, reminiscences can also be affected by what an informant has subsequently learned about an event. As Christopher Thorne has said:

> no matter how self-critical and objective witnesses may be (and obviously they vary enormously in these respects) they cannot 'unlearn' what they've come to know subsequently of what came after the moment or period about which they're being questioned. Their evidence may be first-hand, but it isn't contemporary.[2]

If the evidence does *not* purport to be fact, but is presented as a personal assessment, one needs to know whether it is the informant's own personal assessment, and, if so, for how long, and under what circumstances, the informant was able to make the observation on which his assessment is based – in other words, the *conditions* of his assessment. The distinction between a fact and an interpretation is not clear-cut, but interviewers should still try to be sure that they know which they are asking for and which is being given.

Since the subjective element is more significant in reported than in documentary evidence, therefore, it is helpful to gather as much information as one can about the person supplying the evidence, in order to discover *why* a particular statement has been made. The more strongly people feel about a subject, or the stronger their sense of rightness, or of having been misunderstood, and so on, the more their evidence is likely to be distorted. For this reason some argue that reported evidence can be more valuable the further from the events it is recorded, because, as the feelings ebb in intensity, so is an informant's true testimony less likely to be so distorted by personal feelings. Paradoxically, then, what occurred or was felt at a certain point might, under certain circumstances, be better recorded some years after the events than at the time. So, as with documentary evidence, a consideration of the purpose of any piece of reported evidence is essential in making a correct evaluation.

Similarly, the effect that the recipient of the reported evidence might have on that testimony must be taken into account. Everyone writes differently to different people, of course, depending on the intimacy of the relationship, on whether the recipient is successful or not, and so on. It is more difficult to speak of a 'recipient' when discussing diaries, but nevertheless there always is one, even if it is only the author of them, because diaries are written for a purpose – for companionship, to let off steam, as a working reference book, for publication, etc. Again one must find out in order to evaluate the evidence correctly.

In a contemporary oral history interview, particularly if on radio or television, the recipient is likely to be the public at large and the evidence geared to putting over a particular point of view; whereas, in an oral history interview for an interviewer's own private use, the recipient is usually just the interviewer. As L. A. Dexter has argued:

> [Interviewers] must remember that interviewees, usually, are not engaging in undirected monologues but are, on the contrary, addressing themselves to specific conceptions of a specific audience. And ordinarily conceptions of a specific audience are *in part* determined by the characteristics of the interviewer as perceived by the interviewee.[3]

Dexter cites analytic and experimental evidence to back up this assertion. Because of this central feature of oral history, oral history archives should provide information on interviewers and interview context (including immediate environment), to help one evaluate what has been said. (Is, for example, the interviewer a senior professor or a young journalist?) Interviewers for oral archives should try to be as neutral as possible, to minimize distortion and reaction, and should also ask themselves *how* their presence and questions are affecting the interviewee, and hence the response.

Assessing oral history evidence in particular

Unlike researchers reading already existing reported evidence – be it in the form of a letter, diary or even an oral archive or media interview – interviewers collecting oral evidence can take a number of steps when conducting interviews to aid evaluation. The experience of the legal profession might be relevant here.

In English law, when it is necessary to establish what happened on a particular occasion, reliance is placed almost exclusively on oral evidence. The law of evidence is an established field of law, and comprises rules that have been developed over many years. The concern is to establish facts, rather than the witness's interpretation of those facts, and three general principles may be extracted from the procedures employed for this purpose.

1 According to the 'hearsay' rule, second-hand evidence is not admissible. English law stresses that evidence must be based solely on direct personal experience.
2 More significant, perhaps, for oral history, is that English law does not generally find acceptable evidence that has been written down after careful reflection. The principle is that the witness wherever possible should be present in person to be questioned, and that he should not produce and read a prepared statement (i.e. written evidence).
3 English law does not permit a witness to volunteer evidence; it can be extracted only by direct question and answer. Cross-examination (questioning of a witness by counsel for the party who did not call that witness) modifies a main danger of oral evidence – that a partisan witness can present the evidence in the way he wishes.

English law sets so much store by *oral* evidence partly for historical reasons, and partly because in many cases no documentary evidence can be found. But its main justification is that, experts argue, seeing someone answering questions at the time provides good opportunities for evaluation, and much better than when a witness presents or reads written evidence.

The claim of contemporary and recent oral history to serious consideration has much to do with the ability of researchers to question and assess eye-witnesses while the evidence is being given, and the following methods can be used by interviewers to help them evaluate that evidence.

1 They can continually ask the follow-up question, 'Is that what you felt at the time?'
2 They can return to asking about the same issue from different tacks at different stages in the interview.
3 They can mark out in advance some specific facts – such as dates, names and places – to ask at some stage during the interview, to test out how precise the informant's memory is in general and, if necessary, for specific periods in the past. Bernard Crick suggests that a way to test accuracy of memory might be 'even feeding them with

false information to see whether they readily agree'.[4]

4 They can observe the interviewee with close (but not too apparent) attention. Although the informant is not in the witness box, and one should therefore guard against putting him on to the defensive, nevertheless, by maintaining eye contact as suggested in Chapter 4, one can gauge his responses. Hearing the informant's voice and observing his physical reactions, one can gain a 'feel' for the interviewee which often would not be apparent from reading what he has written. The degree of anxiety on the informant's part can, with most people, be a guide to the quality of his testimony: if his eyes are continually avoiding your own, or if he is struggling to convince you of a certain point, one should generally be more suspicious. Often it is when the interviewee is not *trying* to convince you of anything nor going out of his way to offer strong opinions, but answering your questions in a calm, direct and constructive way, that the testimony is at its most reliable. Over-anxiety on the informant's part is not always prompted by sinister intent, however. As Philip Williams found, a genuine desire to please can be a hazard: 'helpfulness could itself be dangerous, leading some people who had no idea of the right answers to questions to guess wildly instead of saying that they did not know.'[5] Need for caution on a similar front was pointed out by another respondent in our survey: 'The ones who are keenest to be interviewed, who approach the researcher rather than vice versa, are likely to have a particular axe to grind.'[6]

5 Interviewers, with their ability to summon evidence into being, can compare and contrast accounts. Without saying 'X says this; what do you think?', they can simply ask 'What do you think of this proposition?' Charles Raab describes an approach he and Andrew McPherson found successful when researching into the Scottish education system:

> People tended to know each other and to have interacted over a long period, and could tell us not only about themselves but about others. We could thus 'triangulate' interviewees' accounts of the same events or issues which they participated in or observed from different vantage-points. This helped us on specific areas where we sought information in some depth. We could try out interpretations and hypotheses on different people and see how they reacted.[7]

In the last resort, however, after all these questions have been considered and taken into account, researchers will be left with their own judgement, which explains why oral history can be so challenging.

Using oral history

There are two main types of book or article using oral evidence: interview-based works, where oral evidence forms the greater part of the text; and works for which oral evidence is just one source among many and where the authorial presence is far more in evidence. It is the latter which are more prevalent in academic writing and on which our attention will focus, but brief reference will first be made to the former.

Interview-based works

The form has not been as widely exploited by academics as one might have expected. The authorial element can never be absent from these books and articles, because even if interviews are printed verbatim, with the interviewer's questions edited out, the very fact that certain questions have been asked (and certain people interviewed) means that some selection has taken place. Yet the extent of the authorial element varies – from works like *Felix Frankfurter Reminisces*, where the presence and character of the subject/interviewee emerge from the interview without interference, to interview-based articles such aş John Mortimer's, where the author/interviewer tries to evoke some of the atmosphere of the interview by describing the scene and the interviewee's reactions. If the authorial presence is too intrusive, it can stifle the subject and communicate rather more of the author than the person interviewed. Other works strike a balance. One example is *The Politics of Education* (1971), which examines the role of the Education Minister by means of interviews between Maurice Kogan (an academic and former official at the Department of Education and Science) and two former Ministers of Education, Edward Boyle and Anthony Crosland.[8] The book is divided into three sections of approximately equal length: in the first the author/interviewer surveys some of the issues to be discussed by the ministers, separately, in the following two sections. A clear authorial statement of views and objectives is thus followed by the evidence of the two specialists, who respond to fairly short questions such as 'What impact do MPs have on educational policy making?', 'Who decides whether an issue gets to Cabinet or not?', 'But can Ministers be run by civil servants?' In this way, the opinions of both author/interviewer and interviewee are presented, and the context of the interviews is made apparent, but the evidence itself is not cluttered by authorial comment. Whether the material is presented in an unbiased way as possible, and whether the author/interviewer's presence is minimal or very much in evidence, what is important is that readers should be able to discover what is going on and that the status of the evidence be clarified.

Non-interview-based works

There are six main ways in which authors can present oral evidence.

1 Absorbed into the text without any reference to sources. This is the usual form in political science, 'instant' or contemporary histories and journalism.
2 Absorbed into the text but with an anonymous source in a footnote or endnote indicating that in an unspecified way oral evidence had been used as a source in the sentence or paragraph; for example, 'Interview with a junior minister in the Wilson government', or simply 'Private information' or 'Private interview'. This form is used most often in contemporary or recent history.
3 As 2, but with the name of the interviewee mentioned, as 'Interview with Lord Smith'. This system is the most commonly used in recent or modern histories. The name can also appear with the place, and sometimes with the date, of the interview, as 'Interview with Lord Smith, Tunbridge Wells, 1.1.83'. Some authors also like to indicate that it was a *personal* interview, or an archive interview, and to this end some oral archives specify the form in which their material, if cited, is to be used.
4 Direct quotation from the interview (or a paraphrase) can be made in the text, with footnote or endnote references to the interview are usually provided. If an author does find it advantageous to quote, the interviewee's permission must be sought (unless the author has *carte blanche* in an interview's use). Authors quoting (rather than paraphrasing) need to decide whether they will quote verbatim, in the spontaneous but erratic form of human speech, or in polished prose. Nikolai Tolstoy, for example, writes: 'I always quoted absolutely word-for-word from the tape.' He did this not just when informants were giving general views about the past but also when they were reconstructing a conversation. 'This is, of course, to some extent pedantry,' he does, however, point out, 'since accounts of firsthand speech after thirty years cannot be accurate, even when it is the protagonist talking.'[9] The advantages of paraphrase or quotation over merely incorporating the evidence in one's own text are that it provides variety and colour, especially when a text is suffering from a mass of detailed and impersonal factual material, and it can help to make a point more emphatically.

5   As 4, but the fact that oral history evidence is employed is specifically
    mentioned in the text, as in the form 'Lord Smith later recalled in
    interview that . . .' (when paraphrasing) or 'As Lord Smith later
    recalled in interview . . .' (when quoting). This form has been used
    by Martin Gilbert,[10] and also by Bernard Crick, who writes: 'I was
    vastly impressed with the unreliability of human memory, and
    formed the view that if one does have to rely on memory alone, one
    should make the point very clear in one's text.'[11]

6   Answer *and* question can be included in the text. This form is rarely
    used in non-interview-based works, though it was adopted in Nigel
    Nicolson's *Alex* (1973).

The form found most satisfactory will depend upon the individual
author and the circumstances. Journalists or writers of 'instant' history
can no more be expected to write in their text 'As the Chancellor told me
in the corridor at the Commons last week . . .' than writers of modern
history (if they have interviewed) should be forgiven for providing
extensive references to written evidence but omitting all reference in
their sources to oral history evidence. However, if interviews are to be
mentioned, and where it is not clear whether an interview was a personal
one or for an archive or the media, it is useful to indicate who conducted
the interview; it may also be helpful to state where an interview took
place and, even more so, *when* the interview took place – with Lord
Smith when still in office, soon after his retirement, or a long time after,
for example. Multiple interview references (e.g. 'Passage based on interviews with Lords Brown, Jones and Smith) can save space while revealing the range of sources, but they provide no clue as to the exact role of
the evidence from each interview; for that reason, they should perhaps be
avoided. Finally, some references to oral evidence where this has not been
directly quoted do not make it clear whether the sentence or passage to
which the note applies is what the interviewee actually said or believed,
or whether evidence from the interview was merely used or considered
by the author when writing the passage in question. Wherever possible,
the role of each piece of oral evidence should be made clear.

Hugh Trevor-Roper has written:

> The main purpose of footnotes is to indicate the documentary source
> of a statement, so that, if it should be doubted or need revision in the
> light of other evidence, it can be checked and any error isolated. But
> where the source is an oral interrogation of which only the author has
> the text, anything more than a general reference seems pointless:

what is the point of recommending a reader to check a source which is out of his reach?[12]

But this argument, although logical, does not take into account the interview which might be available elsewhere, in an oral history or media archive; or indeed the author might have decided to preserve a recording, transcript or notes of his interview for eventual consultation by interested scholars. Indeed, even if others can never see or hear the original interview, footnotes, whether general or specific, reveal what the source was, and indicate to readers that it was not a printed source that they might want to consult. To retrieve oral history from its under-the-counter and 'not quite academically respectable' taints, it is desirable for authors to provide reference notes for oral evidence just as meticulously as for written evidence.

Increasingly, authors mention in their acknowledgements those who rejected the offer to be interviewed. But this practice makes the implicit assumption that the author has a right of access to subjects, and that they do not have a good reason for declining; it is therefore, we feel, to be avoided. A brief description of interview methodology – in acknowledgements, notes on sources, or elsewhere – should not, however, be avoided. Even in works of contemporary history where it might be inappropriate to give the names of interviewees in the main body of the book, it is still helpful to mention (even if not by name) the numbers of those interviewed, the approximate length of interviews, how names were selected, the role of interviews in the research, the method of recording, whether interview transcripts or notes were kept and, if so, whether in due course they can be made available to other researchers.

Authors who have decide to paraphrase or quote from interviews should, if neither *carte blanche* nor 'strictly no quotation' rulings were given, return their extracts for comment. The most suitable way to do this might be to offer in a letter one of four options: extract(s) (1) all right as they stand; (2) require changing (if so please specify); (3) all right in unattributed form only; (4) to be removed altogether (some authors might not wish to suggest that as a possibility). The letter should also explain again the nature of the final product, and provide publication or completion dates where possible. One should also give some indication of the range of research sources employed, include photocopies of the page on which the extracts appear so that the interviewee can see the context in which his remarks have been presented (since the context can affect the meaning), and so that any changes can be made on the photocopy; to avoid replies where no comment is necessary it might be worth giving a time limit after which it will be assumed that the extracts are satisfactory. The best stage to do this task (which might take up to two months) is probably when the first draft is completed: a fair percentage of interviewees are likely to want changes, which can be incorporated into a subsequent or final draft.

Some authors find it helpful to work up the testimony into some form of a narrative very soon after the interview. Ben Pimlott is one such author: 'I think the main thing is that one needs to use interview material very quickly, otherwise the stimulus it provides fades. If I allowed it to lie fallow for a bit, then I tended to lose a lot of what I had acquired.'[13] However, for the many authors who will not be able to write drafts soon after interviews because the research will be incomplete, it may be helpful to write down the ideas that the interview stimulated, so that at least some of the flavour can be retained.

PART III

Case studies:
individual books

8

Modern and
recent history

To what extent do authors of modern and recent history – of periods for which all or some archival material is available – rely on oral history evidence, and how far is it used only by contemporary historians and biographers to compensate for gaps in or unavailability of primary source material? In what areas do authors writing in the branches of history described below find interview evidence helpful? How did they use the material in practice – do they include direct quotation and footnote (or endnote) references, or do they absorb oral evidence into the main text in such a way as to make it difficult to assess the contribution that it has made to their work? The following three chapters will explore how authors have tackled these questions in practice by discussing its use in their books, and to a lesser extent, to survey the literature in each field. We do not seek to make value judgements about the books in question; nor do we aim for a comprehensive coverage of the literature.

Political history

Many authors writing political history have not formed a very favourable impression of oral evidence. Stephen Koss, who conducted a few (six to ten) interviews for his *Nonconformity in Modern British Politics* (1975) and *The Rise and Fall of the Political Press in Britain* (1981), found 'interviews most useful – illuminating would be saying too much – in either confirming or disproving interpretations of character or perception'. But, Koss continued,

I suppose that, in its own way, an illuminating aspect was the way in which the memories of several interviewees resisted hard evidence that qualified or contradicted their strong recollections. One politician-lawyer, for example, pounded the table, and, clinging to his version of events, refused to acknowledge photocopies of letters as being items he could ever have written.[1]

In his book on nonconformity, which runs from Victorian times until the Second World War, Koss thanks those who 'granted interviews, of inestimably greater value than they were perhaps able to perceive'.[2] His endnotes, however, refer to but a handful of interviews as sources. Oral evidence was used even less in the first volume of his work on the political press,[3] covering the nineteenth century; although for the second volume (on this century), a few dozen survivors were interviewed, he was not impressed by the reliability of journalists as sources of information. Koss concluded his comments on his experience of interviewing: 'I never miss an opportunity to conduct an interview, though I rarely find the experience as instructive as I would hope.'[4]

G. C. Peden, for his *British Rearmament and the Treasury 1932–39*, conducted six interviews. The notes show that the author had conducted a thorough and systematic examination of the public record. How, then, could interviews aid an author of a modern historical monograph orientated towards a policy rather than a biography? Peden records in his 'Note on Sources': 'The writer was fortunate in that a number of Treasury officials allowed him to interview them, and these interviews proved extremely useful in helping to understand the significance of various documents.'[5] He subsequently commented:

> Interviewees could rarely remember day-to-day events accurately, but they could recall the atmosphere, attitudes, characters, relations between characters and general background of (as the case might be) the Prime Minister's Office or the Treasury of the period. . . . [they] could *sometimes*, but not always, recall the significance of events or friends as they appeared then without hindsight. . . . All seemed very reliable, and sometimes what an interviewee said would be subsequently backed up by examining documents in the PRO.[6]

In one example of a recent history, written without the benefit of official records, Anthony Seldon conducted 225 interviews, mostly with retired ministers, civil servants, journalists and party officials, for his *Churchill's Indian Summer*.[7] He analysed the first 160, which broke down into 55 with former politicians (40 ministers and 15 parliamentary private secretaries), 80 former civil servants (including 44 former permanent or deputy secretaries and 17 private secretaries) and 25 miscellaneous. The interviews were graded from A (large yield of fresh material unavailable in contemporary sources) to E (no value at all). The grades were aggregated and produced the following percentage results:

	A	B	C	D	E
politicians	18	36	29	15	2
officials	35	49	5	6	5

There is much that is arbitrary in such an analysis; nevertheless, the figures revealed that one particular researcher found interviews with former officials (of which 84 per cent were in the top two grades) more rewarding than those with former politicians (54 per cent in the top two grades). Further analysis revealed (principal) private secretaries to be the most valuable single group.[8]

For his book, Seldon asked for permission to quote from interviews with the individuals concerned. About 50 per cent asked for changes or added fresh information, and 5 per cent or less rejected the requests. Where permission was refused, the reference in the endnotes is to 'Private information'. Where permission was granted, references in the footnotes read 'Interview with X', undated, and without specifying whether the note refers to a fact given or an opinion, or whether a whole paragraph or just a sentence was based on material gleaned from interview with the particular person.

Although probably only 10 per cent or less of the book was based on oral evidence, oral history and its efficacy was a subject to which most reviewers referred. David Carlton wrote in the *Sunday Times*:

> could it be that the oral recollections are excessively self-serving, selective, and above all, 'safe'? Certainly, very few discreditable policy secrets, derogatory to what is left of our national reputation, have come to light. . . . Not one [permanent secretary] emerges as lazy, stupid, embittered or cantankerous, still less as prone to such human frailties as would titillate readers of popular newspapers. Instead, we are fed a diet of deferential blandness.[9]

Enoch Powell referred in his review in *The Times* to some errors he had detected in matters pertaining to his own experience: 'it is a worrying specimen of the reliability and quality of the interviews which have contributed so largely to the content'.[10] Both viewpoints contain much justice. The information on individuals' roles in the book *is* bland, and, although the author tried to eradicate errors by having each section of the book read by at least one expert witness (fifty in total), and by cross-checking with other sources, errors still slipped through. Some of the fault undoubtedly lay with the author, and in his inexperience (the interviews were all conducted when he was a postgraduate student), rather than in the method *per se*; nonetheless, they illustrate in practice two major weaknesses (as discussed in Chapter 2) inherent in oral history evidence.

Considerably more use is generally made of oral history by political biographers than authors of monographs. Martin Gilbert, in *Winston S. Churchill*, is writing the most systematic and thorough biography of any British figure; the range of written evidence that he is drawing on is formidable. Yet Gilbert places periodic requests in the press for those with recollections of Churchill to jot them down and send them to him. Besides being an assiduous collector of written reminiscences, Gilbert also cultivates personal relationships with those close to his subject. He distinguishes two distinct types of oral history, the one-off, question-naire-type of interview, and the form he follows: 'I've found it most helpful when I've been able to get to know the people quite well, some-times extremely well, so that I can go back again and again; the more informal discussions become, the more I benefit from them.'[11] In his writing, he sees oral evidence 'very much as one facet of evidence, to be used alongside all the other sources available to a historian'.[12]

Personal testimony has contributed so far only a small fraction of the evidence in Gilbert's Churchill volumes, but the wide variety of ways he uses it is nonetheless instructive. It might be that he has searched out a survivor to provide information about a particular day of Churchill's life. On 27 September 1932, for example, the historian Maurice Ashley travelled to Chartwell to help Churchill with his *Marlborough*:

> That day, although he was not fully recovered from his illness, Churchill insisted on getting up; indeed, he began to walk with Ashley to and fro in the garden. But he was still too weak for such activity, and Ashley later recalled: 'as we were pacing up and down, he got whiter and whiter. Suddenly he collapsed.'[13]

On some occasions, Gilbert uses oral evidence to provide information on his subject's variable, and idiosyncratic, working methods and habits. Bill Deakin arrived at Chartwell for the first time in April 1936, to act as Churchill's research assistant. Forty years later he told Gilbert about 'the ruthless partition of the day, the planning of things all to time. There was never a wasted moment. He had intense control.' Gilbert is not loath to quote at length from interviews, and he gives Deakin full rein to amplify his thoughts. Having described his day, Deakin informs us:

> At midnight when the guests left, then he would start work. Work on Marlborough would go on to three or four in the morning. One felt so exhilarated. Part of the secret was his phenomenal power to concentrate – the fantastic power of concentrating on what he was doing – which he communicated. You were absolutely a part of it – swept into it. . . . Nothing was allowed to interfere with the night work. While he worked he would call up a secretary and start to dictate. I might have given him some memorandum before dinner, four or five hours before. Now he would walk up and down the room dictating. My facts were there, but he had seen it as a politician. My memorandum was a frame. It set him off, it set off his imagination.[14]

On other occasions, Gilbert uses oral evidence to provide information where documentation does not exist. Thus in Volume 5 Gilbert writes: 'Churchill was angered that some of his friends and former supporters had voted for the Government's policy. One of those, Alan Lennox-Boyd, later commented that as a result of his support for Munich, Churchill "regarded me as a renegade".' Patrick Donner likewise recalled, in conversation with the author: 'After the debate Churchill came up to me in the corridor and abused me like a Billingsgate fishwife. I was no longer "Patrick" after ten years, and the intimacy was never recreated".'[15]

Gilbert is meticulous in his attribution of oral evidence. Where he uses it in his Churchill biography, he states the fact in the text, leaving readers to draw their own conclusions about the reliability of the testimony. His 'List of sources' includes 'Author's records of individual recollections', listed alphabetically, with the numbers of the pages where he refers to the interview (or personal correspondence) with them. As his biography progresses, Gilbert is able to draw on a wider range of those with personal knowledge of Churchill: the 1918–22 volume thus draws on the personal testimony of ten people, the 1922–39 volume on twenty-four,[16] and even more references are to be found in Volume 6, which covers the years 1939–41.

Some authors have to rely heavily on oral evidence because of the paucity of written evidence about their subject; this was the case for Bernard Donoughue and George Jones with their *Herbert Morrison*. The great majority of Morrison's private and governmental papers were burned when Lady Morrison moved house in 1960. A literary executor determined to circumvent the consequent dearth of documentation by mounting 'a study of Morrison while people who knew him were still alive. Their recollections [the executor felt] – even allowing for the defects of human memory – would to a considerable extent make up for the deficiencies of Morrison's own papers.'[17] The authors reported: 'With one exception, everyone we approached agreed to talk to us, and we very much enjoyed and appreciated the helpful reception we were given. Without their cooperation this book could not have been written.'[18] That book is thus a markedly different type to, say, Gilbert's *Winston S. Churchill*, and can be seen as a major work displaying oral evidence at its best. Written by two scholars with experience of politicians, the biography appears to display few of the faults latent in the oral history method.

The authors interviewed 300 subjects, usually singly rather than together. Donoughue subsequently wrote:

> The defects of interviews as evidence are obvious and well-known. People's memories are not perfect. But we found that providing the sample of interviews is wide enough, and providing the interviewer is himself the specialist in the field and not using some inexperienced research assistant, then it is possible to check and counter-check statements made and eliminate much of what is doubtful. In any case, with biography the writer is less concerned with precise facts of dates or time (though we often found it possible to establish these details through checking with several interviews) than with perceptions, assumptions and anecdotal requirements.[19]

Not only has the biography been found accurate, but it also makes clear attribution to oral evidence. The endnotes contain several hundreds of references to interviews, sometimes a single interview, at other times indicating that up to six interviews had provided background information for a particular point. Direct quotation is not employed, and instead the oral evidence is merely absorbed into the main body of the text. To take an example: one note reads: 'Interview, Sir Alexander Johnstone. This view was shared by [G. R.] Downes, [Lord] Plowden and, with qualifications, by [Max] Nicholson. Interviews.'[20] This note refers to a passage in the chapter on Morrison's work as Lord President (1945–51): 'In the transport field Morrison dominated the Minister, Barnes, and even himself fixed the salaries of members of the new nationalized boards.'[21] The statement without the footnote would have been of questionable value: with the attribution it carries authority, and helps the reader to evaluate it.

Philip Williams too had to compensate for deficient written evidence, especially on the pre-war period, with interviews in his biography *Hugh Gaitskell*, described by George Jones as 'an academic justification for the use of interviews'.[22] Not only does Williams provide very full references to oral testimony and list in an appendix all the 300 people he interviewed (only two had refused) according to three periods (pre-1939, 1939–51, post-1951),[23] but he is also the only author of a work of political history to have written at length about his experience of oral evidence. His article, 'Interviewing Politicians: The Life of Hugh Gaitskell',[24] charting how the author began 'as a sceptic about the value of interviewing and [ended] as a convert', provides a wealth of illuminating material on his experience and methodology, and is advised reading for any biographer embarking on collecting oral evidence.

Footnotes are always clear, and appear in the plain undated form, either attributed or non-attributed (e.g. 'Interview with an official'). Multi-interview references are also employed. The authority for his statement, 'Privately Gaitskell knew that if the clash continued over a long period, his position would become untenable; he felt he should, and would have to, resign the leadership if Conference went against him again [on unilateral disarmament]', is given in the endnotes as: 'Interviews, Lady Gaitskell, Lord Aylestone, A. Crosland, Lord Gordon Walker, Lord Harris, D. Healey, R. Jenkins, T. Driberg – to whom he said so a year later. Jenkins was almost alone in thinking he would probably have gone out of politics entirely.'[25] Williams cites only half as many footnote references for Gaitskell's later career after he entered Parliament as he does for the period before; but when Gaitskell was in office between 1946 and 1951 the number of references rises because of 'Civil servants' [superior to politicians, etc.] testimony about his style and working habits'.[26] Williams's preferred style was to absorb interview material into the text rather than to quote directly,[27] and it is not always possible to discover exactly what information he did garner from each interview.

More restricted use of oral evidence was made in David Marquand's political biography *Ramsay MacDonald*. The author talked to about fifty former friends, colleagues and acquaintances of his subject,[28] but found the interviews very unreliable for providing facts – though he felt that 'the interviews I conducted were of enormous value to me in reaching impressionistic judgements about MacDonald's personality and character'. Marquand encountered a peculiar difficulty which not all authors face: 'MacDonald was, of course, the victim of much short-term hindsight immediately after the events of 1931; and most of the books written about him in the thirties and forties reflected that fact.' But, he continued, 'contemporaries who survived until the 1960s and who were able to be interviewed then were much more likely to have a reasonably detached view.'[29] Obviously hindsight would still colour their views.

Military and defence history

The source problems confronting a military historian have been discussed by Robert Rhodes James: contemporary written evidence, he suggests, is 'highly suspect' and to establish even the most simple military facts can be difficult. Two of the staple sources for the military historian, the contemporary army war diaries and the naval reports of proceedings, are written, he says, usually 'under severe difficulties'.[30] Ronald Lewin thinks similarly:

> Many young writers go to war diaries and quote from them extensively, but what they do not realize is that in operations the routine necessity of maintaining the war diaries was often a great nuisance, and secondary if you are in the middle of battle to the other things that you have to do. When a period of calm ensued the war diary would then be written from the writer's own recollections and from those of his fellow soldiers: the record can be very accurate – or it can be quite wrong.[31]

Sir Peter Gretton, a retired admiral and naval historian, has written of the naval reports of proceedings:

> I hope that historians will take into account the fact that human nature is weak, and although all the facts may be available, very often the main motive behind the Report of Proceedings will be to show the actions of the ship or squadron concerned in the best possible light.[32]

Rhodes James concludes: 'Official despatches are as untrustworthy as the memoirs of generals. The very nature of war means that, very often, the truth of what really happened is known only to the dead.'[33] Not all military historians would agree with these reservations about contemporary documentary evidence, but few would deny that the strictures of these experienced and authoritative scholars carry some force.

Do interviews help? Rhodes James writes: 'Personal recollections of participants, at all levels, tend to be unsatisfactory.'[34] Nevertheless, it is a medium to which most military historians resort. Montgomery's 'official' biographer, Nigel Hamilton, was concerned to 'fill in the gaps in existing knowledge about Monty's life and career, as well as commenting on the contentious issues concerning him.'[35] Hamilton, who conducted over forty interviews for the first volume of *Monty* (which takes the story up to 1942), uses oral evidence for the standard ends: as 'a supplement to documentary evidence adding the human perspective, balance and colour or as a substitute where no written records survive about a person or period.' In *Monty* 'the extra tone and balance of the interviews helped to personalise an otherwise rather arid account of a man preparing himself for more than thirty years for greatness.'[36]

He differs from many authors in including passages culled verbatim from his interviews, which, again untypically, he always tape-records ('the only serious way to go about the business'). As he explains: 'I have not altered or even 'polished' the extracts I have used, and some readers may be disturbed by the syntax of unrehearsed speech rather than the printed page; but I wanted to abide by my own rules of scrupulous honesty, of not tampering with, or worse still distorting, the often deeply personal nature of such recollections.'[37] For example, he quotes Sir William Mather, who had served in the desert since 1940:

> You see, when he wrote the Operation Order for the battle of Alamein it was like a hen giving birth. He walked backwards and forwards on the sands of Burg-el-Arab all day, backwards and forwards, like Napoleon with his head down, his hands behind his back. And we all said: 'Master is giving birth'.
>
> And he came back into his caravan and in about 4 hours – I remember now it was on 14 sheets of paper – he wrote the whole Operation Order for Alamein. That was it. It wasn't changed, or very few variations were made to it.[38]

This extract from Sir William Mather provided the springboard for what Nigel Hamilton believes to be another unique benefit of oral history: the way that the 'unretouched quality' of these memories encourages the general reader to take an interest in historic documents 'which otherwise would be considered unpublishable . . . I used his Napoleonic simile to encourage the reader to read the entire 42-paragraph battle plan for El

Alamein – which I consider to be one of the seminal documents of the last war.'[39]

A pioneer of one use of oral testimony in books was Nigel Nicolson, who in his biography of Lord Alexander of Tunis, entitled *Alex*, employed a question – and – answer format in the text. In his chapter on the fall of Rome in 1940, for example, Nicolson adopts the following method:

> I discussed [whether General Mark Clark disobeyed Alexander's orders] at length with Mark Clark in Charleston, South Carolina, in March 1970:
>
>> From my readings of the story, General, it does seem that Alexander was very definite in his orders that the break out should be in the direction of Valmontone?
>>
>> Let's get this straight. I had been assigned the mission of capturing Rome. When Alex came to see me before the battle, he said: 'Wayne, I have drawn the boundaries between Fifth and Eighth Armies and you see I have given you Rome.' He joked a bit, and added: 'If you don't take it, I will bring up some more troops and we will take it.'[40]

The cross-examination is continued by Nicolson for several more questions. As Nicolson himself remarked: 'I hope this device [question and answer in the text] will be used more. It sharpens the narrative, dramatizes it, and varies the pace of prose. It is also more authentic', he suggests, 'than the author's own opinions.' General Mark Clark in fact was apparently the only interviewee to raise objections to being quoted verbatim: 'Mark Clark, when I sent him my transcript, rewrote the entire thing in formal military jargon and sent it to me. I managed to persuade him to let me use the original.'[41]

Interviews, however, as Nicolson wrote, 'were only one element of my research. I had a massive archive of Alex's private papers, the PRO documents, published war histories and memoirs, etc.' What, then, did interviews give the author that other sources could not? 'Often the most useful things were negative, like Lord Harding's remark that Alex had little compassion about the death of his soldiers in battle. Others were able to recall very graphically the details of battle crises.'[42]

Not all military historians are as enthusiastic about oral evidence. Brian Bond, who has written widely on the army[43] and regularly sees about ten subjects per book, looks to interviews to help him track down 'surviving documents and secondly for any light they might throw on my subject – usually "atmosphere" and personal insights rather than new facts. . . . personal relations in the making of policy is an aspect which seldom features in official records.' By way of example, he cited 'the relations between Hore-Belisha, Liddell Hart and the General Staff, 1937-9'.[44] Over all, Bond found his interviewing 'just about' worth the effort, 'but it is impossible to quantify. What is most valuable is not perhaps the evidence but gaining some notion of what "important" people, e.g. Monty, Alex, Mountbatten and Yadin, were like.' He concluded: 'Most of my interviews have been with members or ex-members of the armed services. I would say that nearly all were anxious to help and tell "the truth", but many had little notion of what historians do and what scholarship is about.'[45]

Denis Richards, the author of the three-volume official history *Royal Air Force 1939-45* and the biography of Lord Portal of Hungerford, Chief of Air Staff during the Second World War,[46] has had long experience of both documentary and oral evidence. Richards interviewed about a hundred per volume for his official history of the RAF during the Second World War, and seventy-five for his biography of Lord Portal, published over twenty-five years later. He finds interviewing an essential adjunct to written evidence, particularly for the information it provides on personal relations, which he finds are not included in official records. For Richards, to fail to interview a major and accessible witness, 'is to fail in research – to ignore a potentially important source of information.' Nevertheless he has strong reservations: 'Most prominent people have a self-justificatory line to sell – quite understandably. The really objective interviewee is a rarity.' However, 'a written document may also lack objectivity,' and Richards believes that the historian must 'scrutinize all the evidence, written or spoken, with equal care.' He makes the interesting observation: 'Leaders who have been so good that they occupied one prominent position after another usually remember less about past events than leaders who have been sacked and have had ample time to dwell on their past experiences.'[47]

Stephen Roskill, the official historian for the Royal Navy in the Second World War, conducted a handful of interviews for virtually all his books. He was not greatly impressed by their efficacy: 'I find one nearly always had to be on one's guard against highly subjective views for which documentary evidence is lacking or insubstantial', and thus 'I prefer to use written sources except in special cases when they are inadequate or missing.'[48] A fellow naval historian, the American scholar Arthur Marder – whose work according to Rhodes James (in 1966) has 'made us acutely conscious of the inadequacies of recent military history in this country'[49] – was described by Ronald Lewin as a 'nonpareil in the use of oral history for legitimately academic purposes'[50]; interviewing was a prominent feature of his work. Marder's reliance on oral evidence (alongside full consideration of documentary sources) has not, however, gone without challenge, and it played a significant part in a long-running dispute between Marder and Roskill over Sir Dudley Pound's role as First Sea Lord during the first part of the Second World War. More recently, Christopher Thorne has queried two assertions made in Marder's last book, *Old Friends, New Enemies*[51] – that the Imperial Japanese Navy (IJN) was reluctant to go to war with Britain in the Second World War, and that the attention of the IJN was so focused on the US navy that it thought little about the problems of a war with Britain. 'It seems possible', writes Thorne, 'that Marder's confusion over these issues . . . springs from the extent to which Marder relied upon the testimony (perhaps of a somewhat bland kind?) of retired IJN officers.'[52]

The controversial nature of the source can be seen because the importance and status of oral history continues to be a matter of disagreement amongst military historians. But as the last total British war, that of 1939–45, recedes in time, it is likely that historians will lament the increasing difficulty of being able to sample for themselves this unique source – the eyewitness.

Historians of defence policy, in either war or peace, who are concerned to describe and analyse policy-making at the heart of government, have access after the appropriate interval to the full range of public record sources and other printed material. With regard to interviewing however – and this applies in particular to authors writing on intelligence matters, or whose work discusses similar sensitive subjects – they are likely to encounter a greater degree of reserve than normal among their interviewees. None the less, the problem of sensitivity has not prevented authors of works of recent or contemporary defence history from conducting talks and naming interviewees. Thus three works on post-war defence policy – R. N. Rosecrance's *Defense of the Realm*, A. J. Pierre's *Nuclear Politics* and P. Darby's *British Defence Policy East of Suez* (all published between 1968 and 1973) – are based to an unspecified extent upon oral evidence.[53] Rosecrance tells us, 'Without the guidance of principals in British and American defense policy-making, the study could not have been completed', but then states that 'None of the information or perspectives lent in interviews has been attributed in the text.'[54] Pierre reports that his 'study was considerably enriched and its judgements honed by a number of personal interviews'.[55] Darby claims less for his interviews:

> The inadequacy of published sources made it necessary to draw on discussions and correspondence with persons involved in policy-making. For the most part, this was a matter of amplification of the public record and guidance as to the reliability of published reports.[56]

All three list between twenty and forty people who helped by providing personal evidence, but in none of the three books is it possible to assess the *extent* to which oral evidence has been relied upon, although it must in each case have been significant, since all the studies penetrated behind the White Papers and parliamentary debates.

Diplomatic and colonial history

The records of the Foreign Office are generally felt to be outstandingly useful because developments are well minuted and often reveal, a historian like Geoffrey Warner argues, the assumptions behind a particular policy. It is partly for this reason that diplomatic historians writing modern history (periods of thirty years and more after the events) have not generally made much use of interviews. In addition, their works often discuss the evolution of policy in minute detail, and oral evidence does not generally provide detailed recollection. Geoffrey Warner felt that unless those interviewed were basing their comments on contemporary records, the evidence they provided tended to be vague and unreliable. Occasionally, it was wilfully distorted. He concludes: 'if one considers the time spent, one wonders whether it might not have been more productively employed on seeking out further published evidence'.[57]

Even biographers (as opposed to writers of monographs) of diplomats often have little time for oral evidence: David Carlton, whose biography of Anthony Eden was published in 1981,[58] records: 'I had no high hopes of obtaining specific information in most cases. Usually recreation of "atmosphere" was all I expected, and obtained.' He comments: 'Interviewees rarely appear to have prepared in advance and hardly ever produce any written evidence for their often implausible claims.' The result was 'Very little of concrete value, except that, for example, Malcolm MacDonald was very revealing on Eden's resignation in 1938 and allowed me to quote him at length.'[59] For the last years of Eden's ministerial career (1951–7) Carlton did not have access to official records, but for his war and pre-war service he had access to public record and to private papers, as he did for his earlier book, on the foreign policy of the second Labour government.[60] Although he conducted about a dozen interviews for both books, he found interviews were not of substantially greater value for the later period of Eden's official life when official records were closed than they were for earlier periods.

John Cross formed a slightly more favourable opinion of oral evidence when writing his biography of Sir Samuel Hoare,[61] much of whose political career was dominated by his brief but disastrous period as Foreign Secretary. Cross believes that 'Interviews are clearly indispensable for the writing of modern biography', in particular because of the insights they can provide into the subject's political and ministerial activities, and because they may indicate what to follow up in the public records. However, he considers them again very much secondary to documentary evidence.[62]

Author of works that are known to be taking a critical stance are likely to meet with a diffident response from those being interviewed. Nikolai Tolstoy nevertheless was able to interview approximately a hundred people for his *Victims of Yalta*, which discusses the forcible repatriation of prisoners-of-war to the Soviet Union at the end of the Second World War. Tolstoy reports that his informants were 'very co-operative', and that the only people who declined to be interviewed were Lord Avon (Anthony Eden), Harold Macmillan, and four former Foreign Office officials: 'It is not difficult to see why.' Through interviewing, the author was able to compensate for inadequacies in contemporary public record. He was impressed too by the accuracy of the information he elicited:

> The advantages greatly outweighed the drawbacks. On occasion I interviewed two or more people present at the same event, often of differing nationalities, loyalties and viewpoints, and was generally surprised at the confirmation of the accuracy of their memories which this brought out.[63]

A work falling halfway between recent and contemporary history is a volume entitled *British Foreign Secretaries Since 1945*, written by three authors at Reading University. Their aim was 'to pay special attention to the foreign secretary as an individual; his political status; the organizational context; the domestic setting from which his policies spring; and the international environment in which he operates.'[64] Fifteen interviews were conducted – approximately half of them with former ministers and the rest with former officials. Keith Sainsbury, one of the authors, found these interviews to have been indispensable:

> Some were very good at providing details on human relations, as about Macmillan. Selwyn Lloyd wouldn't expand on Suez but was very informative on the Common Market negotiations, the post-Suez restoration of relations with the United States, and the nuances of his relations with Macmillan, Eisenhower and Dulles.

The three authors adopted a workmanlike approach to the interviews, tape recording where possible, and returning a full transcript in every case for approval and further comment – although few actually provided additional material.[65] In the endnotes, interview evidence is referred to either in the form 'Interview with X' or in the concealed form, for example: 'Opinion expressed to the writer by senior officials of that period (private information).'[66]

D. J. Morgan, the official historian of colonial development, makes only limited use of oral evidence, basing his work as a result substantially on documentary evidence. Morgan found personal evidence most valuable after he had examined the documents and had produced some written work of his own.[67] The aim of the Peacetime Series of Official Histories, as announced by Harold Wilson in the House of Commons on 18 December 1969, was for the history to be written 'while the official records could still be supplemented by reference to the personal recollections of the public men who were involved.' However most of the authors to have written for the series so far appear to have used oral evidence as little as, or even less than, Morgan. One of the few substantial monographs on recent colonial history to have so far been written is David Goldsworthy's *Colonial Issues in British Politics*. His work was based on a thorough examination of political parties' published papers and on interviews with twelve subjects, including four former Colonial Secretaries, Arthur Creech Jones (1946–50), James Griffiths (1950–1), Oliver Lyttelton (1951–4) and Alan Lennox-Boyd (1954–9). All four provided the author with 'a wealth of information and opinion; highly flavoured personalities all, they also conveyed, in distinctive ways, the "feel" of their office.'[68] Goldsworthy found that 'interviewing could illuminate *any* area, sometimes against all expectation'. As to limitations of the method, he felt it had 'very few drawbacks, provided you approach interviews realistically – i.e. with solid background knowledge before you start, and making due and tactful allowance for human factors.'[69]

Clearly in a subject like colonial history, where one is concerned not just with the activities of Westminster, Whitehall, parties and pressure groups in Britain, but with developments in the colonies themselves, and where one has to consider the aspirations and policies of peoples of widely differing outlook, interviews can have an especial importance in locating papers and informing historians of the issues involved, which may look very different from the point of view of the indigenous population or the white settlers on the spot. Charles Douglas-Home, when writing his biography of Sir Evelyn Baring – much of whose official life had been spent in the colonies and culminated in his period as Governor of Kenya (1952-9) – travelled widely in India and Africa. He interviewed a hundred colonial officials, soldiers, diplomats and politicians (although not native Africans) who had worked with his subject, and corresponded with a further sixty. Douglas-Home's interviews consisted of 'usually a chat, with note taking afterwards'.[70] In the text he does not refer to interviewees by name; neither does he in the endnotes, although he provides a list in 'Source material' at the end of the book.[71]

Any author of the period of decolonization in Africa will benefit from exceptionally good contemporary journalism, associated with two names in particular, Colin Legum and Oliver Woods, the material for whose journalism inevitably came largely by word of mouth.

History of economic and social policy

Economic policy

Samuel Brittan's *Steering the Economy*,[72] which has gone through three editions, is one of the few texts in this field to have drawn avowedly on oral evidence. For his second and third editions Brittan benefited from the fourteen months he spent as a temporary civil servant at the Department of Economic Affairs from November 1964, as well as receiving 'official' guidance from the civil service: 'The Treasury itself went out of the way to give me all the information it properly could.'[73] But he also relied heavily on 'informal' oral evidence, gleaned in the normal course of his journalistic work (he was Economic Editor of *The Observer* from 1961 to 1964 and Economic Editor of the *Financial Times* from 1966) and from specially arranged interviews, some sixty to seventy for the first edition alone.[74] Brittan was able to combine a rare background of experience of Whitehall from the inside with his journalist's craft of extracting information, to produce a book which gives vivid portraits of chancellors and officials, and an account going far deeper than contemporary published sources.

Industrial relations

One finds rather more use of oral evidence in books on employment policy and labour relations. Oral evidence has been found to be a very useful adjunct by authors writing about single episodes, or about the broad span of historical development. Eric Wigham used interview evidence in his *Strikes and the Government 1893-1981*,[75] the early sections relying exclusively on written evidence, the latter almost solely on oral evidence, obtained either as part of Wigham's normal work as labour correspondent of *The Times* (1946–69), or culled from special interviews for the book. In his *Government Versus Trade Unionism*[76] as in others of his books Gerald Dorfman made use of interviews and includes, at the end of the book, a two-page section entitled 'Personal interviews', in which he names some fifty people interviewed, their official position, and the date of the interview. Underneath the last-named individual, 'Woodcock, George, former General Secretary, TUC', etc., and a list of the three dates when he was interviewed by Dorfman, are the words 'Plus other members of the TUC staff, union leaders, politicians and civil servants who wish to remain anonymous.' In his endnotes, Dorfman either employs the form 'Interview with X', and the date, or, the anonymous form, 'Unattributable Interview with Parliamentary Private Secretary'.[77] In *The Voice of the Past*,[78] Paul Thompson makes the general point that, in economic history, oral history has encouraged a renewed interest in *people*, their working methods and experience, rather than a reliance on cold statistical evidence. This is clearly of particular relevance to labour history.

Business history

This branch of economic history is concerned, as are studies of individual trade unions, with micro- rather than macro-economics. Although some histories have been written about whole industrial sectors, or on themes, most business histories have dealt with single companies or groups. This is largely because individual companies are prepared to pay historians, and often research assistants as well, to do this work; however, many volumes have interest far beyond the particular company. The studies enjoy a position akin to 'official' histories, authors being granted access to recent internal records. Because many authors of business histories have used oral history and employed it in a variety of different ways, their

writings will be considered at length. However, as most of the authors of
business history aim to write a study of policy making at the top, few
have availed themselves of the opportunity for interviewing those lower
down the hierarchy, and thus have denied themselves part at least of the
potential of oral history.

Only in the last twenty years, has the writing of business history
become widespread in Britain, and authors and companies were slow at
first to follow the lead given by Charles Wilson with his history of Unilever, and Allan Nevins with *Ford: the Times, the Man, the Company*,
which were published in 1954 in Britain and in the United States
respectively. As the founder of the world's first modern oral history
archive at Columbia University, Nevins not surprisingly made full use of
oral evidence 'to establish Ford's own personal work habits, like his
strict avoidance of office work and letter answering; and to separate the
various roles in the team-work that contributed to the development of
the important Model T design.'[79]

When Sir Norman Chester wrote *Nationalization in Britain 1945–51*,
he found that the fullness of the records obviated the necessity for much
oral history fieldwork.[80] Private company records, however, are often far
from full. In 1960, long before oral history came into vogue, a pamphlet
published by the Historical Association entitled *Business History*
recorded:

> As one approaches the present, business policy records tend more and
> more to contain only what was decided and not how decisions were
> reached. Important discussions over a meal, on the telephone or
> during a game of golf, often pass unrecorded. There is more likely to
> be written evidence of these behind-the-scenes activities before the
> coming of the telephone and the typewriter, when partners had to
> discuss matters more by correspondence and wrote their own letters.
> At that time, too, it was more common to keep detailed private
> diaries and to take more revealing minutes. In more recent times,
> however, the historian will be lucky if he finds much in writing about
> how decisions were arrived at. He is, therefore, largely reliant on
> interviews with senior or retired executives.

The pamphlet continues: 'Such interviews will be more valuable after
the historian has read the documents and knows the questions he wants
to ask about events and about personalities.'[81]

However, despite the general agreement on the value of interviewing,
a survey of the major works in the field reveals that authors of business

history have been coy about attributing sources. This habit stems in part from the fact that business archives, unlike the public record or private papers, rarely, if ever, become open to the general public, and thus writers of business history do not feel obliged to provide comprehensive source references.

Stanley Chapman, author of *Jesse Boot of Boots the Chemists*, observes that 'Boots is a typical business in one respect at least: that the records relating to its early history are meagre.' He remarks that 'there are the usual company accounts, directors' minutes and shareholders' reports, but more detailed records appear only as fortuitous survivals which cover the ground very imperfectly. Consequently I have had to rely heavily on oral evidence.' However, Chapman maintains that 'this has not been an inferior source of information':

> The business historian is particularly concerned with the origins and effectiveness of new policies and these are often only revealed in memories of telephone conversations, unminuted conferences or vacation discussions, which may very well be passed over in letters, books, reports and other written records.

And in an eloquent statement of the importance of contemporary or recent history Chapman writes: 'Clearly these memories will not be available indefinitely and to rescue them now is to save an important British business from historical oblivion.'[82] Chapman has absorbed the interview information within his text, and provides endnotes solely for 'external' sources – mainly books and newspaper articles. However, he lists those he interviewed in the 'Sources and acknowledgements' at the end of the book: four family members of Jesse Boot, twelve current directors and managers, and twenty-seven retired employees of Boots.[83] Although it is not possible to assess the extent and precise areas where Stanley Chapman relied on interview evidence, he has provided a fuller statement of his approach and sources than many authors.

Charles Wilson wrote a pioneering study of business history, *The History of Unilever*; the first two volumes, which were published in 1954, covered the period up to 1945, and the third volume, published in 1968, covered the period 1945–65. Wilson had access to a formidable array of written evidence – but is not without criticism of it. He informs us in the preface to Volumes 1 and 2:

> One lesson the task of writing recent history teaches the historian: the inadequacy of documents as the sole source of history. True there is no better single source for history, but where there is opportunity – as

there is here – for the historian to take personal testimony not from
one but from many actors in the play itself, where recollections can be
checked and counter-checked, one becomes acutely aware of the complexity of human motive, the fugitive nature of historical 'truth', the
gaps in the evidence, the sometimes tenuous relationship of word and
deed.[84]

Wilson thus goes further than many in attacking the documentary
evidence that is often regarded as sacrosanct. Yet again it is not possible
to assess the precise extent and areas in which Wilson found oral evidence
valuable, because, as he explains, references and source notes have
generally been avoided on the grounds that they 'could serve no useful
purpose', since primary sources are unavailable to the public.[85] He does,
however, in his bibliography, specify twelve people who provided
'reminiscences – for example, H. G. Rushton (whether by letter or in
interview is unspecified) on 'Personalities in the Lever business'. He
further lists over 300 names of people who 'have assisted with information, advice and criticism'.[86] In Volume 3 such a list is dispensed with
because 'The number of those who have, formally or informally, given
me the benefit of their knowledge and experience is far too large to be
printed.'[87] However, Charles Wilson has carefully recorded and preserved for future reference a note of his written and oral sources.[88] In the
absence of clear source notes, this is undoubtedly the next best practice.

Leslie Hannah, director of the Business History Unit at London
University, is rare among business historians, in that he does provide
extensive source notes, his *Electricity before Nationalization* containing
sixty-four pages of such notes. However, although Hannah makes many
references to reported evidence in the form of newspapers and memoirs,
he omits references to interviews (except where, as he says, interview
evidence pointed to a different conclusion to the documents, or where it
added to documents in a significant manner). But he has adopted a useful
and comparatively unusual practice: he lists fifty-six names in his 'Note
on sources' of those who aided in 'the interpretation of documents' by
'correspondence and interviews', and he provides an additional and
informative note in brackets after each name – of the organization with
which they were connected, or the area on which their comments were
found to be of most help. We thus learn, for example, that Sir J. H.
Wedgwood provided material on the Central Electricity Board and
railway electrification.[89] Hannah prefers to adopt an informal approach
to interviews rather than formal tape-recorded sessions and, while finding interviews useful in providing atmosphere and personal details, is

more sceptical than many about their value in producing 'fact'.[90]

Another to provide extensive source notes is T. C. Barker, who does refer to interviews in his sources, as indeed one might expect from one of the pioneers of oral history in Britain. In the forty-three pages of endnotes in *The Glassmakers*, a history of Pilkington from 1826 to 1976,[91] Barker refers to oral archive interviews as well as to his own. He found that Pilkington's archives contained a sizeable quantity of correspondence, but mainly for the nineteenth century. Board minutes often concealed as much as they revealed, and he found himself having to rely on oral evidence for the atmosphere of certain key meetings for the background behind major decisions, and for information about personal relationships of key individuals within the company.[92]

The most prolific writer on the history of British business is W. J. Reader, whose commissions include the histories of Bowater, Foster & Braithwaite, Metal Box, Tarmac and, most detailed of all, ICI. His views are thus of especial interest. 'It is useless', he says, 'to rely on the people you see for facts, dates and figures. They compress time, transpose events and forget facts. So I always tell them that I am not after the facts.'[93] The two main problems he has experienced in his interviewing are that the material is provided by and (often) about living people, and has to be handled with care; and that 'at 80 you're not the same chap you were at 50' – in other words, people are prone to say what they think now, rather than what they believed then. Where he does find interviews valuable is less on the financial and technical side, than on the political: the personalities and relationships – who liked whom, and so on – which 'you never get in the documents'. Reader prefers never to quote interviewees by name in his books unless they have specifically told him they do not mind. Thus in his two-volume classic of business history, *Imperial Chemical Industries: A History*, he does not list precise references to interviews in his source notes at the end of each chapter, other than making occasional reference to 'Private information'. He does, however, list in his source-material appendix in Volume 1 the names of those who helped provide 'verbal information' on various aspects, and, in Volume 2, eighty-seven names of those who supplied such information.

The conduct of interviews in a business history is peculiar, as it will be for the historical study of any homogeneous or closed organization, because either the study is commissioned by that body, in which case interviewees may be predisposed towards being frank and helpful, or it will be an outsider's study, in which case the historian as interviewer will be likely to come up against a far colder reception than usual. Where interviews are arranged with senior figures from business, the respondents can be surprisingly forthcoming. One business historian recorded that the directors he talked to were 'appallingly frank'; he hazarded an explanation:

> for many senior figures from industry it is lonely at the top: I think when they get someone listening to them who is interested and knowledgeable – and above all someone like a historian who is not a threat – they are only too glad to have the chance to open their mind.[94]

Such frank information is indeed required if business histories are to avoid being hagiographies.

Social policy

The distinctive contribution that interviews might be expected to make to the history of social policy derives from the opportunity for interviewing those affected by the policy – thus allowing a fuller appraisal of the impact of policy than that afforded by bare statistics. Again, one finds a medley of practices and attitudes.

Roger Smith, the author of *East Kilbride: The Biography of a Scottish New Town*,[95] had access to official records, and was also able to interview twelve 'key' decision makers. They were used to clarify specific issues where the written evidence was unclear or ambiguous. The oral evidence was found valuable, for example, in helping to ascertain the origins of the proposal to build East Kilbride. Documentary evidence alone would not have led to this conclusion.[96] The Health Department of the Scottish Office argued the case for the town with the Home Department (responsible for economic matters in Scotland), who themselves decided to back the plan when they realized its potential for reducing unemployment. While imprecise in its references, Keith Banting's *Poverty, Politics and Policy* (1979) further reveals the potential of interviews, and discusses openly the attitudes and actions of officials in Whitehall. Phoebe Hall, in her *Reforming the Welfare* (on the social welfare services in the 1960s), systematically conducted interviews. Rather than providing sources in footnotes, she gives a list of thirty names under five headings as an appendix, since it was not possible 'to attribute individually many of the views expressed by those involved in the setting up of the social services departments'.[97] From her interviews with all bar one (deceased) member of the key 'Seebohm Committee', she concludes: 'without their cooperation and indulgence, much of the detail of the committee's functioning would have been lost.'[98] Andrew McPherson and Charles Raab, in their forthcoming study of Scottish educational policy making and administration since the war, have found interviews invaluable because the literature on the subject is so thin: they concluded that from their interviewing 'we have learnt a considerable amount about the substance, style, structures, processes, beliefs and values in the public system of Scottish education and its governance at central and local levels.'[99]

History of science

Scientific research is conducted in universities, government organizations and industrial firms, and may be the work of an individual, a small team or a huge interlocking organization. Research in the history of science must therefore deal with many types of evidence at many different levels: oral evidence, private papers and institutional records, which include not only paper records but other matter peculiar to scientific research, such as photographic evidence and machine-produced records.

As well as the diverse spread of sources, the historian of science is confronted by other difficulties. As Nicholas Kurti has pointed out:

> very often the scientific facts are written down in publications or in private or official contemporary reports, but developments can occur very quickly, or erratically. *How* things developed, *who* were the people who really produced the ideas, at what *stage* did a certain idea crop up – these are often not recorded in written evidence.

Moreover, he says, 'scientific developments can progress under great haste. By the time it is written down, much has been forgotten: the anecdotes, the trouble you had been through, the troughs and the failures.'[100] Spencer Weart and Joan Warnow of the American Institute of Physics, which has for some years conducted a number of oral history programmes, observe: 'there are certain kinds of evidence of interest to the historian of science that are rarely answered by the documents', and, as examples, they cite: 'the early biographical background of scientists; how they selected their areas of research; information about certain crucial meetings; personal philosophies and approaches, and personal interactions.'[101]

In one way, however, the history of science differs from the other branches of history discussed here: scientific research is a matter of observation of precise experiment providing empirical data: the 'hard facts' are thus often less open to dispute than they are in the humanities.

The United States historians of atomic energy hold slightly guarded views about interviewing. 'Like all historians, the authors recognized that the memory . . . is fallible,' wrote the co-authors of the first volume in their 'Sources'. Although they found that interviewing was worthwhile, they discovered the importance of a thorough grounding in the documentary evidence:

> We knew that granting the best of memories, an interview is likely to degenerate into random and superficial recollections if the researcher does not ask the right questions. For this reason, we tried to prepare ourselves thoroughly before each appointment. We studied the written record and devised questions that struck at both the central issues and the relevant details.[102]

Historians of science in the United States conduct far more oral history, both on an individual and an archive basis, than their counterparts in Britain.[103] Harriet Zuckeman, for instance, conducted systematic interviews for her book *Scientific Elite*, which examines the careers and research of Nobel laureates in science, focusing on the work that led to their being awarded the prize. She provides a useful twenty-five-page appendix entitled 'Interviewing an Ultra-Elite', which describes her methodology and experience, and includes many pertinent observations.[104]

Oral history interviewing of scientists in Britain has tended to be conducted more by sociologists than pure historians. Professor Margaret Gowing has not, for example, found much need for oral testimony in her official history of Britain and atomic energy. Such work tends to be on periods of recent history, and is concerned to gather information of a kind that is often not documented in the official records. In the early 1970s David Edge and Michael Mulkay studied the development of radio astronomy at Jodrell Bank and Cambridge University. They contrasted the social structures of the two groups, showing that Jodrell Bank was characterized by relatively autonomous teams aimed at specific problems, while at Cambridge researchers tended to work individually within an integrated overall strategy.[105] The twenty interviews they conducted held to a tight format: 'The interviews were structured, in the sense that we had a carefully prepared checklist of questions, all of which had to be asked at one time in the interview.' They found their interviews most useful for 'checking historical details: outlining the *rationale* of scientific developments, and *informal* information about personalities, mutual evaluations, etc.'[106] More source-conscious than many historians, they deposited all the records for which interviewees gave permission for access at the American Institute of Physics in New York.

Three sociologists at the Polytechnic of North London, Peter Glasner, David Bennett and their research fellow David Travis, have conducted some fifty interviews in their project on the development and operation of genetic manipulation regulations in Britain:

> we were after a detailed knowledge of how the organizations in the field operated. In the early stages the interviews were exploratory – we wanted to develop a 'feel' for the area and we encouraged anecdotal replies. We wanted to know *who* was important at different stages, *how* the policy evolved as it came through various committees, and to pinpoint *when* a particular prevalent attitude changed, and who was influential in changing it. In the later stages we were able to cross-check interview accounts with each other, and with documents acquired from respondents. The documents helped us to be more precise about events, but the interviews were vital for interpreting the documents.[107]

From this cursory examination it would appear that historians of science, while finding interviews manifestly less valuable than contemporary documents, do mostly, to varying degrees, find that interviews are an important complement to their work. None the less, the need to treat such interview material with caution has recently been underlined by John Hendry. He cites two papers published in 1977, one based largely on documentary evidence, the other on oral evidence, which offer quite different interpretations of Heisenberg's work around 1924–5. Seldom indeed does the opportunity present itself to make such a direct comparison. Hendry concludes that 'it is [the document-based work] which is now generally accepted by historians as providing the more accurate account.' However, he adds that the problem lay partly in the individual application rather than in the interview methodology *per se*: 'some of the interviews were spoilt by the interviewer playing too dominant a role in moulding or even creating the recollections, while others suffered from the opposite problem, important questions being left hastily or inadequately answered.'[108]

On the other hand, Nicholas Kurti considers that scientists are less likely to change their opinions over time than some other groups (for example, politicians).[109] The potential of interviewing (if not always realised) has been well summed up by Spencer Weart and David De Vorkin: 'An interview is not the end of a topic but the beginning, a conduit from the black-and-white world of published papers to the colourful and chaotic real world of science.'[110]

Interview-based works

Books based solely or primarily on interviews are surprisingly rare in the field of British history. One exception is the work of Kenneth Harris, who has produced two volumes of interviews originally conducted for press or broadcasting: *Conversations* (1967) and *Kenneth Harris Talking To* (1971).[111] By way of a personal philosophy of the subject, he has remarked:

> Conversations can sometimes be the most convenient form of com-
> munication. Sometimes, indeed, they may be the only one that is
> possible. Most men do not wish to talk about themselves; many men
> are willing to answer personal questions. The best use of a conversa-
> tion, in my view, is to give some idea of what a man is like, how his
> mind works, how he sounds, what has happened to him which he
> finds significant, what he believes in, and, if one is lucky, what makes
> him tick.[112]

Interviewees include, in the first volume, George Brown, Lord Butler, Lord Citrine, Edward Heath and Harold Wilson, and, in the second, Barbara Castle and Roy Jenkins. Harris's practice of submitting his record to interviewees and giving them *carte blanche* to make any changes perhaps helps to encourage openness: 'Since the colloquies', Harris explains, 'are not arguments, interrogations or cross-examinations, and nobody is in the dock, I see no harm in this practice.'[113] Material elicited ranges from contemporary history and comment – for instance, Edward Heath speaking in 1966 on his assumption of the Conservative leadership the previous year: 'There was no plot, or conspiracy, no initiative either made by me, or approved of by me, or known of by me, or by my friends' – to recent history, such as Harold Wilson in 1963 looking back over fifteen years: 'In Stafford's [Cripps] case [the Board of Trade officials] played on his strength, not on his weakness. Stafford was an extraordinarily moral person. They played on that.'[114]

Much more of this type of work has appeared abroad. In Australia, for example, John Thompson's *On Lips of Living Men* comprises published recollections about eminent countrymen, including Sir John Monash, who commanded the Australian army in Europe in the First World War, and the Welshman who in 1915 became Prime Minister of Australia, W. H. Hughes.[115] Focusing upon one individual rather than several, Peter Stursberg's two-volume biography of the Canadian premier, Diefenbaker,[116] was published within ten years of Diefenbaker's fall in 1967, and was thus able to capture memories while still fresh. The preface to the second volume explains that fifty-six figures were interviewed in-depth, providing almost 120 hours of recordings. These were made on high-quality equipment and then transcribed, and are listed at the rear of the book.[117] The extracts are juxtaposed with passages of historical explanation and contemporary photographs, providing a well-rounded portrait while in no sense claiming to be comprehensive.

Harlan B. Phillips's *Felix Frankfurter Reminisces* provides a good example of another form of interview-based work: recollections *by* the man himself rather than *about* him. Many memoirs are, of course, based to an extent upon the subject talking to a historian and the conversation being recorded, such as Clement Attlee's *A Prime Minister Remembers* or Lord Swinton's *Sixty Years of Power*,[118] both narrated respectively to Francis Williams and James Margach. But none of these reports direct question and answer, as Phillips's book does. In his foreword Phillips explains:

> When Boswell wrote his life of Dr Johnson he demonstrated how important it is in portraying the varied qualities of his subject to record in detail conversations with him. The Dr Johnson who emerges, however, had to be filtered through Boswell's memory. . . . In these memories of Justice Frankfurter I had the benefit of modern recording equipment and thus was able to capture the words of my subject without the multiple handicaps under which Boswell labored.[119]

While Phillips might overstate the potential of the tape recorder, the benefits it confers are clear. Similar works are Merle Miller's *Plain Speaking: An Oral Biography of Harry S. Truman* (a project that began life as a prospective television series but later became a book)[120] and Michael Teague's *Mrs L: Conversations with Alice Roosevelt Longworth*[121] (Theodore Roosevelt's daughter), which includes an unusual perspective on her father's years in the White House.

Such interview-based works do not provide judgements, and one sometimes wishes for more editorial evaluation of the evidence. They do, however, provide vivid, firsthand material, which, besides any intrinsic contemporary interest, might well prove of more value to future historians than interim or historical biographies based substantially on interview evidence for which no records have been kept.

9

Contemporary history and political science

Times have changed since the day in the not too distant past when, according to legend, the Chinese historian, asked what he believed had been the major consequence of the French Revolution, replied: 'It is too early yet to say.' It is now accepted that events and their significance are now widely studied and debated almost as soon as the events have occurred. Oral evidence is crucial to this writing of contemporary (or instant) history, as well as to political science.

Because of the proximity of events in these fields, material gathered from interviews may not be attributed in the text or notes, with the result that such works often have appear to have more in common with journalism than with history. It is no surprise, then, to find a number of journalists writing works of contemporary history. Moreover, interviews are often found to be indispensable, in the absence of documentary evidence, because without them, authors would have no option but to rely on the 'public print', the press, Hansard, etc. Further, the very nature of, and the response from, the interview are substantially different from interviews for recent or modern history. Not only will writers of contemporary history have to rely heavily on oral evidence if they wish to penetrate behind the public façade, and to know who thinks or who said what (often impossible to tell from the press), but they are also likely to have potential access to all the key figures in the particular episode with which the research is concerned, and memories are likely still to be relatively fresh.

Researchers can benefit from interviewing his informants who are still in office, and from seeing them in their working environment. J. A. G. Griffith has provided an example of how this can operate in practice.

> When researching *Central Departments and Local Authorities*,[1] I might be at the DES talking to an Assistant Secretary and someone would pop their head round the door and say he'd call back later. 'Who was that?' I would ask. 'Oh, he's the Chief Education Officer from such-and-such. He often looks in for a chat when he's in London,' the Assistant Secretary would reply. That's the sort of thing you get from interviews: how the organization or person operated day by day. Interviews can provide a unique opportunity for improving one's understanding.[2]

There are obviously some drawbacks to contemporary oral history, apart from the unlikelihood of being able to attribute points in the text. Key figures may often be less willing to talk ('too busy', 'events too recent', 'too sensitive', etc.) than those approached by the historian writing on earlier periods, and they are often less likely to be frank, objective or entirely honest than those interviewed some years after the events being discussed. As David Marquand has already pointed out, contemporaries of Ramsay MacDonald were far more likely to give valuable oral recollections by the 1960s than in the 1930s and 1940s, when they were highly affected by the passions of the day.[3] J. G. Kellas has commented that there is a 'tendency in political or bureaucratic situations to avoid controversy which might redound against them', and further, that 'Civil servants often give information on the condition that it is not published!'[4]

Other difficulties stem less from the nature of contemporary *oral* history than from that of contemporary history itself. The US historians of atomic energy, Hewlett and Duncan, have described one of the major problems: 'The common criticism of historians writing about the contemporary scene is that they lack perspective, that time has not yet sifted the seed from the chaff. Contemporary historians, it is said, cannot tell what is significant and what is not.'[5] Others question the value of writing contemporary history, when the account will have to be substantially rewritten as more documentary evidence becomes available, and argue that such writing can perpetuate myth and make it harder for recent and modern historians properly to understand developments.[6] Still others contend that contemporary history, in the guise of apparent respectability and objectivity, can become merely the mouthpiece for a particular person or body of opinion represented in oral evidence on which the author might have heavily relied. Bernard Crick, in a review article entitled 'Court History' in the *New Statesman*, has criticized such works: 'One does learn something from such books, but what one is learning is the image the politicians wish to project.'[7] Bias of this kind can, of course, be avoided if researchers are willing to talk to a wide range of witnesses. Political science is perhaps rather less vulnerable than contemporary history to all these weaknesses.

The disadvantages of writing contemporary history are in any case far outweighed by the advantages: an insight today, at greater length than can be provided by the media, into recent major developments, often based in large part on oral recollections (ideally with interview recordings, transcripts or notes retained) that would otherwise fade and blur with the passing years. 'Closeness to events and even commitment can', as John Barnes has pointed out, 'be an advantage and supply an opportunity for insights that might otherwise be denied to subsequent historians.'[8] The historian consulting such works in years to come can allow for lack of perspective on the part of author and witnesses, for the haste with which these books are often produced, and for the limited range of evidence consulted. R. B. McCallum used to say that the Nuffield series of studies of general elections would be immortalized in other men's footnotes: the steady growth of such references in recent books to this series, and to other contemporary histories, testifies to the correctness of his remark, and to the value of the writing of contemporary history. As W. N. Medlicott has argued: 'The most useful function of the true contemporary historian is to provide the first orderly and objective analysis of the confused masses of information immediately released by public events.'[9] David Butler has commented further:

> I believe that it is usually possible to write about events as soon as they occur and to present a balanced account which is comparable in its objectivity and its achievement to the balanced account which the traditional historian, writing about the happenings of past centuries, aspires to provide.[10]

Contemporary and 'instant' history

Contemporary history seeks to record events soon after they have occurred. Although the *Journal of Contemporary History* includes any history relating to this century (and even the late nineteenth century), for the purposes of this book we have narrowed down the definition of

contemporary history (as distinct from modern or recent history) to
works written *at about the same time* as the events being discussed, which
we consider to be within a space of some five years or so; an 'instant'
history might be written within the space of one year. However, a few
books that were published after a slightly longer time interval are
included in this section because they share so many characteristics of
contemporary history.

As David Butler has pointed out, contemporary history is not new,
and has highly respectable early practitioners – Herodotus, Thucydides
and Tacitus in the classical world, and Jean Froissart (in his *Chronicles*),
Edward, Earl of Clarendon, and Gilbert Burnet, the Bishop of the
Salisbury, in the medieval and early modern periods. The first contemporary history to be written this century was probably James Hope's
A History of the 1900 Parliament (1908). Another important early
example was Dean E. McHenry's *The Labour Party in Transition 1931–38*
(1938), published on the eve of the Second World War.[11] McHenry (an
American) tells us how he visited 'two dozen' constituencies throughout Britain in the 1935 general election, and 'interviewed Labour's
opponents ranging from a Cabinet Minister in Downing Street to a
Communist lady in Merthyr Tydfil'. Labour members who helped him
are mentioned by name, including Clement Attlee, Stafford Cripps,
Hugh Dalton, George Lansbury and Malcolm MacDonald. Source notes
are provided only for published works. The writing of contemporary
history has increased dramatically since the Second World War (when
compared to total history books published) in two main areas: histories
of elections, their campaigns and 'run-up' periods; and history of other
specific events or periods.

Elections

In Britain general elections since 1945 have been described in the series
sponsored by Nuffield College, Oxford, The books describe the background of the major political developments since the last election,
examine why the leaders decided to call the elections, provide an analysis
of the campaign at the centre and in the provinces, and include a discussion of the media coverage and a psephological analysis of election
results and voting trends.[12] Extensive systematic interviewing was not
introduced as a major source until the volume on the 1964 election,
written jointly by David Butler and Anthony King. For the book on the
1966 election, also written by Butler and King, the authors conducted
some 400 interviews spread over more than two years, taking trouble to
see 'virtually everybody who was anybody' among party leaders and

party officials, and interviewing some individuals 'seven or eight times'.[13] Butler and his co-authors are able to gain access to anyone they might want to see; interviewees are found to be 'remarkably frank', and evasiveness and one-sidedness are circumvented by repeatedly returning to the same subject with different people and from different angles.[14]

Because of the essentially contemporary nature of their work (each draft with which Butler has been associated has been completed within three months of the election and published well within the year), the authors have benefited from interviews, circulation of drafts, absorption of contemporary atmosphere, and accumulation of press cuttings and election ephemera day by day (the press being, in Butler's words, '*the* major source on events' when writing about elections).[15] Tracking down relevant press cuttings can be very time-consuming if they were not collected at the time, and *The Times* and *The Economist* are still the only major newspapers and weeklies to provide full indexes. The Nuffield volumes are therefore able to utilize contemporary sources to the full and provide an account that is unlikely to be substantially altered, even after the party and private archives have become open to researchers. The series has virtually monopolized the writing about general elections in Britain.[16]

Anthony Howard and Richard West, in *The Making of the Prime Minister* (inspired by Theodore White's *The Making of the President 1960*),[17] discuss the background to the general election of October 1964. These authors too have relied heavily on interviews, and describe how in the period between January 1963 and October 1964 'we have had constant talks with front and back-benchers of both political parties'.[18] The authors conducted approximately twenty interviews, although they held many more discussions which were informal and could not be described as 'interviews'; only 10 per cent or less of those they approached declined to provide them with material.[19] This book was followed by, *The Making of the Prime Minister 1970* (1970), by Andrew Alexander and Alan Watkins, who drew mainly upon their own personal contacts as political journalists.

A comparatively new entrant in the field is the American Enterprise Institute's (AEI) series of studies on elections in selected democratic countries. The first book in the series, published in 1975, described the two 1974 British general elections. The most recent British volume, *British at the Polls 1979*,[20] inevitably covers much the same ground as the Nuffield College studies. Most of the authors appear to have used oral evidence, and one, Anthony King, refers to talks (unattributed) in his footnotes. In common with most collectors of contemporary oral evidence, King conducts informal interviews, with no tape recorder and no set questions, is an attempt to elicit information 'off the record'.[21]

Specific events and periods

Before 1945, contemporary history of specific events or periods had been written only sporadically during peacetime, but it had been far more common in wartime. In the Preface to *The British Campaign In France and Flanders 1914* (1916), Arthur Conan Doyle justified such history and described his methods:

> It is continually stated that it is impossible to bring out at the present time any accurate history of the war. . . . No doubt this is true so far as some points of the larger strategy are concerned . . . many incidents which have exercised the minds of statesmen and . . . many possibilities which have worried the soldiers. But so far as the actual early events of our own campaign upon the continent are concerned, there is no reason why the approximate truth should not now be collected and set forth.

The significance of interviews had not escaped contemporary historians while the next world war was being waged. Gavin Henderson, for example, wrote in 1941:

> We can meet and discuss matters, any day we like, with men who were at Dunkirk. Would not the true medievalist give up his whole life's research for the sake of one interview with one Saxon who fought beside Harold at Hastings?[23]

This form of contemporary or instant history – like that focusing on elections – has burgeoned since the Second World War. A celebrated early example was Hugh Trevor-Roper's remarkable volume of contemporary history, *The Last Days of Hitler* (1947). In the Foreword, Lord Tedder, who had been Deputy Supreme Commander of the Allied Expeditionary Force (1943–5), wrote that the war had shown him the immense and even decisive influence of individual personalities on the course of events. 'In the past', he wrote, 'it has rarely been possible for the effects of the personality and character of individual leaders to be assessed other than by the study of documents.' Such history, Tedder believed, was unsatisfactory because 'the life had gone out of them', and suffered from distortion through bias and 'incomplete evidence'. Trevor-Roper, on the other hand, had been able to produce 'history written from living material', based on 'living testimony' as well as on the flood of documentary material that became available at the end of the war.

Trevor-Roper's oral evidence was from two main sources: evidence given at the Nuremburg trials and other official allied bodies (to provide general background), and that collected by Trevor-Roper himself. Admittedly the circumstances of his enquiry – as an intelligence officer charged with the task of encovering step by step the events of the last few weeks of Hitler's life – are somewhat different from the interviewing undertaken by most authors, but it is contemporary oral history none the less. Although Trevor-Roper does not provide many footnotes to these oral sources, a full 'Note on Sources' at the end of the book lists the forty-two eyewitnesses who provided personal testimony. Trevor-Roper later wrote that he does not see an absolute distinction between oral and documentary evidence: 'After all, an interrogation, being written down, becomes a document.' He continued:

> My evidence was largely 'contemporary oral evidence'; even my documents were, in large part, contemporary oral evidence written down. What makes them more accurate, in some respects, than later reconstructions is this contemporaneity: the evidence was given when it was fresh. But of course it could still be erroneous, biased or perverted. I think that the method of the historian is the essential element, for it is that – not the difference between 'oral' and 'documentary' – which determines which evidence is more reliable.'[24]

Chester Wilmot was able to base his classic work *The Struggle for Europe* largely on the extensive German documents that became available after the war, and had special access to allied documentation; he employed oral evidence chiefly for information on the allied side. As a war correspondent for much of the war (latterly for the BBC, 1944–5) and as special correspondent for the BBC at the Nuremburg trials, he was able not just to undertake contemporary cross-examination but to soak up the atmosphere and witness events for himself. Retrospective interviews were also conducted with many allied officers, such as Lords Dowding and Tedder, Admiral Sir George Creasy and Sir Brian Horrocks. 'Almost every page', Wilmot wrote, 'bears witness' to these interviews. He acknowledged that 'The contemporary historian is in the happy position of being able in many cases to verify and amplify the documentary sources by interrogating the men who were directly or indirectly concerned in their origination.'[25]

A steady but slow stream of contemporary histories followed, describing the events of peacetime. Robert A. Brady, (an American author), when researching for his book on the Attlee government, *Crisis in Britain* (1950), talked to both politicians and civil servants. Moreover, he writes, 'one or more persons in each of the government agencies whose policies are discussed in the following chapters . . . read, criticized, and amended appropriate sections of the manuscript.'[26] The passage of the Independent Television Act of 1954 provoked *Pressure Group* (1961), one of the first books of contemporary postwar history to be based in part on the open and systematic use of interview evidence.[27] The author, H. H. Wilson, states that he relied on the public print – the press, journals and Hansard – but that he also found interviews indispensable: 'Admittedly a difficult and even hazardous method, it is often the only way the student may be able to produce a realistic account.' Some of those he interviewed he does list, although many refused to be cited or even named, and the author even takes the bold and unusual step of naming a civil servant, Sir Ben Barnett, the chief official responsible for the Act at the Post Office (then a Whitehall department).[28]

Suez produced a flutter of contemporary histories, from Paul Johnson's *The Suez War* (1957), whose opening two paragraphs, describing incidents within the US State Department and British Foreign Office, reveal from the outset that oral evidence had been employed,[29] through to Hugh Thomas's later and fuller *The Suez Affair* (1967), which is, by our definition, a work of recent rather than contemporary history. Thomas makes no bones about his reliance on interview evidence: 'In order to investigate the truth, I approached the serving protagonists of that time.' Many saw him, although some declined by dint of 'that curious statute, the Official Secrets Act'.[30] Unlike many authors of contemporary history, Thomas provides endnotes, and goes as far as any author appears to have done hitherto in presenting these references in the form 'Evidence of a Cabinet Minister', 'Comment of a critically placed Minister', 'Evidence of a task force Commander' or 'Evidence of a Foreign Office official'. Only very rarely does Thomas mention interviewees by name, as in the case of Lord Robens and Kenneth Younger (both Labour MPs, and hence not subject to the Official Secrets Act binding on ministers and officials).[31]

Affairs abroad in the 1950s and early 1960s provoked a number of other contemporary histories. Pioneering among these in the use of oral evidence was David Nunnerley's *President Kennedy and Britain* (1972), in which the author declares: 'The chief source of this book has been the systematic interrogation of as many as possible of the principals involved. . . . This process of close verbal questioning was made essential by the absence of most of the official papers.' Boldly situated at the front of the book is a 'List of persons interviewed and office held', mentioning some eighty by name, including many Foreign Office officials such as Lords Caccia and Sherfield. One can only assume that the assassination of President Kennedy in some way precipitated the unprecedented frankness with which British officials agreed to talk and to be mentioned by name.[32] Another episode, the Profumo affair of 1963, prompted the publication in the same year of *Scandal '63*. This was written by a small body of the newly formed *Sunday Times* 'Insight' team, headed by Clive Irving. A forerunner of many subsequent instant histories written by journalists, it offers no guidance on sources but is clearly based to a considerable extent upon oral evidence.[33] This was followed shortly after by another journalist's history, Anthony Shrimsley's *The First Hundred Days of Harold Wilson*. Shrimsley at least provides us with a foreword in which he explains that he constructed the record partly on talks, but that the 'regrettable price of contemporary "history" of this kind is that I am not free to name some of my sources. I therefore name none.'[34]

In more recent years the pace of such books has still further quickened. Stephen Haseler benefited to some extent from talks on recent British politics with senior Labour politicians in his *The Death of British Democracy* (1976), (His earlier *The Gaitskellites* (1969) had been one of the first serious studies to confer respectability on interviews by giving them pride of place in the 'Primary sources' in his bibliography.[35]) It is common practice for periods as well as events to become the subject of instant histories. The Conservatives in opposition, 1974–9, are the subject of Robert Behrens's *The Conservative Party from Heath to Thatcher* (1980). Comparatively unusually for an instant history, the author provides (anonymous) endnotes to interviews, plus the date when the person was seen – a valuable practice which not only gives the reader some idea of the authority on which statements are based ('shadow minister', 'senior Central Office official', etc.) but will make it easier for scholars working on the period in future years to trace authors' deployment of oral evidence, should they at some point in the future deposit their interview records in a library or archive. The journalists Alistair Michie and Simon Hoggart in *The Pact: The Inside Story of the Lib–Lab Government 1977–8* (1978) and Hugh Stephenson in *Mrs Thatcher's First Year* (1980), however, do not provide any indication of interview sources, and these books are thus likely to prove of less value to readers in the future who will have no idea of the authority on which certain statements are made.

Such journalistic instant histories are undoubtedly valuable, although it would be even more useful if a larger number of contemporary histories were written a number of years after the conclusion of each government, when authors felt they could provide more indication of sources employed.

The potential of instant history at its best has been well demonstrated in a book that has been regularly consulted by the media, and will be invaluable in the future to historians writing on the political events of 1981: Ian Bradley's *Breaking the Mould* (1981), on the origins of the Social Democratic Party. Bradley, a journalist on *The Times*, conducted a dozen interviews, without which he says the book could not have been written:

> I wanted firm answers to a lot of basic questions. How the party came to be formed, what were the stages in its development and the break-away from the Labour Party. I wanted to know dates and precise information for myself, rather than reading them second-hand in the press, which could not always be relied upon. I wanted to find out when Roy Jenkins first thought of the Dimbleby lecture theme, and what he was trying to do in the lecture. I was looking for opinions about who was talking to whom at certain key stages, about group-ings at different periods, and relationships between the four main protagonists.

Bradley's personal discussions with these principals were all too brief: Roy Jenkins and William Rodgers could only be talked to on the telephone; a rather hurried hour was spent with Shirley Williams, and a weekend with David Owen at his constituency before Bradley had settled on writing the book. The most useful discussions were with their personal assistants, whom he found to be very accurate on dates and hard facts, and rather more informative about the motives and feelings of the 'Gang of Four' than the latter were themselves. For the talks with the personal assistants, Bradley took his subjects out to lunch, and made notes throughout. 'I'd liked to have taped the talks,' he said, 'so I could have been absolutely sure what they all said. But time was really insuffi-cient.' Bradley summarized his experience:

> In a contemporary study like the birth of the SDP, interviewing was extremely important because I was researching a development which of its nature is not documented. With hindsight one is inclined to see the breakaway as a logical process; interviewing helped make me realize how haphazard and random it all was.[36]

Political science

Political science is concerned with analysing the working of the political system rather than with describing through the passage of time the policy which that system produced. Walter Bagehot used oral evidence to particular effect in his *The English Constitution* of 1867, and the tradition was continued for instance by A. Lawrence Lowell in *The Government of England*. In the preface, Lowell states 'the forces to be studied do not lie upon the surface, and some of them are not described in any document or found in any treatise. They can only be learned from men connected with the machinery of public life. A student must therefore rely largely upon conversations.' This practice, combined with those statistical techniques of which Lowell himself was a pioneer, have lain behind much of the development in the writing of political science this century. Political scientists have been able to compensate for an inherent lack of access to documentary evidence by the use of élite interviewing. This has enabled them to circumvent what David Butler (1968) described as one of the gaps which the authors of the Nuffield Election Studies were aware of in their work in the twenty or so years after 1945: the absence of information on policy decisions in the highest places.[37]

Interviewing of élites has been a tool in the political scientist's research methodology throughout the century. Beatrice Webb, who, with her husband Sidney, criticized Woodrow Wilson's *Congressional Government* for being written 'entirely from the printed documents' – wrote in *My Apprenticeship* (1926): in investigating 'existing social institutions the student finds himself continuously seeking acquaintance with the persons directly concerned with the working of these institutions in order to "interview" them.'[38] Interviews before the 1960s tended to be *ad hoc*, based on personal approaches and contacts, and restricted more to politicians than to civil servants. It has only been since the early 1960s that large numbers of books based in part on systematic interviews on a wide scale, especially with officials, have been conducted – a development that has coincided with the explosion in the number and range of books on political science. This development has enabled political scientists to penetrate far deeper into areas, such as the working of the Civil Service, where the public print itself will not permit a full understanding to be gained. A historian like G. R. Elton, whose research methods are necessarily grounded in documents, can thus write: '[the Cabinet] is a subject for which the materials are exceptionally hard to come by'.[39] The use of oral evidence permits one to overcome these difficulties.

One volume to stand out from the 1945–60 period, for its originality and for its use of oral as well as written evidence, is R. T. McKenzie's *British Political Parties*. Its central thesis is that, despite their different origins and constitutions, the Conservative and Labour parties were fundamentally similar in their activities. Among McKenzie's main non-written sources were over fifty practising politicians who addressed a postgraduate seminar at the LSE, organized by D. G. MacRae, R. H. Pear and himself. He also learnt much, as have so many political scientists before and since, from imbibing the atmosphere of politics, and he remarks: 'I know of no better place to get the "feel" of party activity than in conversation over a cup of tea with a team of canvassers who have spent a chilly evening spying out the land on behalf of their party's cause.'[40] In additions, McKenzie had resort to personal interviews to gain 'firsthand knowledge of the working of British political parties', spending 'hours in conversation' at the House of Commons, party head-quarters, annual conferences, and regional and local offices of the parties.[41]

The early sixties saw a new impetus in the use of oral evidence by scholars. John Mackintosh wrote *The British Cabinet* (1962), a work intended initially to be an updated version of A. Berriedale Keith's second edition of *British Cabinet System*. Mackintosh explained that he compensated for the absence of documentary evidence on recent periods because of the (then) fifty-year rule 'by means of a series of interviews with ex-Cabinet Ministers, Civil Servants, and others who have had opportunities for observing the Cabinet at work'.[42] Officials, he explained, preferred not to be named, but he does list some thirty ex-Cabinet ministers whom he interviewed, including Lords Attlee, Halifax and Salisbury. In the second edition (1968) Mackintosh explains what he looked for in his interviews – 'The object of the interviews was to obtain the general impression of recent practice' – and affirmed what is still the standard convention in political science writing: 'no quotations are used and none of the information is deployed in a manner which could reveal, even to those involved, the source of my information.'[43]

In the same year as the first edition of Mackintosh's *The British Cabinet* appeared the first political science book to be based almost exclusively on the product of large-scale systematic interviewing (written evidence playing very much in subsidiary role); it was written, not surprisingly, by a journalist, Anthony Sampson. The first edition of *Anatomy of Britain* was published in 1962, and although its focus is considerably wider than government, including business, education, and other areas of public life, it may still be considered a work of political science. Sampson explained: 'My method has been fairly strightforward: I have written to about two hundred people, asking to see them, and asking what they were up to.'[44] Sampson's response, to what must then have been a fairly unusual request, was very good: 'the more important the people', he writes, 'the easier, it seems, they are to see.' The Cabinet, senior civil servants and chairmen of the major corporations all agreed to talk, and apparently only three turned him down. Sampson decided to mention them by name; as we have explained, this practice is in our view undesirable.

Despite the increased volume of writing on political science since the early 1960s, there has been little change in the generally agreed practice of not attributing or mentioning witnesses in text, notes or acknowledgements (except, occasionally, for politicians, pressure group leaders, etc., who are not bound by, or not concerned about, the Official Secrets Act). Seldom has a book appeared that has been bold or explicit in its deployment of oral evidence. One such a book is Peter Kellner and Lord Crowther-Hunt's *The Civil Servants* (1980), which contains unattributed verbatim quotations from civil servants and, in the case of Lord Armstrong of Sandersted, attributed quotations.[45] The authors did, however, ensure that, where interviewees were quoted, even without attribution, prior permission had been gained.[46] With increasing interviews of civil servants in the media, as in radio programme like the BBC's *No Minister* (1981), it seems likely that more direct quotation from civil servants will be made in books in the future in both non-attributed and even attributed form.

Personal élite interviewing has enabled not just Whitehall as a whole but also the organization of, and policy-making process within, individual departments to be studied in depth, permitting a far more accurate and profound picture than could be gleaned by studying the New Whitehall Series. Three recent books on the operation of individual Whitehall departments, for example, employed oral evidence in the unattributed form: William Wallace's *The Foreign Policy Process in Britain* (1975), on the Foreign and Commonwealth Office; William Keegan and Rupert Pennant-Rea's *Who Runs the Economy?* (1979), on the Treasury; and Maurice Kogan's *Educational Policy-Making* (1975), on the Department of Education and Science. Interviewing has permitted intra-Whitehall relations to be studied, notably in Hugh Heclo and Aaron Wildavsky's *The Private Government of Public Money* (1974), in which oral evidence played a key part. The authors wrote that 'The political-administrative culture of British central government is a shadowy realm usually left to chance observations in politicians' memoirs or civil servants' valedictories'; the gathering of oral evidence therefore, was crucial. The authors ensured that their interviewees appreciated that they were not writing contemporary history but a work of analysis (i.e. political science):

> We suggested that interviews be granted on the understanding that we would not ask about current cases on personalities, a restriction that widened our entry and avoided the temptation to compete with journalists for current news. . . . Respondents were asked to describe, not who did whom in last week, but how people generally go about doing each other in; not who personally helped them, but where and how they normally look for support.[47]

The judiciary is another area where oral evidence allows deeper understanding. For Alan Peterson's *The Law Lords*, fifteen law lords among others were interviewed at length. Because of this, Paterson was able to write, in the words of Hugo Young, 'a unique book, which advances knowledge about how our country is ruled as well as judged . . . further than any other legal work of my acquaintance'.[48]

The writing on the operation of local government in contrast is one area where interviewing has had a long history. To cite two examples from a vast pre-war literature on local government, John Maud's (later Lord Redcliffe-Maud) *Local Government in Modern England* (1932) was based in part on talks with local government officials whom the author visited over a three-year period;[49] and Herman Finer, for his *English Local Government* (1933), not only interviewed Whitehall officials, who provided material 'with urbane informativeness', but also circulated a questionnaire to several scores of local authorities.[50] Fifty years later such systematic inquiry was continued, for example, by Alan Alexander of the University of Reading, writing on the performance of local government since the reforms that followed the Redcliffe-Maud Report of 1969. Alexander wrote to 101 local government chief executives (out of a total of 487) requesting an interview, and met with a positive response from about 85 per cent.[51] George W. Jones, a leading authority on local government, has outlined the benefits he has derived from interviewing, which can usefully be noted by any political scientist about to embark on gathering oral evidence:

> One, the uncovering of the way things happened and processes, the *how* of politics and government. Two, atmosphere, emotion, the feel

of events. Three, specific anecdotes, illustrations, incidents, to provide authenticity. Four, attitudes to people and events. Five, correcting textbook or conventional accounts. Six, to assess who and what were vertically and horizontally influential at key points.[52]

The development of *systematic* interviewing in political science has not been without drawbacks: Bruce Headey, for example, wrote in our questionnaire that his *British Cabinet Ministers* (1974) suffered from: 'lack of *detailed* case studies/behavioural evidence to test the fit between perceptions and behaviour'. J.D. Aberbach, R.D. Putnam and B.A. Rockman comment in their *Bureaucrats and Politicians in Western Deomocracies* (1981) that: 'The fieldwork was only the beginning of our task. We next have to develop a coding procedure to convert our conversational interviews into quantative data – an extremely delicate job.' But in both cases these books demonstrate the potential for interviewing to peer deep into the realities of the working relationships in government.

The contribution of interviewing to the understanding of government has thus been critical. Few would deny that we have a more accurate perception of government today than we had twenty-five years ago, or that oral evidence has played an essential role in that transformation.

10

Cultural history

We now turn to an examination of some ways in which oral evidence can illuminate understanding of artists and their work. This chapter discusses two literary forms, the biography and the interview-based work.

Literary biography

The use of oral recollection in literary biography is not new. As Alfred Kazin points out in his introduction to *Writers at Work: The 'Paris Review' Interviews*, Boswell at the close of the eighteenth century and Eckemann in the nineteenth conducted interviews when writing their books on Dr Johnson and Goethe respectively.[1] However, the potential of oral history evidence for the biographer has only been fully realized this century.

As Robert Gittings shows in *The Nature of Biography*, 'Biography begins . . . in praise. It is also, whether openly or not, didactic praise.' Thus 'In medieval European times, the Latin Chronicle is almost exclusively the reward of successful secular rulers or of saints.'[2] This style of biography gradually gave way in the first half of the sixteenth century to works that portrayed the man as an ornament to the state, as an example of civic or secular values. The nineteenth century saw the consolidation of biographical tact: the subject's weaknesses were underplayed, and potentially embarrassing material was suppressed. Biography became, in Gittings's words, 'in part, the art of concealment'.[3] Typical might be the life of Dickens by his friend John Forster, concealing not only the novelist's estrangement from his wife but also information about his mistress and his unstable personality, crucial to the understanding of the man's 'life'.

The change to frank (as opposed to concealing) and critical (as opposed to laundatory) biography came in the early twentieth century, and was much associated with the name of Lytton Strachey, whose work, in particular his *Eminent Victorians*, heralded a new style of open biography by detached observers. To the biographer or interviewer the change has been of enormous significance: the detached observer (as opposed to the collaborator or friend) who now writes biography seeks not merely information about the subject and his circle but also facts that might be of a highly personal or critical nature – which oral history evidence can supply in abundance.

Two distinct forms of biography may be singled out: the 'official life' biography, an account of the man's deeds stripped of all details of his private life; and the 'literary biography', an account of the man and his works. It is the use of oral evidence in this second form that will now be examined, a practice reinforced by the sometimes more controversial or unconventional private lives of figures in the world of art compared to those in politics.

The notion of 'frank' biography is expected now not just by biographers and the public but also, it would seem, by those who supply oral evidence. The desire to 'reveal' may, however, paradoxically lead to a distortion of the truth, and the biographer-turned-interviewer should beware of misinterpreting oral evidence for the sake of an apparent 'scoop'. Bernard Crick for his biography of George Orwell, interviewed a female witness who expressed many objections to the way in which Orwell's previous biographers, Peter Stansky and William Abrahams,[4] had 'dolled . . . up' the interview she gave them, and had conveyed the impression that she and Orwell were closer to one another than they in fact were. Her remark that 'only the truth is interesting, and a cosmetic biography is a very great pity', provides a pertinent motto for every literary biographer.[5]

Yet the new frankness is not without its critics. W. H. Auden has argued:

> biographies of writers . . . are always superfluous and usually in bad taste. A writer is a maker, not a man of action . . . no knowledge of the raw ingredients [of his life] will explain the peculiar flavour of the verbal dishes he invites the public to taste . . .[6]

But one cannot hope to write about artists' lives without occasionally exposing some squalid corners of their experience: 'Discretion . . . is not the better part of biography', as Lytton Strachey remarked.[7] Indeed, when one considers that literature, notably the novel, is frequently a presentation of the intricate web of human relationships, one perceives that biography can be faithful to the medium of its subject only by developing its own applied version of that web. For, as Wilfrid Sheed has said, 'gossip [broadly defined] is the very stuff of literature, the *materia prima* of which both books and their authors are made.'[8]

How effective is, in fact, oral history interviewing in supplying information about relationships or other personal matters? Biographers themselves find that in confidential talk the fallible and more human side may emerge, where it would have been left undivulged by the written word. Intimacy is a key factor in the oral history interviewing of this kind. One biographer who frequently employs oral history techniques, Michael Holroyd, emphasizes the important distinction between private interviews conducted for a book, where the rapport established may stimulate candour and trust, and radio or television interviews, where the public element means that 'you become a different person'.[9] Gittings takes a similarly disparaging view of 'public' oral evidence:

> One has only to see or hear a so-called confrontation between two famous people, or an apparently frank statement by a single one of them, to know that the caution imposed by the consciousness of the vast possible audience has reduced such discussions and such statements to meaninglessness.[10]

Roger Berthoud, a feature writer on *The Times*, who has recently published a life of Graham Sutherland,[11] commented on the differences he encountered between the journalistic interviews to which he had been accustomed, and those (approximately eighty in all) he conducted with Sutherland's circle. The latter type was much more leisurely, since, relatively unhampered by time limits on the conversation, Berthoud felt able to let his informant roam. He thought it wise to have extraneous matter on record.[12] Even material that is not used in the book itself may, after all, form part of the subject's archive, if properly transcribed or preserved as a good-quality tape recording.[13]

Just as the interview conducted for private research will differ markedly from a public 'media' interview, so also will the subject of the biography affect the style of the witness. Unlike civil servants and current politicians, who can be evasive and cagey with interviewers,

people in the world of art and letters tend, by the very nature of their profession, to be communicative. There is a price to be paid for such
volubility, however. Michael Holroyd found that many of the
informants for his biography of Augustus John were 'all over the shop'
in interview.[14] A crucial witness for Berthoud's book – an intimate
friend of Sutherland during his student days – gave an interview that
was 'like a page out of Laurence Sterne – diffuse and rambling, yet there
were nuggets of pure gold to be sifted out.'[15]

When assessing witnesses' honesty about personal details, the literary
biographer might bear in mind Gittings's cautionary remark that 'One
lesson every biographer learns is that people's capacity for sexual fantasy
is unlimited.'[16] Michael Holroyd was confronted by this problem when
dealing in his research with Lytton Strachey's homosexual love life. As
he admits in his preface, 'my plan depended for its practicability on the
cooperation of a band of mercurial octogenarians. It was for all of us a
daunting prospect.'[17] Understandably, many witnesses are far from
anxious to comply with the practice of open revelation. The subject's
close family are usually found to be very protective, and, in the case of an
artist or writer viewed as something of an eccentric by the rest of society,
will feel they have a vested interest in rendering him or her more
'normal'.[18] Indeed, those who were active participants in the subject's
life may wish to minimize their involvements, if it was of an
embarrassing nature. Michael Holroyd found people he interviewed for
his biography of Lytton Strachey were reluctant to talk about their
homosexuality – especially since the discussions were conducted before
the publication of the Wolfenden Report. One of his informants, after
reading through Holroyd's typescript, asked if he would be arrested.
'Another, with deep pathos, exclaimed: "When this comes out, they
will never again allow me into Lord's!"'[19] The task of gathering honest
information about a subject's personal life is further complicated by the
frequently encountered problem of jealousy. Roger Berthoud, however,
found that 'fellow artists seem reluctant to comment on the work of a
famous contemporary' – not for reasons of jealousy, but rather 'to avoid
sounding bitchy'.[20]

Despite the pitfalls of oral information in literary biography – and
many difficulties mentioned in Chapter 2 apply with force to this
medium – biographers clearly find interviewing worth the trouble. The
survey conducted for this book revealed that biographers of cultural
subjects – conducting interviews ranging from fewer than ten in
number to 200 and more – all reported that they gained material that

could not have been discovered from other sources. The oral evidence for
a literary biography need not, of course, always be of an embarrassing
nature. Quentin Bell found that the value of most of his interviews for
the biography of Virginia Woolf (with the exception of those with
Leonard Woolf, who provided factual detail and much illuminating
general information) was that they gave him a notion of how people responded to his subject[21] – a particularly significant bonus in the biography
of an artist as complex as Virginia Woolf.

A by-product of clear footnoting of oral evidence is that it can ease the
task of those seeking to analyse the use made of interviews in literary
biography. Alas, the task is obstructed by the fact that, frequently, interview sources are mentioned neither in footnotes nor in the text itself.
One can understand and sympathize with the reasons for biographers'
wishing to disguise their oral sources, in view of the often sensitive
material that is imparted; however, a reference to 'Private interview' can
be better than no reference.

This study of the use of oral history in literary biography must therefore rely heavily on the work of those authors who are thorough in
stating precisely when a piece of information or an idea is drawn from an
interview: good examples are Jeffrey Meyers, in his biographies of
Katherine Mansfield and Wyndham Lewis;[22] Bernard Crick, in his book
on George Orwell; and Paul Ferris, in his *Dylan Thomas*. In the absence
of footnote or textual reference to interviews in many other biographies,
one must turn instead to the authors' acknowledgements. A sample of
twelve biographies of English-speaking cultural figures all give formal
acknowledgement to those who have granted interviews. However, the
authors do not always differentiate between information supplied by
letter and evidence given in interview.[23] Ted Morgan provides one
exception: the acknowledgements of his *Somerset Maugham* specifically
name thirty-seven witnesses who 'allowed themselves to be interviewed',[24] but the actual use of these interviews is clarified neither by the
notes nor by the text itself.

Crick, Ferris and Meyers all include references to interviews carried
out by previous researchers, or by the BBC as part of documentaries.
Crick's notes further include seventy-five references to personal
interviews, and Meyers's thirty-four (*Katherine Mansfield*) and eighty-
one (*Wyndham Lewis*). These two authors offer a model for the use of
oral history in biography. Their references to each interview are informative and precise, giving both date and location. The tone is set by
Meyers's first reference to an interview, noted as 'Interview with

William Craddock Barclay in Wellington, June 17, 1976.'[25] Crick also specifies in each case, whether it was he who conducted the interview or whether it came from an oral archive, as well as quoting at some length from the interviews in the text. A considerable number of references combine interview and letter sources, thus bearing out both the claim that oral history techniques often lead to the revelation of further documentary evidence, and the caution that oral evidence needs to be checked against documents (but not making it easy to see which material came from oral evidence). Paul Ferris mentions over a hundred interview references in his notes – not a large number for the 200 or more interviews he conducted – and sometimes indicates place of interview, but does not always provide dates. He also employs a useful technique, as described in his notes to *Dylan Thomas*: 'Where an informant is named but no context given for the information, it can be assumed it was in an interview with the author.'[26]

Another biography which does give some indication of interview sources is Quentin Bell's life of Virginia Woolf, which has forty-seven footnote references to 'p.i.' ('private information'): these the author defines as 'hearsay evidence'.[27] He follows this abbreviation with the name or initials of his informant. The drawback of this system again is that it fails to distinguish between information conveyed by letter and evidence given in interview.

For his biography of Augustus John, Michael Holroyd conducted nearly a hundred interviews, but he footnotes oral sources only obliquely – for example, 'X to the author'. This method is partly explained, perhaps, by the fact that he does not usually take notes during interviews and is less concerned with verbatim quotations 'the people I interview seem to talk more naturally and I believe truthfully if there is no equipment between us – not even the notebook and pen.' He sits and listens, writing up as soon as possible afterwards 'what has happened between us'.[28]

One factor that full references can indicate is the extent to which biographers had to (or chose to) travel for their material. Meyers conducted interviews in England, New Zealand and the United States for his life of Katherine Mansfield; while Crick's pursuit of the real Orwell took him to rather more humdrum corners, in suburban Surrey and Middlesex, consistent with his overall intention of interviewing as many as possible of the 'ordinary' people who crossed his subject's path. His references show us the *type* of person who was interviewed, thus suggesting the kind of balance the biographer sought to attain.

Oral evidence can be particularly useful for filling in details of an artist's early life. For *Dylan Thomas*, Paul Ferris interviewed many people from the Swansea area, in order to build up a full picture of the poet's family background and youth. A few of these, he admits, 'still grow tight-lipped when asked to reminisce, but this may be irritation with two and a half decades of interviewers.'[29] Both Meyers and Crick sought the reminiscences of old schoolfriends and fellow students in their respective biographies of Katherine Mansfield and George Orwell. Similarly, Michael Holroyd interviewed student friends and acquaintances for his section on Augustus John's studies at the Slade.

A key witness in Meyers's *Katherine Mansfield* was the artist Dorothy Brett, whose friendship with the writer began in 1915. She told Meyers that Katherine Mansfield was so poor during her early adulthood in London that 'she had inadequate shoes and clothing,' and 'could not afford cabs'. This 'poverty affected her delicate health.'[30] When Meyers interviewed Brett in Taos, New Mexico, in March 1976, she was 93 years old, and in Meyers's words 'a lively, frank, kind and responsive woman, [who] spoke generously of Katherine, Murry, Lawrence, Frieda, [Mark] Gertler, [Dora] Carrington, Ottoline Morrell and Virginia Woolf, and made it easy to understand why so many extra-ordinary people liked her and became her friend.'[31] Such an interview is invaluable in allowing the biographer to become acquainted himself with a person to whom the biography's subject was close. It is also often likely to be more reliable than interviews with the subject's closest family, which can be more partial. Thus Paul Ferris implies scepticism in presenting the evidence, by Dylan Thomas's mother, about her son's juvenilia: 'Her account of how these early poems came to be written was a fond mother's view of the precocious boy, happy with pencil and paper. . . . She gave the impression that some of this writing was done before he was ten.'[32]

Quentin Bell is another biographer who found oral evidence valuable in filling in details of his subject's early life. He conducted interviews with, among others, Virginia Woolf's family; some of his principal oral sources were his own mother, Vanessa Bell, and fellow artists such as Duncan Grant. He relies far more on 'private information' in the first volume of *Virginia Woolf*, for which fewer letters exist, than for the second. Much of this 'information' refers simply to what people supposedly said at the time. Even if Virginia Woolf did not make all the witty, sometimes stinging remarks attributed to her, such comments at least demonstrates that those in her family and social circle believed her capable of them.

In retracing George Orwell's schooldays at Eton, Bernard Crick talked to the writer's old tutor, Andrew Gow, in 1976. The schoolmaster's antipathy towards his celebrated former pupil persisted, even after such a long time-lapse: he maintained that Orwell 'made himself as big a nuisance as he could' and 'was a very unattractive boy'.[33] Discussing the fact that Orwell did not try for Oxford because he could not afford to go without a scholarship, Gow stated that he himself has told Orwell's father that the boy did not stand the slightest chance of winning one. 'And sixty years later', notes the biographer, 'Gow fumed that [Orwell] would have brought "disgrace on College" had they even put him forward for a scholarship examination, since he had done "absolutely no work for five years".'[34] Interviewing a figure whom the subject himself may have virtually forgotten once he has disappeared from his own life may, as in this particular instance, revive the violent emotions he aroused in others. When, however, Crick read back to Gow Stansky and Abraham's account of what he had said to them six years before, Gow contradicted several aspects of the account. Crick simply leaves the reader to judge whether Gow's memory or their reporting was at fault.[35]

A further insight is provided by Ruth Pitter's tape-recorded memories of George Orwell's early attempts at writing in the 1920s: 'He wrote so badly. He had to teach himself writing. . . . He became a master of English, but it was sheer hard grind . . . we had to correct the spelling.'[36]

Crick's interviewing research on Orwell also places in a somewhat unusual light his subject's political attitudes. An interview with someone who fought with Orwell in Spain offers an eccentric variation on the writer's politics, as manifested in practice, as opposed to theory: in discussion, apparently, 'Basically [Orwell's] attitude was Fascist, he didn't like the workers. . . . I don't care what he says and what he's written, when you spoke to him he didn't like them, he despised them.'[37] It would be unwise to interpret such partisan opinions as gospel: as Crick shows in dismissing the evidence of another figure in Spain, who 'plainly disliked' Orwell, an interviewee's claims – in this case, that Orwell went to Spain primarily to write a book, not to fight[38] – must be judged cautiously.

Since Orwell sometimes excited hostile reactions, it is therefore essential to Bernard Crick's biography that he includes the impressions of a large number of witnesses. A life as varied as Orwell's, which

involved contact with so many different kinds of people, requires the
dimension that oral history provides – the view from diverse angles.
We thus are provided with not only the view of a former pupil that 'It
was obvious that [Orwell's] head was full of interesting and amusing
thoughts and not infrequently these would get the better of him and his
face would be creased with irrepressible smiles,'[39] but also we are given
the testimony of the poet and critic David Holbrook who, according to
Crick's interpretation, 'saw Orwell as an intrinsically cold and morose
man'.[40]

Other authors beside Crick have found that the relative outsider can
contribute information as stimulating as that supplied by people intimate
with the subject. In his biography of Wyndham Lewis, for example,
Jeffrey Meyers includes material from an interview conducted in 1978
with Henry Moore. This provides insight into Lewis's influence on a
rising young artist:

> The young Henry Moore . . . read *Blast* and *Tarr* with the greatest
> interest and enthusiasm, and felt the salutary effect of their energetic
> strictures. Moore liked the Vorticist emphasis on will and on the self-
> created power of the artist as well as Lewis' insistence on direct
> carving in stone. He found Lewis' intellectual eclecticism a useful
> antidote to Fry and Bloomsbury, who emphasized only one kind of
> French art. Lewis . . . was a model for the kind of artist that Moore
> wanted to become.[41]

Meyers's book on Wyndham Lewis indicates a further way in which
oral history evidence may be advantageous. For the biography of an artist
(such as Lewis) who painted portraits, the author can interview his
sitters. Questions such as 'What was the artist's studio like?', 'How did
he work (for example, how long did his sitters pose)?', 'What, if anything, did he talk about while he painted?' will elicit the kind of detail
that might well not have found its way into a piece of written evidence.
Such testimony may none the less capture the essential flavour of a man
or woman and their environment.

Meyers also uses interviews with Wyndham Lewis's contemporaries
and followers in order to present both sides of the case in some of the dis-
agreements surrounding him. His interview with David Garnett, for
example, gives the latter an opportunity to state whether or not he
thought that Roger Fry and the Bloomsbury circle used their influence
to damage Lewis's artistic career: 'David Garnett, who expressed the
Bloomsbury viewpoint, . . . denied any malign retaliation'.[42] In 1977

and 1978, Meyers interviewed Lewis's later disciples Julian Symons and Hugh Kenner, as well as Anne Wyndham Lewis ('Froanna'), all of whom offered their particular version of Fry's hindrance of Lewis's career although only Anne Wyndham Lewis was a witness to the events recalled. Symons saw it as a 'malign influence'; Kenner detected 'a Bloomsbury art conspiracy' on prices and publicity; and Lewis's widow 'felt that Fry gave Lewis trivial and unsuitable jobs at the Omega, established a boycott in the twenties, tried to prevent Lewis from selling his paintings and forced him to turn to writing in order to exist.'[43] These are highly emotive claims, in the last case, and certainly serious in all three. In view of the fact that Meyers did talk to three (admittedly partial) people, and also to Garnett, on this important question of the Fry/Bloomsbury impact on Lewis, we have a cumulative opinion which may even have gained in value through having been culled in conversation after the event, rather than lifted from letters or diaries written in the heat of the moment.

Apart from their use in helping to establish facts, interviews have been found valuable by the biographer for revealing the subject's character. This, for Quentin Bell, was the chief benefit derived from his interviews with Virginia Woolf's circle.[44] It was also an important aspect of the interviews conducted by Paul Ferris for *Dylan Thomas*. Even when it involves the elaboration of seemingly trivial details, oral history provides completeness, and a three-dimensional effect.

In the Dylan Thomas biography in particular, it also provides an indication of the poet's effect upon others. The widow of the Welsh poet Vernon Watkins claimed, in interview, that she 'regards Dylan Thomas as the most important person in her husband's life. . . . "Vernon thought the drink and the unreliability were only incidental, that he'd go on to be an old man writing poetry, like Yeats . . .".'[45] The composer Elisabeth Lutyens thought Thomas 'the funniest man in the world', and considered five hours in a pub with him as 'five hours of incredibly funny conversation'.[46] A rather different reaction came from the American scholar Norman Holmes Pearson, who recalled Thomas's uneasiness in the academic surroundings of Yale when he visited the United States in 1950:

'When I met Dylan before dinner', he says, 'I thought he was extraordinarily tense. Then, and again during the dinner, he spent a good deal of time explaining how he could have gone to university, to Cambridge. There was a feeling – this may have been snobbishness on our part – that he was not at ease because he wasn't a university man.'[47]

Passages such as this, apart from their vivid amplification of individual personalities and behaviour, also contribute to the quality of literary bio-graphy in much the same way that dialogue – that element which Alice in Wonderland felt to be so essential to an interesting book – broadens the appeal of a novel. Transcribed interview extracts, as used throughout the Thomas and Orwell biographies, give the books a different level of expression, inject into them the spontaneity of direct speech, and help to vary the pace of the text. By incorporating the tone of the interviews within the fabric of the book, the literary biographer can reflect, however obliquely, some portion of the artist's own talent.

Special problems arise for the biographer with the choice of a living subject. Close co-operation with a willing interviewee can, notoriously, produce oral testimony so partisan as to turn the work into a simple apologia. Michael Holroyd has pointed out how contemporary bio-graphers of his current subject, Bernard Shaw, were misled by Shaw's eloquence into an uncritical acceptance of the information he presented to them.[48] Conversely, a biographer's refusal to be drawn into the orbit of a dominant personality can result in a cold and distant image of a powerful living figure. Iain Hamilton's life of Arthur Koestler is derived largely from letters and printed sources. According to one critic, its limitation is 'not that its subject has collaborated too closely but that he has held himself too remote.'[49]

A final example will help to highlight both the value, and the risk, of the extensive use of oral evidence in literary biography. Richard Ellmann's much-praised life of James Joyce employed a wide range of interview material to establish, for the first time, a reliable chronology of his subject's career and the specific Dublin context of Joyce's fiction.[50] For Ellmann, professional doubt about the veracity of some spoken evidence is matched by an overriding belief in its worth: 'You are more likely to get the truth in an interview than in a formal written statement.' However, in a sceptical review of the revised edition of *James Joyce*, the Joyce scholar Hugh Kenner takes issue with the biography's dependence on uncorroborated anecdote – the 'Irish Fact' – in its attempt to find historical origins for many fictional incidents. 'Substantiations you'll get with ease in Dublin,' Kenner asserts, 'but you'd best be wary lest they be Irish Facts.' In defence of his approach, Ellmann claims that all his oral evidence has been assessed with due reserve, and that 'the distinction between what may and may not be true' has been made clear.[51]

Interview-based works

Equally effective secondary material on the arts is provided in books (or articles) composed wholly of interviews with one person or one group. Such interview-based works provide a useful alternative or supplement to conventional autobiography.

An excellent example, in the field of music, is *Conversations with Menuhin* by Robin Daniels, first published in 1979.[52] The choice of the word 'conversations', rather than 'interviews', suggests the essentially informal nature of these sessions. Robin Daniels, a music critic and psychotherapist, conducted his interviews during the violinist's sabbatical year (a natural time for reflection), at Menuhin's Highgate home, over a period of six to nine months. The author felt an 'intuitive rapport' between Menuhin and himself,[53] which allowed for a gradually evolving relationship between the two men, based on mutual trust. In consequence, the interviews come across as fresh and candid. Each interview was tape recorded and never lasted more than one and a half hours; because each was one in a sequence, Daniels was able to break off before the momentum had been exhausted. He generally tried to ask broad questions, in order to give his interviewee 'a lot of space', and this method is apparent in the book itself, where one short question will elicit a discursive reply that continues for several pages.

Robin Daniels used 90 per cent of the interview material in the book itself. Although Menuhin was not shown the full transcripts of the interviews, he saw the manuscript, and made only a very few alterations. Topics covered in the 'conversations' include the formative influences in Menuhin's life, the composers with whom he feels special affinity, his routine on the day of a concert, the principles on which the Yehudi Menuhin School is founded, and his attitude to money. Finally, he is asked what ideals he holds dearest. What emerges is a picture not simply of a virtuoso musician but of the whole man – his beliefs, his values, his personal qualities.

Daniels sees himself, in the role of interviewer, as 'a fairly blank screen, so that people can project on to me. . . . I want to reveal, but not expose.' He hopes that, in the process, he may also reveal his interviewees to themselves. His questions are both allusive and concise, allowing the interviewee to 'come into the question in his own way'. It is from this stance of openness, awareness and sympathy that a three-dimensional self-portrait of the artist emerges, providing a valuable lesson in what can be achieved when interviewer and subject are working together harmoniously.

A different style and product, conceived also as an interview-based work, is exhibited in David Sylvester's *Interviews with Francis Bacon*.[54] The book resulted from a series of interviews conducted between 1962 and 1974, which the author taped and transcribed. Unlike Daniels's work, only a small proportion – approximately a quarter – of the transcribed material was actually incorporated in the book; and the sequence of the remarks was, in some cases, rearranged. David Sylvester justifies his editing by explaining that his chief aim was 'to present Francis Bacon's thoughts clearly and economically – not to provide some sort of abbreviated record of how the taped interviews happened to develop'.[55] The version that emerges is consequently less discursive than *Conversations with Menuhin*, and is framed rather within a question-and-answer structure. The interviewer appears to be asking many questions, some of which are longer than the actual answers, rather than making a few suggestive remarks that might stimulate the speaker to make long, perhaps rambling replies.

One effect of Sylvester's method is that, at several points in the text, some might feel that he is actually putting an idea into the interviewee's mind; for example, Bacon responds to a lengthy hypothesis put forward by the interviewer with the simple comment: 'Well, I'd never thought of it in that way, but when you suggest it to me, I think it may be so.'[56] In a later interview, however, Bacon refuses to accept the implications of a particular question: when the interviewer tries to make him admit that the reason for his preoccupation with Velázquez's *Pope Innocent X* may be traced to an 'obsession' with his father, Bacon remarks that many other artists have been moved by this, 'one of the most beautiful pictures in the world'. Sylvester, however, persists: 'I don't think other painters have continued to make versions of it over and over again.' 'I wish I hadn't' is Bacon's short reply.[57] Nevertheless, by being rather aggressive in his questioning and provoking a smart response, in this instance Sylvester elicits a sense of his subject's manner and character, which more than compensates for the evasion of definite fact.

Subjects covered by the interviews include Bacon's interest in the image of the human mouth ('I've always hoped in a sense to be able to paint the mouth like Monet painted a sunset');[58] his preference for working from photographs rather than from life when painting portraits of his friends; his habit of throwing paint on to the canvas, and his use of rags and scrubbing brushes; the meat-like quality of his figures; and an explanation of why he distorts the image in his paintings. The juxtaposition of the interview text with illustrations of paintings by Bacon and those who influenced him adds a further dimension.

This kind of interviewing, which is based on the methods of journalism but operates in a much more expanded form, is evident also in the work of the *Paris Review*. This literary journal pioneered interviews with celebrated writers during the 1950s and has published, with systematic regularity, interviews with most of the leading modern literary figures from the English-speaking world, as well as with foreign writers such as Jean Cocteau and Jorge Luis Borges. These have been collected and published in this country under the title *Writers at Work: The 'Paris Review' Interviews*.[59] The interviews, although conducted by many different people, are all published in a similar form. In each case, the transcript is preceded by a description of the writer – his or her physical appearance and general manner – and of the interview setting, which is either the writer's home or place of work (occasionally, a hotel), thus allowing a prior glimpse of the writer's personality and environment.

It is, perhaps, appropriate that the *Paris Review* interview conducted by Julian Jebb with Evelyn Waugh in 1962 should have taken place in the author's bedroom at the Hyde Park Hotel, with Waugh sitting in bed wearing white pyjamas.[60] During the interview conducted with Robert Graves by Peter Buckman and Willian Fifield, the poet was variously 'setting the table, correcting a manuscript, checking references, cutting his nails with an enormous pair of scissors, picking carrots, singing folk songs, and slicing beans. He was not an easy man to keep up with.'[61] The interview with Allen Ginsberg was conducted in even more challenging circumstances. The interviewer, Thomas Clark, fortuitously met Ginsberg in a bar in Bristol in 1965, and hitchhiked with him to Wells, Glastonbury, Bath and London. Finally Ginsberg settled down to be interviewed in Cambridge. The words in the published version 'are his, with little alteration save the omission of repetitive matter in half a dozen places'.[62]

A rather different version of the original resulted from Gordon Lloyd Harper's interview with Saul Bellow in 1965, in the writer's University of Chicago office. Unlike the Ginsberg transcript, Bellow's was the product of much careful revision. Tape-recorded interview sessions were held over several weeks, and Bellow was sent a typescript of his remarks after each interview. 'Bellow worked over these typed sheets extensively with pen and ink. . . . Frequently, there were slight changes in meaning. . . . Other alterations tightened up his language. . . . Any sections which he judged to be excursions from the main topic were deleted.'[63] Passages in the final transcript read as though they were written rather than spoken by Bellow – as was probably the case. A revised interview may be more appropriate in the case of an author such as Bellow, in that it imitates his own method of writing. In contrast, Allen Ginsberg's interview (left virtually unchanged), although it shows the poet expressing himself with eloquence, does read very much like spontaneous, 'off-the-cuff' conversation. The spontaneity of Ginsberg's interview is obviously more appropriate to a poet of his background; while the disciplined approach of Bellow's accords with the method of a meditative novelist.

In this way, the essential truthfulness of oral history is demonstrated; points of information may be hidden, exaggerated, distorted by the interviewee; yet the intangible portion of the subject – the effect of a personality on others, the interplay of relationships, the flavour of the atmosphere at a certain time in a certain place – can all be amply conveyed.

PART IV

Case studies:
oral archives

11

Oral archives in Britain (non-media)

Although gaps and deficiencies in documentary evidence could to some extent be compensated for by oral archives for the benefit of future researchers, the formal establishment of oral history archives in Britain has been a slow and fragmented process. It might be argued that an 'older' nation is likely to be more reluctant to acknowledge and apply new techniques in recording and presenting its own history than 'younger' nations, which are more forward-looking and adaptable, and readier to exploit new tools. Thus, when the tape recorder came into existence, it was the United States which first seized on the opportunities it offered; and oral archives are now the norm in libraries and institutions there. Certainly Israel, where oral history programmes abound, testifies to the theory that a new country is more likely to catalogue its history by the most up-to-date method available.

In Britain, there is no one central oral archive. The BBC Sound Archives contain only a selection of broadcast material, and access is restricted to bona fide researchers. The general public is referred to the British Institute of Recorded Sound (BIRS), the closest approximation in this country to a national sound archive; but its contents, apart from its large gramophone record collection, consist mainly of radio and television material. An interviewing programme is not regarded as part of its function; indeed, it is doubtful whether its present funds, supplied almost entirely by the government, could be stretched to include such a policy.[1]

It is therefore left to enterprising archivists to take the initiative. As the ensuing description of British oral archives will illustrate, most collections are on a small scale, conceived and launched by one individual and, all too often, restricted by lack of money and staff. It is regrettable that, at a time when the definition of a library as a place housing only books is swiftly being revised to include a wider variety of research material, more thought is not being put into the position of oral history archives. An imbalance also exists in the importance attached to oral history by different disciplines. Medical and scientific establishments, for example, are much more vigorous in creating oral archives than political or cultural institutions – a tendency that is consistent with the pioneering nature of the medical and scientific professions, as against the innate caution of political and administrative bodies. Libraries that house colonial archives are, however, more alert to the need for oral records, presumably because they are dealing with countries where the written word is not as widely used as in Britain.

Social historians, as has been shown, have long recognized that the spoken word should be systematically recorded. Thus the Oral History Society of Britain has encouraged individual researchers and even libraries to collect verbal records of ordinary people.

This chapter offers a brief survey of a selection archives in Britain that hold oral records by or about eminent British figures as already defined. It does not claim to be an exhaustive history of oral archives in Britain. The Oral History Society has started to do this by issuing a published *Directory of British Oral Collections* (Volume 1, 1981)[2] focusing on social history. Our aim is to underline the problems encountered by both the oral archivist and the researcher who wishes to consult oral archives, and to suggest guidelines. As with individual authors who conduct interviews, we have also sought to gather and publish the views of oral archivists themselves, quoting from a variety of experiences. To have included information on individual experience would have been laborious, and as a rule only peculiar methodological details are given. The summary therefore focuses on content.

Regional and local history

Regional and local oral archives, often based in local libraries, proliferate in the United States. With the growth of interest in local history in Britain, some recording of eminent local figures has taken place. One of the most interesting oral history projects in this category has been undertaken by the West Devon area of the Devon County Library,[3] dealing with the blitz and rebuilding of Plymouth. Questions were drawn up by library staff, and interviews conducted by Joe Pengelly,[4] a presenter for BBC South West and Honorary Research Fellow in Oral History at Exeter University. The aim of the questions asked in interview was, as J. R. Elliott, the Area Librarian, explains, 'to "get behind" the official council minutes and to get the background leading up to decisions and the role of members and officers in arriving at these decisions. The relationship between officers and between members also figures in the questions.'[5] Most of the tapes in the collection are not, however, accessible to the general public, since the contributors spoke frankly on the understanding that the tapes would not be available for a certain period.

On a broader front, Nottinghamshire County Library has a collection of tape recordings of Nottinghamshire figures in its Local Studies Library. These include interviews with Kenneth Adam, the Director of BBC Television during the 1960s; the authors Stanley Middleton, Alan Sillitoe and Geoffrey Trease; and the artist Dame Laura Knight. There are also reminiscences of D. H. Lawrence by, among others, his brother George. Most of the recordings last approximately half an hour. Some of the tapes were deposited with the former city library as early as 1955, but these records have deteriorated badly, some irreparably. Some tapes are copies of programmes broadcast by BBC Radio Nottingham. The D. H. Lawrence collection was begun in the mid-1960s by David Gerard, former City Librarian. Excellent facilities exist for examining this collection. Typed manuscripts are available for most of its contents. The oral material is listed in the form of a card catalogue, and listening facilities are in the library (on headphones).[6]

The largest regional oral history programme in England is the North West Sound Archive,[7] run by Ken Howarth, Sound Archivist at the Manchester Museum. The NWSA seeks to 'make, collect and preserve sound and related visual recordings of the life, character, history and traditions of the North West; to make them available for use, and to encourage member organizations and individuals to do the same.'[8] A small number of the recordings are of 'eminent' figures, including Sir Harold Wilson[9] and the pioneer educationist Edward O'Neil. Most of these recordings were made for use in local radio; but Ken Howarth is currently conducting a series of interviews with distinguished members of the University of Manchester, in conjunction with the Communications Department. There are also tape recording of the artist L. S. Lowry, in which he talks about his early feelings for the industrial landscape. As the NSWA is essentially a depository, material by people from a wide variety of fields is collected together under the one regional umbrella. However, it is pledged to establish a public service, which will make cassette copies of recordings available through the North West Regional library Bureau in Manchester.

Scotland's Record[10] is the brainchild of its Director, John Dundas, who was motivated by his former Scottish Office colleagues' dying or retiring to distant places without leaving behind a personal record of their experiences. With three Scottish trustees, Dundas launched the national project in 1977.[11] In view of the fact that it is a 'one-man show' run by John Dundas, he has to be selective when deciding upon his subjects. Most of the recordings are in the form of a continuous narrative rather than interviews. The speakers are asked to talk on topics related to Scotland's industrial, economic and social history over the past fifty years, and they are always people who actually participated in events. Some recordings were made in a studio, but most took place in the informant's own home or office. In this way, John Dundas has found, many people who would never normally leave a written account have been persuaded to record their experiences in the relaxed atmosphere of familiar surroundings. By the end of September 1981, eighty-six titles (seventy-six hours of listening time) had been recorded. Projects of interest include reminiscences on the Scottish Office (formerly the Scottish Home Department), spanning a period of more than thirty years since 1939; the Toothill Report on the Scottish Economy; Scottish Industrial Policy in the 1930s; the Scottish Land Court; the making of Strathclyde University; and surgery in Edinburgh 1937–77.

Every tape is deposited in duplicate in the National Library of Scotland, where it is available to scholars under the normal conditions of a copyright library. Scotland's Record, as a venture in oral history, stands as a monument to the initiative and dedication of one man, and the loyalty and enthusiasm of its members. In view of the fact that it provides a constant supply of material for a national library, it seems a pity that it receives no government grant.

Politics and administration

Gillian Peele, Tutorial Fellow at Lady Margaret Hall, Oxford, has written: 'The deficiency [in post-war written evidence] can partly be remedied by systematic oral history. . . . Unfortunately, however, Britain has been slow to encourage the formation of oral history archives [for] the political historian.'[12] Gillian Peele's statement accurately reflects the position in Britain today. The lack of continuous work in this field is all the more remarkable because of the large amount of academic study on political and administrative history, the near-universal agreement on the inadequacy of written evidence, and the focus in other countries of gathering oral history evidence on this branch of modern studies.

A number of projects have been discussed but have failed to materialize. For example, certain bodies within Parliament, like the House of Commons Library, the House of Lords Library and the Sound Archives, have all debated whether to establish oral history archives. John Palmer of the House of Commons Library has written:

> we did discuss [an oral history] project some years ago, since one is very much aware that the memories of many Members could usefully be tapped before they retire: they seldom write down their reminiscences and often leave little behind in the way of papers . . .[13]

In fact, one series of interviews did take place, with the former Labour MP and miner Lord Taylor of Mansfield. These interviews inspired Lord Taylor to produce a volume of memoirs, *Uphill all the Way* (1973), but no interviews have since been conducted.

Unfortunately, Parliament, like the BBC, does not feel it can affort to spend money on oral archives that will be of interest to outsiders, and sees its oral archival work primarily as a service for internal use. Nevertheless, the case for recording reminiscences of elderly and/or retired members is significant, and a project – for example, along the lines of the United States Former Members of Congress oral history project – would not be hard to organize and would be cheap to run with existing equipment. In particular, since there were no sound recordings of Parliament before April 1978 (bar two short experiments in 1968 and 1975), oral history interviews could be used to record on tape unique material about the atmosphere of particular debates, and indeed whole Parliaments, before sound recording began, and could also provide information about other significant changes to Parliament throughout the twentieth century.

Among the survivors are a few who sat in Parliament at the time of the first Labour government in 1924, significant numbers who sat during the 1930s, and even more who recall at first hand the debates during the Second World War. And it is not just members of both Houses who could be taped but parliamentary clerks, stenographers, secretaries and attendants. Indeed, at the time of writing, the man who was private secretary to the Chief Whip in the House of Commons for many years from 1919 is still thriving. To record such people, no less significant in its way than recording parliamentary debates – for which a written record (Hansard) is already kept – may prove simpler and more straightforward than the various parliamentary bodies have appreciated.

   Three potentially major projects in this field were begun, but all foundered through lack of funds. The Granada Historical Trust (considered in Chapter 12) differs from the other two in that it was based on a television company rather than an academic institution. The second archive was set up by Nuffield College, Oxford. The project originated with a group including a young research student, Edmund Ions, who in 1960 returned from the United States where he had worked for some time with the seminal Oral History Research Office at Columbia University. When the group began preliminary recordings, it was decided to focus attention on inter-war politicians, since it was felt the younger ones could be interviewed later; a few recordings were made – for example, on the 1929–31 Labour government. The programme was not extended, and an opportunity of recording the leading surviving political figures from the inter-war years was thus missed.[14] The initiative was continued by David Butler, who presided over some twenty interviews on post-war subjects, including a twenty-hour interview with Tony Benn on the renunciation of his peerage (which is still perhaps the longest contemporary oral history interview with a politician on a single subject). But by the mid-1960s, because of funding problems, the time it took to transcribe tapes, and above all difficulties in finding people to conduct the interviews who would ask the right questions, the project was abandoned.[15]

   The third oral archive in Britain devoted specifically to this subject is the British Oral Archive of Political and Administrative History, attached to the London School of Economics (LSE).[16] The archive was the idea of Anthony Seldon who, like Ions, had been struck by the work in oral history in the United States, and its potential in Britain. The establishment of the archive was made possible by Derek A. Clarke, a librarian, who housed it in the British Library of Political and Economic Science, attached to the LSE, and it was funded by the Social Science Research Council (SSRC). Derek Clarke became the director, and Anthony Seldon the administrator. Detailed plans and timetables were drawn up to conduct 250 interviews with surviving senior ministers, civil servants and chiefs of staff from the years 1945–75, gathering information not just on political and administrative history but on post-war social and economic policy, and military, colonial and diplomatic history. It was intended to have neatly catalogued, in one institution, a battery of recorded and transcribed information on all major post-war developments, on relationships, personal working methods, personal assessments, policy processes, atmosphere and a wealth of other aspects of history which would have been unlikely to have found its way into the Public Record Office. In other words, it would have conducted searching and confidential interviews with the post-war equivalents of Chamberlain, Baldwin, Lloyd-George, Warren Fisher, Hankey and Vansittart.[17]

The first (pilot) stage of the archive was completed by the end of 1980, and consisted of forty-nine interviews with thirty different subjects. Interviwees included former ministers, Lords Amory, Boyle of Handsworth, Home and Shackleton, and former permanent secretaries, Lord Croham (Sir Douglas Allen), Lord Sherfield (Sir Roger Makins) and Sir Antony Part. The average length of talk with each subject was one hour and forty minutes, giving an average transcript length of forty-two pages. Transcripts are neatly bound with full contents information, details of interviews and biographical notes; a search guide, bound separately, contains a fourteen-point guide to the methodology employed in the pilot project.

The tapes of the interviews are available to researchers, but little demand to listen to them has yet been shown. A more likely source of interest to scholars are the typed transcripts of the interviews. Over half the transcripts are immediately available for examination, and can be inspected in the library's manuscript room.

The work had to cease in 1981 because the SSRC discontinued its funding on the grounds that the criteria for the selection of interviewees were inadequate and the interviews were too open-ended.[18] It is probable, however, that, in financial circumstances where only 25 per cent of projects could be funded, the SSRC felt unable to support a historically based project for which there is as yet little interest among academics.

Colonial history

Colonial history is a subject that naturally lends itself to oral history, since it records the British experience in countries where written accounts have not, traditionally, proliferated. Colonial oral archives have been established at both Oxford and Cambridge, and a few smaller collections are also in existence.

A specialized archive is housed with the India Office Library and Records.[19] The IOLR has been associated with two oral history projects. The first was conducted by the BBC for its radio series, *Plain Tales from the Raj*. Michael Mason, the producer, secured the BBC's agreement to a proposal that copies of the original taped interviews, only parts of which were used in the broadcasts, should be deposited in the IOLR, the Department of Sound Records of the Imperial War Museum, and the Library of the School of Oriental and African Studies. About seventy-five interviews were conducted, mostly by Charles Allen; although the speakers were mainly British people, there were also some Indians who recorded their memories of life under British rule.

It was realized, however, that there were many more people still living whose recollections would be worth recording. Accordingly, a further series of interviews has been conducted under the auspices of a committee known as the British in India Oral Archives Committee, based at the School of Oriental and African Studies (SOAS), Malet Street, London. Another sixty or so interviews – with, among others, Lord Mountbatten and Field Marshal Sir Claude Auchinleck – resulted from this project. There is a full catalogue of tapes which can be consulted at SOAS, the Imperial War Museum or the IOLR, all of which have listening facilities. However, the field of those with experience of life in India during the closing period of British rule is still far from being fully covered, and the IOLR hopes to mount a further project, which is still in the early planning stage.

The largest colonial history oral archive in Britain is at the Centre of South Asian Studies at the University of Cambridge.[20] The tape-recorded collection forms only one part of the holdings in this library, which was established as a distinct institution in 1964. In October 1981 it contained 274 recordings, which consist of interviews conducted by a number of different researchers. There is an important collection on India, including interviews with a wide variety of people connected with Mahatma Gandhi, and with the freedom movement. Uma Shanker made 115 recordings on the late 1960s and early 1970s, interviewing former Indian freedom fighters, but his work has had to be terminated – again, through lack of funds. Other interviews on life in India have been carried out by the centre's staff, and the work is still in progress. Although this archive has no brief to interview those who were leaders in recent Indian history, it is nevertheless a valuable source of information for scholars who wish to hear a firsthand account of those who participated in events, and who were familiar with the men who forged them.

The Oxford Colonial Records Project[21] was established in 1963, with the aim of collecting the private papers of people who had worked in the colonial service, and three years later an oral history programme was included as part of its work. The interviews conducted at this time were chiefly with colonial governors and secretaries of state for the colonies. As Patricia M. Pugh, a former archivist on the project, remarked:

Retired colonial officers are always pleased to talk about their experiences to others with some knowledge of their background and the problems with which they were faced in their working lives. From the very first inception of the scheme the committee of the Project realized that many valuable details of colonial history could be preserved if such people were asked to record their recollections on tape. This part of the Project's work was very much secondary to the collection of written records in the first two years. Funds were so short that none could be diverted to this purpose even though, as Jack Tawney [the project's first director] realized, 'memories were in even greater peril than written material'. At first he merely carried with him his own tape recorder when visiting certain willing, prospective donors of papers and recorded their conversation in an informal manner. . . . A method was evolved for creating an oral history branch of the Colonial Records Project, with interviewers selected for their knowledge of the relevant area of experience. Questions to be asked were carefully prepared in advance and the person to be interviewed was asked if he would be prepared to answer them as well as to speak on those particular aspects of colonial history with which he was known to be familiar.[22]

The tape and transcript of each interview, along with all the other material from the project, are stored in the Rhodes House Library (part of the Bodleian). The library has a complete list of the eighty-four interviews recorded up until 1975; but access to most of these is restricted.

The work fell into abeyance for a number of years, but in 1976 William Beaver, a doctoral student in colonial history, expressed an interest in expanding the oral history programme, to cover people who had been involved in colonial life in a capacity other than the purely administrative – for example, in the private sector and the armed forces. The scheme was established in October 1977, with the new name of the Oxford Development Records Project. William Beaver was its first executive director, and the project received a grant from the Ministry of Overseas Development. Although the collection still consisted chiefly of papers – on specific projects such as the role of the British armed forces in Africa, the development of African agriculture in Kenya, law enforcement and education – tape recordings continued to be made.

Anthony Kirk-Greene, the project's current director, stresses that, in conducting these interviews, painstaking research and carefully considered questions are of prime importance.[23] He still tries to maintain the system whereby interviews are prepared and carried out by someone who has worked in the interviewee's colonial territory. In Oxford, which has access to a rich supply of retired colonial staff living in the Cotswolds, this is not too much of a problem! One or two days' research in preparation for the interview is generally considered necessary. Kirk-Greene always emphasizes to interviewees that the material is for the use of a university library, not for public consumption; this encourages them to talk freely. Confidential material is restricted, according to the wishes of interviewees, who are asked to complete a form on conditions of access. As a result, some cannot be seen until the year 2000. It is strictly for the use of genuine researchers, and certainly not for the media – although the ODRP has taken the trouble to follow the Imperial War Museum's practice of using 'long-life' reel-to-reel tape, which is then transferred on to cassette for those researchers who wish to listen.

The number of pages in a transcript may vary from thirty to over eighty. Unfortunately, since not all the transcripts are available to researchers at present, the collection will not be a general tool for historians for some time. Interviews with such eminent colonial figures as Lord Chandos (formerly Oliver Lyttelton), Lord Boyd of Merton (formerly Alan Lennox-Boyd), Lord Caradon (formerly Hugh Foot), Sir Hilton Poynton and Malcolm Macdonald are thus waiting in the wings for tomorrow's historians.

If there are no further cuts in government aid, the ODRP is funded until the end of March 1984. Anthony Kirk-Greene doubts that they will be able to complete all their oral history programme by that date. Co-ordination in oral history work generally is rare, so it is gratifying to report that the ODRP is careful not to overlap with the work carried out at the Centre of South Asian Studies in Cambridge. While the latter concentrates on India and South-East Asia, the Oxford project covers African countries, excluding the Sudan, which is dealt with by a special section at the University of Durham.

Military history

Oral archives in Britain seem to be at their most flourishing in the field of military history. The most celebrated collection is at the Department of Sound Records at the Imperial War Museum[24] (keeper of the department, David Lance). This work was established in 1972, to supplement and complement the museum's reference and audio-visual collections. Among the aims of the new department were the acquisition of broadcast recordings from radio and television collections and direct off the air; the recording of relevant speeches, sound effects and music; the establishment of an oral history programme, with projects developed chronologically from the beginning of this century, as well as individual interviews with people of significance who do not fit neatly within any one project.[25]

Although interviews were conducted for nineteen of the projects undertaken, and 6000 hours of interviews have been recorded to date, only a small proportion of these are with the men and women 'at the top'. For the 'Military and Naval Aviation 1914–1918' project, forty-four interviews with former members of the Royal Flying Corps, Royal Naval Air Service and Royal Air Force were conducted. The 'Mechanization of the British Army 1919–1939' project comprises thirty-nine interviews with officers who were involved in various aspects of mechanization – for example, the development of the Tank Corps. For 'Britain and the Refugee Crisis 1933–1947', interviews were conducted with refugees from Europe and with British subjects who were involved in the organization of the refugees and their internment as 'enemy' aliens. Another project, which illustrates the broad range of the IWM's work, is 'British Service Cameramen 1939–1945' (still in progress), which includes interviews with cameramen who served with the Army Film and Photographs Unit and with the Royal Navy and Royal Air Force during the Second World War.

The oral history work of the IWM looks at war in its widest context, as it impinges on civilians as well as on military personnel, and provides a unique document of twentieth-century life. Complete listings of interviewees may be obtained from the museum. Broadcast recordings – copies of which may, in many cases, be purchased by members of the public – are another aspect of the museum's oral records. Included in this category are 250 unedited interviews recorded by the BBC for its series *The Great War*, and a large collection of recordings made during or immediately after the events of the Second World War, as covered by the BBC; interviews connected with BBC's *Women at War* series;

contemporary speeches and other broadcasts by British public figures between 1930 and 1950, from the BBC Sound Archives (including Lloyd George, Chamberlain, Attlee, Montgomery and Mountbatten); and 400 unedited interviews recorded by Thames Television for its series *The World at War, 1939–1945*.

Included in its 'miscellaneous recordings', the IWM has contemporary recordings of speeches made by wartime leaders, including Churchill, Hitler, Mussolini, Roosevelt and Truman, speeches by Nazi leaders, and the proceedings of most of the Nuremberg Trials.

For its own oral projects, the IWM selects informants who, it is felt, will provide a representative cross-section of speakers for each topic. The interviews – which are conducted by staff interviewers (there are normally three of these) and by trained freelance interviewers chosen for their particular subject knowledge – range from a quarter of an hour to sixteen hours, the average length being about two and a half hours. Master copies of the tapes are preserved in a purpose-built, temperature-controlled store outside the museum. Copies for internal and research use are kept at the museum.

The Department of Sound Records regards the tapes rather than transcripts as its 'product', and records to broadcasting standards; but it does transcribe as many interviews as time and money permit (approximately half). Both tapes and typescripts may be purchased by the visiting public.

The oral history programme at the IWM is rather different from most of the other archives described in this chapter: it is carried out by a museum, and the fact that copies of most of the material are for sale underlines its function as an accessible service, as well as a research body and repository. We do not, therefore, come up against the barrier of confidentiality and secrecy that surrounds so much oral history work – partly, no doubt, because only a small percentage of interviews conducted are with the people who actually directed events.

The Royal Air Force Museum at Hendon provides an example of an oral archive at the opposite end of the scale to the IWM collection. The RAF Museum has a small oral archive, consisting of twenty-two interviews with retired servicemen recalling their experiences. The recordings are unedited and, with regard to both sound and content, vary in quality. The museum does not like to publicize the collection, and does not make transcripts of the tapes – a definite sign that not much use of the material is anticipated in the near future.

The most significant oral archive run within the armed forces themselves is at the Air Historical Branch of the Ministry of Defence.[26] The programme started in 1974, with the aim of obtaining both historical information not documented elsewhere and material that would complement and amplify existing evidence, and of recording the memories and opinions of personnel who had unique experience of certain specialist operations. These objectives, as stated by the AHB's current head, Air Commodore Probert,[27] seem to encapsulate the way in which an institution may best exploit oral techniques in recording its recent history.

J. P. McDonald, who was present at the outset of the project, recalls how they started off using a Sony taperecorder, little better than a toy. Now a Uher machine is employed, which offers better monitoring and superior recordings under a wider range of conditions. When the programme was first mooted, it was hard to convince the Ministry of Defence of its value, and a further problem was the interviewing staff's lack of experience.[28] It was decided that three broad groups of people should be interviewed. One such group are senior commanders, whose recollections need to be captured before detail is forgotten; they discuss their careers, their colleagues, and the issues in which they were involved. Fourteen of these interviews have been conducted, including those with five former Chiefs of Air Staff, Sir John Slessor, Sir William Dickson (also Chief of Defence Staff), Sir Dermot Boyle, Sir Thomas Pike and Lord Elworthy. Secondly, a history of the Royal Air Force College, Cranwell, was undertaken: this included tape-recorded reminiscences. Lastly, to supplement written material, specialists in, for example, engineering, military intelligence and helicopter development have been systematically interviewed.

The interviews with senior RAF commanders – those who were the policy makers – are conducted by the head of the branch. He works at the rate of approximately one every six months, and concentrates on the time when his subjects held high office, rather than asking for reminiscences of their career as a whole. Ten years, he believes, is an optimum time-lag between retirement and the oral history interview. The length of interviews varies between one and five hours, the average being about two hours. Interviewees are generally willing to talk freely, since AHB guarantees to interviewees that what they say will not be revealed to outsiders except with their express permission.

Although it does not advertise itself as a facility for outsiders, genuine researchers writing on RAF history are encouraged to visit the AHB, who will guide them on sources. Subject to the restrictions of confidentiality, and if it is considered worth while, they may be allowed to listen to any relevant tapes, some of which have yet to be transcribed.

A rather different type of oral archive is housed at the Royal Air Force Staff College at Bracknell, and is of particular interest because it is one of the very few centres to make video recordings of interviews. The archive was established for use on staff training programmes, and interviews for such a purpose cannot, of course, touch upon the sensitive material recorded for the Air Historical Branch. It is, however, an interesting enterprise, described by its instigator, Group Captain Mason, as 'a rather diffident attempt to capture a little of the personality and character of distinguished men who have been personally associated with, or have influenced, the evolution of British air power.'[29]

The Royal Navy Submarine Museum at Gosport[30] runs a small oral archive. The museum aims to enlarge this steadily, and is at present giving priority to capturing on tape the reminiscences of early submariners, now in their eighties and nineties. The oral archive collection was initiated because people are generally unwilling or unable to write their reminiscences, and it was found to be the only way to record intricate details.[31] Although 'responsible' researchers are granted access to them, the museum describes itself as 'very selective'.[32]

At the Royal Marines, Eastney (Southsea, Hampshire) an oral history archive is beginning to materialize. A pilot study has been carried out, to assess the feasibility of an oral programme. The one guiding principle, as with most oral history archives, is to record material in fields where documentary evidence is poor or nonexistent. Owing to stringencies in defence expenditure, the Marines are unable to include past events (the Second World War and earlier) within their purview; neither can they cover events within the experience of personnel still serving, as they would have liked. The one area in which they plan to pursue oral history is in relation to current events. However, as these will be 'official interviews' (the term used by the RM Corps Secretariat),[33] access to the information obtained will be covered by the Public Records Act, and material will not be available for ordinary research with prior permission from the Ministry of Defence.

A large collection of tape-recorded interviews – chiefly with merchant seamen, and members of contingent groups such as shipbuilders and dockside workers – is held at the National Maritime Museum in Greenwich. The interviews were conducted by Campbell McMurray, partly for the historical record and, in some cases, for the BBC Radio 4 series *The British Seafarer*. The material is regarded as 'modern private documents', and theoretically comes under the thirty-year rule for recording and access. In practice, however, all enquiries are treated on their merits, and access may be granted in certain cases, subject to the usual constraints of confidentiality. The museum does not ask informants to sign a clearance forfeiting their right to influence material, since McMurray believes this would be to take undue advantage of the position gained by the interviewer.[34]

Cultural history archives

In contrast to military oral archives, those on cultural subjects are relatively thin on the ground. No central body such as the Arts Council has seen fit to establish an oral history programme, and such records have, therefore, been left to individual archivists.

Oral archives containing interviews with British writers are particularly scarce outside the BBC's collection. With such a broad field, and so many outstanding twentieth-century creative authors, the absence is remarkable. Almost alone in the field is David Gerard, whose interviews with contemporary novelists are available commercially rather than as an archive. His oral history archive on D. H. Lawrence is available at the Nottinghamshire Local Studies Library (see above). Gerard located and interviewed people in the area who had known Lawrence in his boyhood and youth, including Lawrence's friends and family, as well as literary critics. Included in the sixteen hours of tape recording are interviews with Rebecca West, Compton Mackenzie and David Garnett. A full list of these will appears in Keith Sagar's forthcoming *D. H. Lawrence Handbook*.[35]

British artists and people associated with the international art world are better represented in oral archives outside the BBC than British authors. The Tate Gallery Archive[36] has, next to the BBC, the largest oral archive on cultural subjects in Britain. Its audio-visual holdings, acquired and on loan, total 425 accessioned items by 1982, including tapes, transcripts (many from the BBC), films (mostly offcuts) and video tapes. Material comes from two sources: those that the gallery conducts itself, interviews with subjects including David Hockney and Bernard Leach; and from outside interviewers, including foreign sources, who donate tapes. The Tate Gallery Archive is open only to bona fide researchers (those working for a higher degree, or for a definite publication, film or exhibition), by written application and special appointment. Only such conditions encourage artists to talk reasonably freely about their lives and their work.

An oral archive containing interviews with artists is also to be found in one of the projects carried out by the Department of Sound Records at the Imperial War Museum (see above) and is entitled 'Artists in an Age of Conflict'. This consists of interviews with artists who have considered the subject of war in the twentieth century. Those recorded were mostly associated with the Official War Artists' schemes during the two world wars; but the collection also includes interviews with artists whose work has been concerned with events in Vietnam and Northern Ireland. Over fifty interviews have been recorded; the project is still in progress.

Scientific history

The richest source of oral history archives in the scientific field is to be found in medical institutions. The British Medical Association has a small collection of audio recordings and films, some of which come into the 'oral history' category;[37] it provides a good example of how much valuable material can be recorded and preserved by institutions with little experience of oral history. The collection includes the 'medico-political reminiscences' of Sir Guy Dain and Dr S. Wand, and a film made in 1961, of a twenty-minute conversation between Professor Brian McFarland and Lord Platt about Sir Robert Jones, the founder of ortho-paedic surgery. (The BMA considers the film, which is intended for general medical audiences, as being of historical value, not only because it is about Sir Robert Jones but because it portrays two eminent ortho-paedic surgeons.)[38] There is also a short interview with Sir Henry Dale (1961), who talks about his career. This film, in which the BMA holds the copyright, is listed as a 'Valuable film record of one of the great men of medicine – despite some technical imperfections.'[39]

On a larger scale, the Royal College of Physicians[40] has a small but significant collection of tape-recorded reminiscences of distinguished fellows. Interviews (bar one recorded in 1981) were conducted between 1969 and 1977, and supervised initially by a doctor with broadcasting experience. Subjects include Sir Charles Dodds, Lord Moran, Lord Platt (formerly Sir Robert Platt), Sir Kenneth Robson and Lord Rosenheim. The archive was established because members of the medical profession frequently expressed interest in listening to a record of events, given at first hand by a witness to some particular development in medicine. Those normally selected for interview are senior fellows who are known to have been concerned personally in such developments – for example, the discovery of penicillin, the partial elimination of tuberculosis, and the establishment of the National Health Service.

The library does hold some notes on the contents of the tapes, in order that particular subjects may be traced, and it is hoped that full transcripts will be available for examination; some of these might be edited and distributed in pamphlet form. Sir Gordon Wolstenholme, the present Harveian librarian, does have plans to interview other elderly fellows but finds them reluctant to co-operate, as though this would be some kind of admission that their days are numbered (a not uncommon experience).[41] Were the interviewing programme established more firmly as a continuous part of the library's work, fellows might be more inclined to participate.

An embryonic oral archive is being formed at the Technology Policy Unit at the University of Aston,[42] which participates in the International Project in the History of Solid State Physics. Its work differs from that of most other archives described in this chapter, it is in that primarily motivated by recording material for a book rather than for internal or external consumption,[43] and also because of the international dimension to the work. Some of the tapes are sent to the American Institute of Physics for transcription and editing. Several dozen taped interviews have already been recorded with pioneers in the field, including those from both academic and industrial spheres. Funds for the project have been provided by a number of institutions in Britain, Germany and the United States, including the Leverhulme Foundation and IBM. The project has been running since October 1980, and it is hoped that, on its completion in 1983, a suitable repository for the tapes will be found, where they can be consulted by future historians.

On a more extensive scale, at the Imperial College of Science and Technology[44] the Archive Office and Television Studio have combined to produce video-taped interviews, lasting between fifteen and twenty minutes, with, for example, the physicists Lord Flowers and Lord Penney. Copies are kept in the archives strongroom, where temperature and humidity are strictly controlled. They have so far been used only by members of the college, but it is theoretically open to bona fide scholars, by appointment.[45]

Generally speaking, in Britain, unlike in the United States, the initiative has gone into preserving the *written* records of individual scientists, rather than in capturing new oral records. In 1973, under the auspices of a Royal Society committee, Margaret Gowing founded at Oxford the Contemporary Scientific Archives Centre, concerned solely with documentary evidence. The difficulties of securing continuous funding of the centre suggest that attempts to raise the much larger funds necessary for an oral history project in the present economic climate would fail. The Wellcome Institute for the History of Medicine does analogous work to the centre's for those individuals and organizations connected with medicine. But, again, like other records projects in the history of science – by the Institution of Electrical Engineers, and on the chemical industry by the Open University – it is primarily concerned with documentary records.

Conclusions

This brief survey shows, with one or two bright exceptions, a sorry state of oral archive work in Britain by the early 1980s. The work, while all of value, is of uneven quality, and there is as yet little evidence of learning from others' experience, or of learning from any of the literature on the subject – for example, David Lance's booklet *An Archive Approach to Oral History*.[46]

Some critics, while agreeing with the need for the type of oral archive discussed in the next chapter (storing material already produced), would question the need for oral archives whose *raison d'être* is the creation of entirely new material. At this point it might be useful to consider the arguments for and against the existence of such archives. Apart from general doubts about the value of oral history itself (as discussed in Chapter 2), the following criticisms have been made.

1 Undoubtedly the major criticism is the expense, and these archives, if properly run, are highly labour-intensive. At 1983 prices, even conservative estimates suggest that a one-hour interview can cost £500 if properly transcribed and stored. Critics ask how one can justify the expenditure of scarce resources on this kind of activity, especially at a time of cuts in finance for research, when money might be devoted more wisely to locating and preserving contemporary written evidence.

   This is a persuasive argument against oral archives, but written evidence is not the only source that is liable to be destroyed if not located in time. People die, and memories of those still living fade. As Brian Harrison, whose use of interview evidence is always subordinate to his reliance upon written evidence, found when he undertook a research project on the women's movement in Britain:

From beginning to end, my overriding purpose was one of con-
servation. For this objective, I had arrived late on the scene. I never
ceased to resent that historians had not seized the opportunities
presented by the tape-recorder many years before for interviewing
major participants. . . . Many prominent activists were eager to
preserve their recollections, yet they received all too little
encouragement from scholars to do so. . . . When beginning on a
study of British women's organizations since the 1840s, the first
priority in the mid-1970s seemed to be to preserve information that
was, so to speak, perishable: the documentary and other work
could safely be postponed.[47]

Many others have felt, or are likely to feel, similarly. The answer
might be that we should spend scarce resources on locating and
preserving all extant documentary evidence, but that a question of
balance is necessary when considering reported evidence. Not all
reported written evidence is of a high grade, and it might well be that
interview programmes could yield more material of historical value
than yet more contemporary written evidence.

2 Some critics believe that oral history has value as a source only when
interviews are conducted by authors themselves rather than by a third
party. Thus Donald Watt has said:

an interview conducted by the historian himself can yield three
main benefits: it can help him when he is totally stuck, it can
provide a useful link up with documentary evidence and it can
provide the all-important social background which the documents
do not provide. But interviews conducted by a third party for an
'oral archive' are only of limited value because they reflect the
questions in the mind of the interviewer.[48]

It cannot be denied that a personal interview is bound to be more
valuable than one conducted by a third party for an oral archive, who
will be unlikely to focus on those questions of concern to the particular
researcher listening to or reading them. Moreover, much of the
benefit of an interview is meeting the people for oneself and being able
to form an impression at the time of speaking of the reliability of the
evidence given. This doubt about oral archives is telling; supporters
would reply that an oral archive interview might be a second-best
solution, but it is better than no autobiographical record at all being
preserved (which, sadly is often the case).

3 Some people doubt whether serious researchers will actually want to

consult oral archives. Others say that oral archives will be used too much: researchers will flock to them as a shortcut to forming their own conclusions from a more arduous consideration of the documentary evidence. Although oral archives do indeed produce much 'quotable' material, often of a personal nature, and such extracts may well be employed, even out of context, written archives can be abused too.

4 Some critics feel there is too much uncertainty in the production of oral archives. According to this argument, individual interviewers *know* what areas they want to explore, but oral archives have to anticipate. How do they decide whom to interview and what areas to concentrate on? Should they interview x many people, and talk for $2y$ units of time, or talk to $2x$ many people for y unit of time? The very arbitrariness of the procedure is to some a source of concern. Documentary evidence is given: it either exists or it does not. Oral history evidence, however, is summoned into existence, and differing methodology employed to produce this evidence can yield different results. To this criticism we would say that more informed debate should produce certain codes of practice that could circumvent such problems.

5 The final objection to be mentioned is perhaps the most straightforward. It is that the written material produced is already so vast – and even more so for the post-war years, with the plethora of information recorded by the media – that to produce still more information is unwarranted. It is certainly a great problem for oral archives to know what subjects have already been sufficiently well documented. There is a real need for closer collaboration between academics, archivists of written documentation (including those in the Public Record Office) and oral archivists in order to establish where the gaps are, and how they can best be filled by oral evidence.

Convincing arguments can, however, be put forward for the creation of new oral archives, and the expansion of those already in existence.

1 Oral archives can compensate for gaps in written evidence, and for subjects which documents do not cover. The case has been put forcibly by Nigel Nicolson:

> With the present dearth of private letters and diaries, the oral interview may come to be a major method of recording the unpublished details of contemporary events. I believe it should be systematically pursued, not left to the chance of authors using it for their own purposes.[49]

The potential of oral archives has been pinpointed by Milton Meltzer in the United States, whose discovery of a collection of oral history interviews with the photographer Dorothea Lange led directly to his writing the biography *Dorothea Lange: A Photographer's Life*.[50] Meltzer wrote subsequently:

> So long as the historian or biographer doesn't accept uncritically the oral history produced by another, or use it as a substitute for his own research in every kind of source, he can only be grateful to those institutions and individuals who are carrying on the work of oral history.[51]

Such use is not a minority occupation. Arthur Schlesinger, Jr, for example made extensive use of the John F. Kennedy and Robert F. Kennedy Oral History Programs in his 1978 volume, *Robert Kennedy and His Times*.[52]

As Lord Blake put it: 'Think how much one would give to talk to someone who actually knew Disraeli, Palmerston or Pitt!'[53] Had it been possible to establish a political oral archive last century, we would have been able to read not only the recollections of colleagues, subordinates and historians talking about these statesmen, as well as others, but the replies of the statesmen themselves to critical cross-examination.

2 Oral archives help to verify – or disprove – rumour and supposition, and can thus establish facts for future historians. Formerly, historians had to rely on rumour which might have found its way into contemporary letters and diaries, or into newspaper accounts, where sources are often unattributed. By ascribing points of view to individuals by name, oral archives can make clear on whose authority certain statements have been made. Equally, a sceptic might say that oral archives are bringing new rumours and suppositions into existence.

3 Oral archives produce material in a non-literary form, namely sound (or film). Where sound recordings have been made, it no longer is so important whether the substance is available elsewhere in the written evidence. With the development of oral and audio-visual aids in teaching, there is likely to be an increased demand for good-quality oral history recordings upon which programme compilers can draw.

4 Oral archive interviews have value even before the death of the interviewee. Oral archives commonly find that researchers wish to use their records before they themselves interview a subject, in order to

learn something about the subject's personality and memory, and to
discover which questions have already been covered in the archive
interview. Sir Stanley Hooker, a pioneer of aeronautical engineering
and an enthusiast of oral history, has written:

> There have been endless efforts in researching into the contribu-
> tions of various people after they are dead, when an interview
> during their lifetime would, at least, point the way to the contribu-
> tion which they themselves consider to be their most important
> efforts.[54]

Oral archives also ensure that interview records are preserved of those
who have been so often troubled by interviewers (a small but significant minority) that they no longer agree to meet researchers. In-
depth interviews preserved in oral history archives contain far more
satisfactory information for historians than the relatively superficial
press or television/radio interviews, which are often the only surviving autobiographical records.

Tapes versus transcripts

Among practitioners of oral history, the issue of whether in oral history
the primary product is the transcript or the tape is hotly disputed. While
oral archives geared for lecture, broadcasting or linguistic purposes
consider transcripts to be very much secondary to the tapes, oral archives
catering primarily for academic users regard transcripts as the primary
product, sometimes to the extent that they do not even keep the tape
recordings.

However, since even open-reel tapes are relatively small and provided
they are stored under certain very feasible conditions (see Chapter 5,
pp. 100–3) should endure indefinitely, there seem to be no serious
grounds for destroying tapes because no one at present wishes to listen to
them. As Louis Starr has written, 'so far as possible [transcript *and* tape]
should be preserved, allowing researchers to choose for themselves.
Future generations may prove more aurally oriented.'[55] At the Oral
History Research Office at Columbia University, of which Starr was
director (1956–80), the staff 'have never had more than a couple of
requests [to listen to tapes] a year',[56] and other United States oral
archives, like the American Institute of Physics, find the ratio of requests
for transcript to tape lies in the region of 1000:1.[57] It is not surprising,
therefore, that oral archives should sometimes not wish to keep tapes;
but future needs cannot be predicted.

Moreover, tapes provide, like gold to pound notes, an ultimate guarantee of validity. If tapes are destroyed, there is no way of cross-checking that a certain person did indeed say what is in the transcript: the typist might simply have made a mistake. It is important, then, not just to *keep* tapes but to produce very good-quality recordings. It is highly probable that demand for sound material will increase in the future, by broadcasters and teachers (as well as lecturers) wishing to produce programmes in which the voices of those who forged or witnessed events is recorded.

Oral archives that gear themselves primarily towards academic users should in addition ensure that top-quality transcripts are produced which have passed through a number of recognized steps (initial typing, return for correction to interviewee, retyping, indexing and contents-paging, binding, copyright and access clarification stages). Further reading on the preparation of transcripts can be found in Cullom Davis's *Oral History: From Tape to Type*.[58]

Funding

For individual researchers, the costs incurred when interviewing are not normally prohibitive and can generally be absorbed in their general running expenditure. If they undertake a long series of talks and interview expenditure does become excessive, they can obtain small grants from fund-giving bodies like the British Academy or the Nuffield Foundation. In contrast, the question of finance is absolutely central to oral history archives. Expenditure will vary considerably, according to whether records are transcribed (a major cost), the degree of pre-interview preparation, the quality and fullness of transcription, and the provision of sound technicians and equipment. At 1983 prices an oral archive might expect to pay in the region of £500 per hour of new interview, through to transcription, binding and storage.

How this expenditure might break down for a transcript-orientated oral archive has been described by Louis Starr for a year's work of the Columbia Oral History Archive: administrative and clerical salaries, 29.2 per cent; interviewers' salary, paid by the hour, 24.1 per cent; transcribing, 20 per cent; travel, 14 per cent; printing and supplies, 5 per cent; indexing and extra typing, 3.5 per cent; extra clerical help, 1.8 per cent; tape recorder maintenance, 1.6 per cent; telephone and postage, 0.8 per cent.[59] For the type of oral archive which, like the Imperial War Museum, devotes considerable energy to preserving and reproducing high-quality sound recordings, expenditure on technical staff and equipment will take a large slice of the budget.

In Britain, as elsewhere, many oral archives have faltered because of funding problems. Active oral history archives often continue only because they are sponsored by a wealthy institution (e.g. a business), rather than conforming in response to a realistic estimate of what recording work is likely to be most needed by contemporary and future researchers. The best hope for securing regular funding in the future is for academics and archivists, as well as those concerned with planning the future needs of broadcasting, to discuss the *role* of and *future development* of oral history, so that it can be established on a firmer foundation. With a clearer understanding of the content and role of, and need for, oral history, funds may increase, partly from both governmental bodies but more likely from private organizations.[60]

Recommendations

In order to ensure that oral history is effective, and that material recorded does not merely duplicate existing records, interested parties from at least the following ten fields of history should meet to discuss the peculiar source problems of each discipline and to identify the major lacunae in the written evidence: political, administrative/legal, economic policy (including business and labour relations), social/social policy, colonial/commonwealth, defence/military, foreign policy, scientific, cultural, intellectual/religious. Such meetings would also ensure that academics, broadcasters and other users of oral history could identify areas of likely future interest, for the benefit of active oral archives. It is essential for oral history archives to remain close to those who know about the written evidence extant in a particular field, as well as to keep in constant touch with broadcasters academics and educationalists, the twin users of their products.

In addition, there is also a clear need for a national oral history advisory centre, which could not only advise on technical problems but act as a clearing house for enquiries on the whereabouts of recordings. Such a central organization could also instigate the development of specialist depositories for oral history recordings and transcripts from each of the branches of history listed above. Further, it could issue a set of guidelines, similar to the US Oral History Association's *Oral History Evaluation Guidelines* (1980) or the Canadian Oral History Association's *Code of Ethics and Responsibilities* (1982), but with specific application to oral history in Britain.

12

Oral archives in
Britain (media)

The richness of recorded sound in Britain is to be found in archives run by or connected with the broadcasting media. However, there is little interchange between academics, those interested in oral history and broadcasters. In his otherwise precise and informative source book, *Great Britain since 1914*, C. L. Mowat offers only the vaguest of advice to modern historians about the contribution of media archives to their research: 'Radio and television broadcasting have obviously produced a vast amount of material recorded on discs or tapes, though most of this is doubtless not retained for long.'[1] This chapter seeks to describe the kind of material to be found in media archives, and to indicate which archives contain material of interest to outside researchers and, if so, how one might have access to it. It focuses on oral history records (those obtained by question and answer) of both contemporary and retrospective kinds, and also looks at the preservation and possible contributions of historically interesting non-interview material in media archives.

With regard to preservation and access, a major problem is that, since both the BBC and the independent broadcasting companies are primarily producers and disseminators of material, the sound material they preserve is held principally with a view to future internal use, and the intrinsic historical value of a piece is no guarantee for its selection. Only a small percentage of broadcast material is kept at all; and offcuts (produced but not actually broadcast, and comparing at an approximate ratio of an average 8:1 with broadcast material) almost invariably move straight from the cutting-room floor to the dustbin. To the historian in search of oral records and oral evidence, such material can, however, have immense potential value.

Such a loss has not, however, passed without comment. In 1978 the Labour MP Brian Magee drew attention in the House of Commons to the amount of potentially valuable archival material that was being discarded each year from Broadcasting House and beyond. His motion stated that

> we as a society have not yet woken up to the fact that, with the development of audio-visual material, chiefly used on television and in film, we have acquired a form of historical source-material which is comparable in bulk, interest and importance with the printed record, and that because we have failed to wake up to this fact, we make nothing like the necessary institutional arrangements for its preservation, nor do we make the necessary financial arrangements for its preservation.[2]

Magee complained that the BBC failed to make its archives freely available to the public, and called for 'something in the audio-visual field that is similar to the British Library – in other words, a national sound archive, much more fully comprehensive than the British Institute of Recorded Sound, the nearest equivalent. The chief objections to his proposals raised in the debate were that the large-scale preservation of sound material would prove much too costly an operation, and that in any case we were in danger of 'swamping ourselves' with too much archival material in this country.[3]

Whereas it may legitimately be doubted whether all radio and television material is worth preserving, most agree that more thought is needed to be given to preservation procedures. Magee's recommendation that the BBC and ITV should have a statutory requirement to deposit material in the National Film Archive, treating it as something of a copyright library,[4] was very similar to that put forward just over a year later by the Advisory Committee on Archives, chaired by Lord Briggs. The committee reported that, while its members were 'all greatly impressed by the range, richness and variety of the BBC's archives and by the extent to which they represent a national, as well as a purely BBC, asset',[5] it was alarmed at the somewhat haphazard fashion in which the existing BBC archives operated, and was particularly concerned that 'not nearly enough material is being retained by Sound Archives in relation to the amount and value of the material being broadcast daily'.[6]

Some progress has been made in implementing the recommendations of the Briggs Committee. Contractual and copyright problems, however, and lack of both storage space and finance (especially since the BBC's charter places no formal obligation on the corporation to keep archives), mean that changes in archival policy take place fairly slowly. None the less, of the fourteen recommendations in the Briggs Report, twelve have been acted upon, and Briggs himself believes that one benefit derived from his report was to 'raise the archival consciousness of the BBC, amongst producers'.[7]

The BBC sound archives

The BBC Sound Archives at Broadcasting House have been collecting and preserving broadcast material since the 1930s, and include more than 100,000 catalogued items. Mark Jones, the Sound Archives Librarian, estimates that around 12–15 per cent of new broadcast sound material is preserved in some form – on commercial gramophone recordings, or Transcription Service and Sound Archive recordings.[8] One must bear in mind that the BBC Sound Archives are not the only repository of such material. Institutions such as the British Institute of Recorded Sound, the Imperial War Museum, the India Office Library and Records, the School of Oriental and African Studies and the Greenwich Maritime Museum keep BBC recorded material. In addition, most BBC local radio stations deposit material in local libraries.

In view of the fact that the archives are intended primarily for in-house use, the potential of material for future programmes is as much a criterion for selection as that of historical value. According to Mark Jones, however, the Sound Archives do aim to capture a wide range in their selection, which includes both the weighty and the trivial. Although they do not permanently keep all complete sequences of such news programmes as *The World at One* and *Today*, they do preserve some programmes in their entirety.

The archives are open to bona fide researchers, while casual members of the public are generally directed to the British Institute of Recorded Sound,[9] which offers superior facilities for on-the-spot listening. The fee for use of the Sound Archives in 1982 was £10 per session, plus VAT. The £10 charge will be considered by many as disconcertingly high, and one might be forgiven for suspecting that it is a deliberate means of fending off a glut of researchers, for which the BBC has neither sufficient space with listening facilities, nor staff for dealing with enquiries. On average, three or four outside researchers a week listen to material in the Sound Archives.

In view of the impressive system of cataloguing and storage at the archives, they have great potential for wider and more frequent use. Of the material in the repositories at Broadcasting House, there are usually four copies on disc and, for some material, a copy on tape. For extra security, duplicates of all preserved material are held at the BBC's Evesham centre. As well as a comprehensive cataloguing system, which is being transferred to microfiche, the department has also published catalogues under a number of subject-headings, including, for example, *BBC Sound Archives: Catalogue of Recorded Talks and Speeches*, which runs to four volumes, covering the beginning of the archives to 1970 (April) when financial stringencies stopped further publications.

In order to discover the nature of the material in the archives, we surveyed it as catalogued in September 1981. An eminent politician, R. A. Butler, was selected as an example. He appeared in a total of forty-eight catalogue entries, the earliest being a speech made in 1941, when he was parliamentary under-secretary at the Foreign Office. Of particular interest are two examples of political oral history – an interview Butler gave to Kenneth Harris in 1966, and a profile broadcast in 1978, presented by Anthony Howard, for which the people interviewed included Julian Amery, Humphry Berkeley, Enoch Powell and William Rees-Mogg. For Lord Mountbatten there are seventy-nine entries, the earliest being a 1944 Christmas message to the troops. Other features of interest as oral history include Mountbatten's reminiscences of Gandhi, Nehru and Churchill; his account, thirty years later, of the Dieppe raid of 1942; a 1978 interview with Ludovic Kennedy broadcast on BBC 1 the following year; and Denis Healey's comments after Mountbatten's assassination.

On figures from the arts one finds rather fewer entries per person. For T. S. Eliot, however, there are thirty-six entries featuring talks on or by him (not including recitals of his poetry). The earliest entry is a reference to him by W. B. Yeats in a 1936 lecture on modern poetry; there are also recollections of him by John Betjeman (1964), and a talk by Valerie Eliot on *The Waste Land* (1971), which would be classed as an 'oral record'. Benjamin Britten features in forty-eight entries related to talks, the earliest dating from 1947. Of note is an interview with the composers John Ireland and Sir Lennox Berkeley on their careers, in which discussion of Britten is included, and a joint interview with Britten, E. M. Forster and Eric Crozier on the making of *Billy Budd*.

Henry Moore (who is listed seventeen times) has his earliest entry detailed as follows: 'Int. on sculpture Unknown Political Prisoner, example of unsuccessful INTERVIEWING.'

In the field of science, there are nineteen entries for Albert Einstein, the earliest being a talk by Sir William Bragg in 1936. Of particular interest are an appreciation by Bertrand Russell (1954), and Einstein himself speaking on 'America since the Bomb' (1966).

These random samples indicate something of the range and wealth of material in the archives. At the same time one can only regret that even more material is not preserved, and that access to the archives is not facilitated. The more the public becomes aware of the calibre of the archive, the more pressure will build up for more funds to be devoted it.

The BBC written archives

The BBC Written Archives are housed at Caversham, near Reading, and include *inter alia* extensive BBC transcripts. The scripts of nearly all nationally broadcast radio talks, dating back to 1923, are kept on microfilm, but there are fewer samples from local radio and the external services.[10] Transcripts of some formally scripted television programmes and of recent television interviews, such as those with Lords Boothby and Brockway from *The Twentieth Century Remembered* are also kept.

The Written Archives include all 'programme as broadcast' scripts – logs of production details, which do not, however, include verbatim records of what actually went on the air. It is important to remember that the broadcast interview *per se* on a wide scale is a relatively new development: before about 1955, most words were scripted. The 'presenter's script' record for interviews on current programmes (contemporary oral history) may, in view of the essentially spontaneous nature of interviews, contain no more than questions and cues: the flesh of the interviews – the answers – are lacking.[11]

It is because they had to be scripted, and presented in the form of talks, that early radio programmes were so much shorter than they are today; the script often runs to only a few pages. What one reads is precisely what was broadcast, since there were no ad libs. A speaker might, however, make handwritten alterations to the script after it had been typed: these are visible on the microfilmed scripts of some of Neville Chamberlain's 1939 speeches.

As with sound archives, the BBC does not have extensive facilities for outside users. It is necessary to book ahead, because the centre has only two microfilm-reading machines. Yet so conditioned are historians to the written word that the Written Archives receive many more visitors than the Sound Archives. Approximately three or four outside researchers – including many biographers – consult the centre each day. The staff emphasize that they want the archives to be used: not infrequently books are published which, they realize, might have benefited from the additional material they could have provided, had the author only thought of consulting them.

Examples of some of the microfilmed programme scripts held by the Written Archives include a wealth of transcribed oral material: talks by Sir Thomas Beecham on Delius (1951), Sir William Beveridge on 'Unemployment' (1931), Winston Churchill on 'Causes of War' (1934), E. M. Forster wondering 'What would Germany do to us?' (1940), David Lloyd George on 'Responsibilities of Empire' (1937), Field Marshall Montgomery on 'NATO as I see it' (1954), Bertrand Russell on 'Science and Democracy' (1947) and H. G. Wells on 'World Peace' (1929). Such items qualify as 'oral records' (rather than oral history) and, as such, add a valuable dimension to the evidence on recent British history.

The National Film Archive

Difficulties that outside researchers may encounter in gaining access to sound and written archives are but a shadow of the problems of inspecting television film. The BBC and IBA television networks simply do not cater for outside researchers in their film archives. Individual researchers may, with some success, contact their regional network and receive permission to consult their television archives, but such *ad hoc* arrangements are not an official function of these authorities.[12] The BBC Film and Videotape Library at Brentford, Middlesex, is the largest such archive in Britain, but it is strictly for internal use and does not generally choose to co-operate with members of the public.

The quest for film collections is likely to lead one to the National Film Archive in Dean Street, which since 1935 has been the British Film Institute's national repository. In 1961 its brief was officially extended to include television. It has tended to include far more items from independent television than from the BBC, since the latter runs its own archives, while the independent networks rely more on the NFA as their repository and grant it a large annual subsidy for this purpose.[13] Currently it acquires approximately 2000 items a year, including videotapes,[14] and it selects items for both their artistic and their historical value. The NFA's holdings have been computerized since August 1979, and complete catalogues can be purchased; those catalogues housed in the NFA may be consulted free of charge, but a fee is charged to researchers who wish to view material.

The researcher will find much potentially valuable material in, for example, the renowned John Freeman television series of the late 1950s and early 1960s *Face to Face*. People interviewed include Augustus John, C. G. Jung, Evelyn Waugh, Sir Roy Welensky and Victor Gollancz. From London Weekened Television's *Weekend World* series, we find a rich source of contemporary oral history, with contributors including Edward Heath, Dr David Owen, Michael Foot, Margaret Thatcher and James Callaghan. These interviews from the late 1970s and early 1980s will provide a real insight into the way politicians presented themselves to the public, and the way in which interviewers such as Peter Jay and Brian Walden sought to draw them out.

The NFA also contains a great variety of miscellaneous interviews culled from a wide range of television sources, which unfortunately are seldom specified on the index cards. For one year, 1959, there are interviews with, for example, Aneurin Bevan, Hugh Gaitskell and André Maurois. Like the BBC Sound Archives, the NFA holds only a small proportion of all the material that has actually been produced, and interview records are undoubtedly much fuller for politicians than for artists. Within these limitations, however, it offers important source material, both as oral history (interviews) and oral record, including much newsfilm. Since television, in particular, provides evidence of the society that creates it, it is important that its material should be preserved, in complete units, as well as in extracts. Then, in a hundred years time, the hope expressed by Lord Briggs that 'historians can plug in and see a whole day's television' may, perhaps, be realized.[15]

The Granada Historical Trust

Valuable though broadcast oral history is, it has the inherent weakness that people rarely speak as frankly on the air, and that interviews are often geared more to extracting entertaining recollections than to obtaining fresh information. It thus seemed a very promising development when, in November 1960, a novel plan was announced in the press:

Men and women who have influenced the history of our time, and others who have been close to great events, are to be invited to record, on film or a sound tape, a personal assessment of their lives and work, and of the age in which they live, for the Archives of the Granada Historical Trust, a non-profit-making organization, which will be responsible for their preservation and safe keeping.[19]

The intention was to make the recordings in absolute secrecy, and none of them was to be broadcast or even publicized until after the death of the contributor. The hope was that, by establishing the principle of secrecy, interviewees would feel able to talk and divulge their opinions and comments with complete candour. Contributors were further to be allowed to make any corrections or additions they wished (a possible but complex business for film), and records were not to be added to the archive until contributors were entirely happy with their product. This was an important proposal, with clear objectives and a design that would require little modification in the light of over twenty years of subsequent experience of 'oral history' interviewing.

The 1960s saw only six interviews being shot, mostly with politicians, but one was with the political commentator and editor of the *New States-man* (1931–61), Kingsley Martin. His interview is the only one to have been made public, when extracts from it appeared in the *Sunday Times* after Martin's death in February 1969. Martin's contribution was recorded on film, as were all other interviews except one.

Barrie Heads, managing director of Granada Television International, was a producer on some of the interviews:

> We shot in the region of seven to eight hours for each programme. We found that by the end of the second day of filming we had uncovered about all the worthwhile material we were likely to obtain. . . . We were putting some fascinating stuff down on film, and we were constantly surprised at how frank some people were prepared to be.[20]

A number of problems account for the phasing out in the 1970s of this important work (although the trust is apparently dormant rather than extinct).[21] Although intended eventually to make programmes contain-ing 'highlights' from the interviews (as in the BBC's *The Twentieth Century Remembered*), no such programmes were in fact made, partly because of restrictions on usage placed on them by interviewees in the 1960s. Some momentum was lost when Sir Gerald Barry,[22] an executive of Granada and a leading force behind the trust, died in November 1968. Moreover, the nature of the work – archival storage for 'the can' rather than for immediate consumption – did not appeal to the journalistic temperament: enthusiasm for the project, high in the early 1960s, dwindled as staff moved on.

Conclusions

Media archives, like other oral archives, suffer principally from lack of funding and lack of consensus on how much material should be preserved. Non-media oral archives have far greater potential for recording valuable material for historical purposes (confidentiality, knowledgeable interviewers, more time), but media archives are still a major and under-appreciated source of serious oral history. One looks to media archives to do more to preserve offcuts, to ensure that valuable broadcast material is not lost, and above all to make their wares more accesible to outsiders. Lord Briggs himself feels strongly that the BBC's responsibility should be in actually fostering the demand for such archives:

the BBC has an obligation to make its material available. . . . The more an article is used, the more willing they should be to build it up; so I think the best way to increase archive material is to increase its availability.[23]

Appendix A:
Legal considerations

The vexed question of copyright is one that remains somewhat ambiguous with regard to oral evidence, but that must nevertheless be faced by individual researchers. It is rare to find that scholars who use interviewing methods have actually made specific copyright arrangements for their tapes or transcripts. Nor is it a matter on which oral archives hold a unanimous policy.

It must be emphasized, however, that there is no copyright in the spoken word. As the standard legal work on the subject explains: in order to qualify for copyright protection,

> the work must be expressed in some form of notation. Thus, a speech or lecture, even if recorded on a dictaphone, sound film or other recording device, would not be entitled to copyright protection as a literary work, though the recording itself might be protected as a sound recording under section 12 of the [Copyright] Act of 1956.[1]

Thus copyright comes into being when a note is taken. The speaker cannot claim copyright in a text, unless he is actually dictating it to someone who is taking it down at his request. In any attempt to interpret whether a piece of material may be published, three main areas of restriction are involved: copyright, breach of confidence, and the contractual aspect. Libel and contempt of court must also be taken into consideration.

If, however, the material exists only as a sound recording or on film, copyright is, according to section 12 of the 1956 Copyright Act, vested in whoever has paid for the recording to be made, be it a film company, a commercial or educational producer of taped material, or a broadcasting organization. Accordingly, the individual author who tapes an interview in the course of his research owns the copyright in the recording. The interviewee cannot claim copyright in the final product. Technically, as he is the instigator, rather than someone taking dictation at the speaker's request, the interviewer owns the copyright in the transcript; but he would be rash, nevertheless, to quote from it without first clearing it with the interviewee.

As David Lance has emphasized, the issue is a complex one; and the interviewer must still seek his informant's permission if he wishes to publish remarks made in interview:

> the consent implicit in agreeing to be interviewed does not represent a legal right for the interviewer to publish or otherwise reproduce the information he has recorded. To secure this right in law the informant's explicit and written consent is necessary.[2]

Archivists such as David Lance ask oral informants to assign their copyright to the institution: this transfers all rights and licences in the recording, but in order to be legally binding the assignment of the copyright has to be in writing, and signed by the informant.[3]

For a broadcasting organization such as the BBC, copyright problems are largely resolved by the making of contractual arrangements. The standard contracts the corporation draws up for its staff generally enable it to use contributions made in the course of their duty without any further clearance, but with regard to outside contributors the wording of the particular contract will govern the extent of the corporation's rights. The BBC's standard contracts with outside contributors generally grant the corporation broadcasting rights, non-paying (e.g. educational) audience use, and the right to sell the programme overseas. Other rights may also be included, such as the option to publish a transcript of the material in *The Listener* within twenty-eight days of the broadcast, or to permit the British Institute of Recorded Sound to make recordings. In addition, rights are taken to permit schools and colleges to record specifically educational programmes off the air (although the tapes have to be wiped after a certain time). There are thriving operations dealing with permissions to use BBC material for commercial purposes, run respectively by BBC Records (covering radio and television sound tracks) and BBC Enterprises (for television film), but it will frequently be necessary for additional permission to be obtained from a contributor before material can be released.

The BBC has therefore organized itself thoroughly with regard to potential copyright hazards. The private individual must, however, endeavour to be as scrupulous as the public corporation. The term 'off the record' can bear legal emphasis, although the more direct issue is that it is a morally binding one. 'Breach of confidence' is, however, a well-recognized cause of legal action. Points such as these should be treated with due circumspection by the person who has recourse to oral evidence. It is not simply a question of the letter of the law: there are also considerations of personal integrity and conscientiousness, and one's reputation among past and potential oral witnesses, which it would be unwise to neglect.

Appendix B:
Video and oral history

Some people have always felt that one should not stop at recording one dimension of an interview – namely, the sound – but should also record the only other sense perception that it is possible to record – namely, sight. As long as film was the only medium on which the visual dimension could be recorded, the feasibility of wide-scale visual recording was bound to be restricted because of the cost of film and cameras, and the need for elaborate lighting to record indoor interviews. The position, however, has changed dramatically with the advent of video, which falls in real cost almost yearly, while the video cameras (which record visual images on tape as opposed to film) become lighter and hence more manageable, and low-cost models become better able to film in the lower-light conditions of indoor interviews (indoor locations are always advisable for interviewing because of the noise problems of interviewing out of doors).[1]

Why, then, should not all oral history interviews be recorded on video? The arguments for doing so are many. One enthusiast for video, the American Richard Whitaker, has pointed out that many people in broadcasting in the 1940s argued that television would never replace the radio because the narrative element would be sacrificed to the visual, and he believes that sound recording will in turn be overtaken by videotaped oral history.[2] In the same way that tape was seen to give much more of an interviewee than note taking, so video manifestly gives one more than tape. An interviewee's reactions, facial, body and manual gestures can be easily observed. If the interviewee is being evasive, this can be more readily perceived, and it is far harder to lie convincingly to a camera than to just a tape recorder. Pauses, which are usually meaningless on tape, can be crammed full of significance if one is observing the interviewee's face. Such aspects as age and background can often be taken as read when one sees an interviewee.

Critics of videotaped oral history, however, acknowledge the value of seeing the face of interviewees in contemporary and cross-questioning oral history interviewing but question its relevance for retrospective oral history interviews. If a person is being interviewed about his recollection of the House of Commons during the First World War, or of Attlee's Cabinet after the war, it might be more useful just to hear his voice and conjure up one's own images, rather than seeing him as he was in the interview, years after the events he is describing. The counter-argument is that, if one can see the person talking, one is reminded more forcibly that this is only a recollection and not the reality, and one has more information to help in assessing the reliability of the witness.

More substantial arguments for sound recording rather than videotaping interviews are the cost of the latter, which, although falling in price, will never be as cheap as sound tapes and a tape recorder. An argument noted in the main body of the book against tape recording interviews was that some found that the obtrusiveness of the recorder inhibited a free exchange of information, and to most individual researchers the frankness of the information conveyed should always take precedence over the vehicle of recording. Video, despite its technical improvements and its superiority over film cameras, is still more obtrusive than a tape recorder and to be used properly requires two people present (one asking the questions, the other holding the camera) – although, if the interviewer and cameraman are fully confident and proficient, even those with no previous experience of being filmed are found to relax before the video camera. Some have found that an interviewee in a videotaped interview is more self-conscious, and more likely to 'put on a performance', than when just the sound is being recorded. A further drawback with video for both individual researcher and oral archive is that often it is merely the transcript that authors want to consult, and it is thus questionable, for purely scholarly use, whether the additional burdens and expense of videotaping oral history are justified.

Again we find there are no easy answers, merely a selection of arguments for and against. Much, however, would appear to revolve around the *end* for which the interviews are being recorded: if purely for private research, then sound tape would appear the most suitable vehicle; if, however, it is envisaged that recordings may be used as part of educational films as a teaching aid, or by television, then it might well be sensible to record interviews on video. A halfway house would be to record the interviews judged likely to be of the greatest long-term interest, or, while recording the whole interview on sound tape, to record just a portion of the interview on video.

An area where video can be useful to *all* collectors of oral history, however, is as suggested by Paul Thompson. When learning how to interview, it can be very useful to see oneself on film interviewing a subject in a mock interview.[3] This technique of seeing onself, and thereby enhancing one's awareness of one's own approach, has been found helpful in training all manner of people in personal encounters, be they doctors, solicitors or teachers, and it is a method which any oral history interviewer would benefit from too.

Notes

Chapter 1   Oral history and this book

1 This is not to say that this description of oral history is more valid than others; it is merely the one we find most useful. The Library of Congress defines oral history as 'A record of information gathered in oral form, usually on tape, as the result of a planned interview' (National Union Catalog of Manuscript Collections, Information Circular No. 7, Library of Congress, Descriptive Cataloging Division, Manuscript Section, May 1971). As a description, we would prefer Louis Starr's 'Oral history is primary source material obtained by recording the spoken words – generally by means of planned, tape-recorded interviews – of persons deemed to harbor hitherto unavailable information worth preserving' ('Oral History', *Encyclopedia of Library and Information Science*, 20 (New York, 1977), p 440). We would differ from some, however, in arguing that a tape recorder is not an essential adjunct to oral history: too much oral history has been, and is being, recorded direct on to paper to permit such a restrictive interpretation.

2 The definition of documentary evidence rests upon the archivist Hilary Jenkinson's definition:

> A document . . . is one which *was drawn up or used in the course of an administrative or executive transaction (whether public or private) of which itself formed a part; and subsequently preserved in their own custody for their own information by the person or persons responsible for that transaction and their legitimate successors.* (*A Manual of Archive Administration*, 2nd rev. edn (London: Lund Humphries, 1965), p. 11)

3 Some notable British contributions on the subject, however, have appeared – notably Brian Harrison, 'Oral History and Recent Political History', *Oral History* [1], 3 (1972); Philip Williams, 'Interviewing Politi-

cians: The Life of Hugh Gaitskell', *Political Quarterly*, (1980); Ken Young
and Liz Mills, 'Public Policy Research: A Review of Qualitative Methods'
(London: Social Science Research Council, 1980); Charles D. Raab, 'Elite
Interviewing as a Tool for Political Research: The Case of Scottish Educational Policy-Making', conference paper (1982).

4 C. L. Mowat, *Great Britain since 1914* (London: Sources of History, 1971)
p. 175. Patrick O'Farrell, Professor of History at the University of New
South Wales, puts the same point more bluntly: 'What is worrying from an
agnostic's viewpoint is how little rigorous thought appears to have been
given to the nature of oral "history", what it is, what it can properly do and
be' ('Oral History: Facts and Fiction', *Quadrant* (Sydney), (November
1979) p. 5.

5 Paul Thompson, *The Voice of the Past* (London: Oxford University Press,
1978), p. 25. This book is the standard work on non-élite oral history.

6 Brian Harrison, 'Paul Thompson, *The Voice of the Past*: Oral History', *The
Pelican* (Oxford: Corpus Christi College, 1979–80), p. 78.

7 L. A. Namier, *Diplomatic Prelude 1938–39* (London: Macmillan, 1948), p. v.
But see D. C. Watt's comments in chapter 2 on Namier's use of oral
evidence, pp. 28–9.

8 Letter, H. Montgomery Hyde to authors, 10 November 1981.

9 The conference was held in London, in October 1966. Reprinted in D. C.
Watt (ed.), *Contemporary History in Europe* (London: Allen and Unwin,
1969), pp. 42–3. John Barnes was a pioneer of political oral history.

10 David Butler, *The Electoral System in Britain 1918–51* (Oxford: Clarendon
Press, 1953), p. 214.

11 Personal interview with David Butler, Oxford, 28 November 1981.

12 Oral archives first became popular in the United States (where, ironically,
the transcript is seen as the primary product). Today in the United States
there are over 500 oral history archives and projects. There is a thriving Oral
History Association (founded in 1967) which issues an excellent journal,
Oral History Review. Columbia University, where an Oral History Office
has been established, is a focal point for oral history in the United States.
Seventy years before its establishment, H. H. Bancroft instigated the collection of oral history memoirs of leading 'Westerners' by sending stenographers out to talk to them. For an interesting discussion of the history of
oral history in the United States, see Charles T. Morrisey, 'Why Call It
"Oral History"? Searching for Early Usage of a Generic Term', *Oral
History Review* (1980), pp. 20–48.

13 David Lance, 'An Up-Date from Great Britain', *Oral History Review* (1976),
p. 63.

14 David Lance has written the standard work on oral archives, *An Archive
Approach to Oral History* (London: Imperial War Museum, 1978).

15 As stated in the Introduction, the book originally contained an extended
chapter that discussed interviewing in the broadcasting media, in theory and

in practice, and it is with some regret that we decided that its inclusion would make the book too long. Media interview material that finds its way into archives is discussed in chapter 12.

16 David Lance, 'Oral History in Britain', *Oral History Review* (1974), p. 64; T. C. Barker, 'Oral History in Britain', 15th International Congress of the Historical Sciences, Bucharest, 10–17 August 1980, Report, vol. 1, pp. 555–6.

17 The development of this and other branches of oral history is outlined in Anthony Seldon, 'Learning by Word of Mouth', *The Times Higher Education Supplement* (20 August 1982).

18 Quoted in Barker, op. cit., p. 560.

19 *Oral History in Schools*, by Sallie Purkis, and the *Directory of British Oral History Collections* (compiled by Anne McNulty and Hilary Troop) were published in 1978 and 1981 by the Oral History Society.

20 Letter, Paul Thompson to authors, 17 March 1982. We are also very grateful to John Tosh for turning our attention to the significance of oral tradition. John Tosh is author of *The Past in Question* (London: Longman, in preparation), on the scope and methods of history.

21 There is an excellent literature on the subject: for example, the now somewhat dated Jan Vansina, *Oral Tradition: A Study in Historical Methodology* (Harmondsworth: Penguin, 1973); David Henige, *The Quest for Chimera: The Chronology of Oral Tradition* (Oxford: Clarendon Press 1974); and Joseph C. Miller (ed.), *The African Past Speaks* (Folkestone: Dawson, 1980).

22 Thompson, op. cit., p. 49.

23 Brian Harrison, 'Paul Thompson, *The Voice of the Past*: Oral History', p. 78.

24 This trend is discussed in Anthony Seldon, *Churchill's Indian Summer* (London: Hodder & Stoughton, 1981), pp. 424–25.

25 Robert Gittings, *The Nature of Biography* (London: Heinemann, 1978), p. 59.

26 Roy Jenkins, 'The Development of Modern Political Biography 1945–70', Don Carlos Coloma Memorial Lecture 1971, reprinted in R. Speaight (ed.), *Essays by Diverse Hands*, new series, 37, 1972 p. 74.

27 R. G. Hewlett and O. Anderson, Jr, *A History of the United States Atomic Energy Commission*, vol. 1: *The New World 1939–46* (University Park: Pennsylvania State University Press, 1962), p. 664.

28 Personal interview with Martin Gilbert, London, 5 November 1981.

29 Captain Stephen Roskill, oral history questionnaire, August 1981.

30 Brian Harrison, 'Oral History and Recent Political History', p. 38.

31 Interview with Ian Bradley, 29 October 1981.

32 Interview with Anne Sloman, 3 September 1981; *see* Hugo Young and Anne Sloman, *No Minister* (London: BBC Publications, 1981).

Chapter 2   Criticisms of oral history

1 Nathan Reingold, *A Critic Looks at Oral History: The Fourth National Colloquium on Oral History* (Oral History Association, USA, 1970), p. 215.

2 Peter Oliver, 'Oral History: One Historian's View', Canadian Oral History Association *Journal*, 1 (1975–6), p. 17.

3 Seventy-five questionnaires were sent out, and we received replies from fifty-five authors, of whom twenty also provided additional information in interview.

4 Bernard Crick, oral history questionnaire, November 1981.

5 Roy Jenkins, 'The Development of Modern Political Biography 1945–70', Don Carlos Coloma Memorial Lecture 1971, reprinted in R. Speaight (ed.), *Essays by Diverse Hands*, new series, 37, 1972 p. 73.

6 Keith Middlemas, oral history questionnaire, September 1981.

7 Letter, David Marquand to authors, 9 September 1981.

8 Quoted in Brian Harrison, 'Oral History and Recent Political History', *Oral History* [1], 3 (1972), p. 34.

9 Philip Williams, 'Interviewing Politicians: The Life of Hugh Gaitskell', *Political Quarterly*, 51, 3 (1980), p. 310.

10 Lord Blake, oral history questionnaire, August 1981.

11 Stuart Sutherland, 'All in the mind' *Sunday Telegraph*, 2.1.83. Sutherland's article is a review of the Baddeley book. Sutherland has been Professor of Experimental Psychology at the University of Sussex since 1965.

12 Williams, op. cit., p. 310.

13 Private letter to authors, 11 December 1981.

14 Nigel Nicolson, oral history questionnaire, August 1981.

15 Richard Clutterbuck, *Britain in Agony* (Harmondsworth: Penguin, 1980), p. 17.

16 Alan Butt-Philip, oral history questionnaire, September 1981.

17 Private information.

18 Richard Lochead, 'Three Approaches to Oral History', *COHA Journal* (1975–6), p. 8. This view is not Lochead's own.

19 Barbara Tuchman, 'Distinguishing the Significant from the Insignificant', *Radcliffe Quarterly*, 56 (October 1972), pp. 9–10. Quoted in Ron Grele, 'Can Anyone Over Thirty be Trusted: A Friendly Critique of Oral History', *Oral History Review* (1978), p. 38.

20 David Irving, oral history questionnaire, 1 October 1981.

21 The authors are indebted to John Macnicol, of Bedford College, University of London, for bringing this point to their attention.

22 F. W. Winterbotham, *The Ultra Secret*, (London: Weidenfeld and Nicolson, 1974).

23 Personal interview with Martin Gilbert, London, 9 December 1981.

24 Personal interview with Ronald Lewin, East Horsley, 23 October 1981.

25 Captain Stephen Roskill, oral history questionnaire, August 1981.

26 Personal interview.
27 Personal interview.
28 Reingold, op. cit., p. 217.
29 George Jones, oral history questionnaire, 28 August 1981.
30 Philip Williams, op. cit., p. 311.
31 Stephen Koss, oral history questionnaire, September 1981.
32 Brian Bond, oral history questionnaire, August 1981.
33 Quoted in Harrison, op. cit., p. 46.
34 Personal interview with Martin Gilbert, London, 9 December 1981.
35 Harrison, op. cit., p. 36.
36 Lochead, op. cit., p. 8.
37 Paul Thompson, *The Voice of the Past* (London: Oxford University Press, 1978), p. 17.
38 Noël Annan, in *London Review of Books*, 15 October–4 November 1981, p. 4.
39 Quoted in Harrison, op. cit., p. 37.
40 Ben Pimlott, oral history questionnaire, September 1981.
41 Brian Bond, oral history questionnaire, August 1981.
42 Grele, op. cit., p. 41.
43 Denis Richards, oral history questionnaire, August 1981.
44 Brian Harrison, 'Paul Thompson, *The Voice of the Past*: Oral History', *The Pelican*, p. 79.
45 Anthony Howard, oral history questionnaire, October 1981.
46 Peter Davies, oral history questionnaire, October 1981.
47 Personal interview with William Moss, Boston, Mass., 14 December 1981.
48 Enoch Powell, 'Old Men Forget', *The Times*, 5 November 1981, p. 11. Powell was reviewing Anthony Seldon's *Churchill's Indian Summer* (London: Hodder & Stoughton, 1981).
49 Francis King, *Sunday Telegraph*, 3 January 1982, p. 12. King was reviewing a volume of interviews with novelists, *The Imagination Trial*, edited by Alan Burns and Charles Sugaet (London: Alison and Busby, 1981).
50 Private oral history questionnaire, August 1981.
51 L. J. Tivey, oral history questionnaire, 10 October 1981.
52 Personal information.
53 Charles Raw, in *London Review of Books*, 17 December 1981–20 January 1982, p. 20. Raw was reviewing Anthony Sampson's *The Money Lenders* (London: Hodder & Stoughton, 1981).

Chapter 3   Advantages of oral history

1 Michael Holroyd, oral history questionnaire, August 1981.
2 Martin Gilbert, *Winston S. Churchill*, Vol. 3: *1914–1916* (London: Heinemann, 1971), p. xxvi. Quoted in Brian Harrison, 'Oral History and Recent Political History', *Oral History* [1], 3 (1972), p. 35.

3 Nikolai Tolstoy, oral history questionnaire, October 1981.
4 Bernard Crick, oral history questionnaire, December 1981.
5 Personal interview with Professor Nicholas Kurti, London, 4 December 1981.
6 Ronald Lewin, letter to the editor, *The Times*, 4 June 1981.
7 Background evidence to Harrison, op. cit.
8 Michael Holroyd, oral history questionnaire, August 1981.
9 British Oral Archive of Political and Administrative History (BOAPAH) interview with Sir Robert Scott, Peebles, 16 June 1980.
10 As in *The Pathology of Leadership* (London: William Heinemann Medical Books, 1969).
11 J. A. G. Griffith (with T. C. Hartley), *Central Departments and Local Authorities* (London: Allen & Unwin, 1966).
12 Personal interview with J. A. G. Griffith, London, 3 November 1981.
13 Denis Richards, oral history questionnaire, August 1981.
14 BOAPAH interview with Lord Boyle of Handsworth, London, 23 July 1980.
15 BOAPAH interview with Lord Harlech, London, 26 June 1980.
16 BOAPAH began to exploit this aspect.
17 Personal interview with Lord Selkirk, Wimborne, 13 August 1981.
18 Personal interview.
19 Harrison, op. cit., p. 38.
20 Sixteen volumes have been published in the series so far (London: Allen & Unwin). The series began with the *Home Office* (1954), and the most recent volume is on the *Department of Education and Science* (1979).
21 Ben Pimlott, oral history questionnaire, September 1981.
22 David J. Mitchell, 'Living Documents: Oral History and Biography', *Biography*, 3 (Winter 1980), p. 284.
23 John Barnes, in D. C. Watt (ed.), *Contemporary History in Europe* (London: Macmillan, 1969), pp. 41–2.
24 L. A. Namier, *Diplomatic Prelude 1938–39* (London: Macmillan, 1948), p. v.
25 Personal interview with Martin Gilbert, London 5 November 1981.
26 Personal interview with Martin Gilbert, London 9 December 1981.
27 David Irving, oral history questionnaire, October 1981.
28 John Barnes, in Watt, op. cit., p. 42. Keith Middlemas and John Barnes, *Baldwin* (London: Weidenfeld & Nicolson, 1969).
29 Personal interview with Michael Holroyd, London, 11 September 1981.
30 Background evidence to Harrison, op. cit.
31 Personal interview with Roger Berthoud, Hampstead, 17 September 1981.
32 Michael Holroyd, *Lytton Strachey: A Biography*, rev. edn (London: Heinemann, 1973), Preface, pp. 11–17.
33 Philip Williams, 'Interviewing Politicians: The Life of Hugh Gaitskell', *Political Quarterly*, 51, 3(1980), p. 313.

34 Personal interview with Martin Gilbert, London, 3 November 1981.
35 Personal interview with Laurie Leavitt-Kahn, London, 14 January 1982.
36 Quoted in Harrison, op. cit., p. 32.
37 Personal interview with Sir Norman Chester, Oxford, 28 November 1981.
38 Letter, Martin Gilbert to authors, 16 December 1981.
39 Nigel Nicolson, oral history questionnaire, August 1981.
40 Robert Rhodes James, oral history questionnaire, August 1981.
41 Personal interview with Lord Hill of Luton, London, 4 August 1981.
42 Mitchell, op. cit., pp. 284-5.
43 Volume 2 by F. H. Hinsley, E. E. Thomas, C. F. G. Ranson and R. C. Knight (London: HMSO, 1981).
44 Nigel Hamilton, in *London Review of Books*, 5-18 November 1981, p. 16. See also review in *The Times*, 10 September 1981.
45 Quoted in Harrison, op. cit., p. 32. See also Paul Thompson, *The Voice of the Past* (London: Oxford University Press, 1978), p. 76.
46 Phillip Whitehead, *Sunday Times*, 14.2.82.
47 Personal interview with Lord Briggs, Oxford, 27 November 1981.
48 Denis Richards, oral history questionnaire, August 1981.
49 Roy Jenkins, 'The Development of Modern Political Biography 1945-70', Don Carlos Coloma Memorial Lecture 1971, reprinted in R. Speaight (ed.), *Essays by Diverse Hands*, new series, 37, 1972 p. 73.
50 Nigel Nicolson, oral history questionnaire, August 1981.
51 Bernard Crick, oral history questionnaire, December 1981.
52 Harrison, op. cit., p. 41.
53 John Colville, *Footprints in Time* (London: Collins, 1976), p. 70.
54 Andrew Boyle, *Poor, Dear Brendan* (London: Hutchinson, 1974). C. E. Lysaght, *Brendan Bracken* (London: Allen Lane, 1979). Bracken was an *éminence grise* after 1945, not just to Churchill, but also to many other senior Conservatives, including Oliver Lyttelton and Sir Walter Monckton. Bracken had been Minister of Information, 1941-5. Sir Philip Sassoon was Conservative MP for Hythe from 1912 until his death in 1939. He held office as Parliamentary Under-Secretary of State for Air 1924-9 and 1931-7. A man of great wealth and hospitality, he entertained many of the leading figures from the worlds of art and politics.
55 *The Times*, 8 January 1982.
56 *The Listener*, 5 November 1981, p. 542.
57 Michael Holroyd, oral history questionnaire, August 1981.
58 Brian Harrison, describing his project on the British women's movement in the twentieth century, deposited in the Fawcett Library, London, in 'Introduction to the Tapes', p. 1. Harrison concludes the 'Introduction' with these words: 'Insofar as interviewing extends the historian's understanding of human personality and the breadth of his perception, it makes its own distinctive contribution towards what must surely be the overriding purpose of all humanistic study' (p. 15).
59 David Irving, oral history questionnaire, October 1981.

Chapter 4 Methodology for individual researchers

1 The classic source on interviewing must be the four-page appendix to Beatrice Webb's *My Apprenticeship* (London: Longmans, Green, 1926), entitled 'The Method of the Interview', pp. 423–6. An outstanding longer account is to be found in Paul Thompson's *The Voice of the Past* (London: Oxford University Press, 1978), ch. 6 ('The Interview'), pp. 165–85. Also highly recommended are L. A. Dexter, *Elite and Specialized Interviewing* (Evanston, Ill: Northwestern University Press, 1970); George Ewart Evans, 'Approach to Interviewing', *Oral History*, 4 (1973); W. J. Langlois (ed.), *A Guide to Aural History Research*, Victoria, BC.: Aural History, 1976); Stanley Payne, *The Art of Asking Questions* (Princeton, NJ: Princeton University Press, 1951). Two further works at least could be consulted with profit: Peter Honey, *Face to Face: A Practical Guide to Interactive Skills* (London: Institute of Personnel Management, 1976), and Arthur Kaiser, *Questioning Techniques* (Farnham: Momenta, 1979) (with thanks to David Reid for bringing these works to the attention of the authors). The authors also benefited much from reading unpublished papers by Margaret Brooks, 'Conduct of the Interview', and Alan Shuttleworth, 'Being Interested in People', again from the thoughtful written and spoken comments of Brian Harrison.
2 Quentin Bell, oral history questionnaire, August 1981.
3 There is much overlap between both, and individual researchers could with profit read Chapter 5 as well, particularly if interested in tape recording and in sound quality.
4 See Chapter 2, note 3.
5 Dexter, op. cit., p. 11.
6 Dexter himself refers readers to Eugene Webb, D. Campbell, R. Schwartz and L. Seechrest, *Unobtrusive Measures: Non-Reactive Research in the Social Sciences* (Chicago, Ill: Rand McNally, 1966), for alternative ways of gathering evidence.
7 This point was expressed by several of those interviewed.
8 These, and subsequent percentages based on the oral history questionnaire sample, are only approximate and rest on a subjective categorizing of the respondents' written statements.
9 Personal interview with Martin Gilbert.
10 Personal interview with Lord Briggs, Oxford, 27 November 1981.
11 Philip Ziegler, oral history questionnaire, August 1981.
12 David Irving, oral history questionnaire, September 1981.
13 Robert Rhodes James, quoted in Brian Harrison, 'Oral History and Recent Political History', *Oral History* [1], 3 (1972), p. 34.
14 Roger Berthoud, oral history questionnaire, August 1981.
15 Dexter, op. cit., p. 76.
16 Webb, op. cit., p. 424.

17 Philip Williams, 'Interviewing Politicians: The Life of Hugh Gaitskell', *Political Quarterly*, 51, 3 (1980), p. 303.
18 See Chapter 8, p. 00.
19 John Cross, oral history questionnaire, August 1981.
20 Private information.
21 Nikolai Tolstoy, oral history questionnaire, 6 October 1981.
22 H. Montgomery Hyde, oral history questionnaire, September 1981.
23 Anthony Howard, oral history questionnaire, August 1981.
24 Stephen Koss, oral history questionnaire, September 1981.
25 Personal interview with Janet Morgan, London, 31 March 1982.
26 Williams, op. cit., p. 306.
27 Ibid., p. 313, and comments from questionnaires.
28 Dexter, op. cit., p. 31.
29 Paul Ferris, oral history questionnaire, August 1981.
30 Thompson, op. cit., pp. 175–6.
31 Private information.
32 Paul Ferris, oral history questionnaire, August 1981.
33 Private information.
34 Alan Butt-Philip, oral history questionnaire, September 1981.
35 Bernard Crick, oral history questionnaire, December 1981.
36 Dexter, op. cit., p. 37.
37 James Kellas, oral history questionnaire, September 1981.
38 Webb, op. cit., p. 423.
39 Thompson, op. cit., p. 166.
40 See, for example, Cullom Davis, Kathryn Back, Kay MacLean, *Oral History: From Tape to Type* (Chicago, Ill.: American Library Association, 1977), p. 11; Langlois (ed.), op. cit., p. 10.
41 Margaret Brooks, 'Conduct of the Interview'. She feels that preliminary meetings nevertheless are a necessary step for oral archives.
42 Harrison, op. cit., p. 44.
43 Webb, op. cit., p. 425.
44 Private information.
45 Private interview.
46 Webb, op. cit., p. 426.
47 Dexter, op. cit., pp. 56–7.
48 Ibid., p. 57.
49 Thompson, op. cit., p. 173.
50 Nikolai Tolstoy, oral history questionnaire, 6 October 1981.
51 *Oral History*, 4, pp. 62–3, Evans is quoted in Thompson, op. cit., 1973 p. 168. Paul Thompson has a particularly useful discussion of questions on pp. 167–72.
52 Peter Kellner, oral history questionnaire, September 1981.
53 Letter, David Marquand to authors, 9 September 1981.
54 Bernard Crick, oral history questionnaire, December 1981.

55 See, for example, David Lance, *An Archive Approach to Oral History* (London: Imperial War Museum, 1978), pp. 36–9; *Oral History Evaluation Guidelines* ((US) Oral History Association, 1980); and the forthcoming *Code of Ethics and Responsibilities* produced by the Canadian Oral History Association.

56 Hugh Heclo and Aaron Wildavsky, *The Private Government of Public Money* (London: Macmillan, 1974), p. xviii.

57 Private information.

58 Webb, op. cit., p. 425.

59 Herbert Butterfield, 'Official History, Its Pitfalls and Its Criteria', *Studies* (June 1949), p. 143 (in postscript to the article).

60 Dexter, op. cit., p. 36.

61 Heclo and Wildavsky, op. cit., p. xviii.

62 Nikolai Tolstoy, oral history questionnaire, 6 October 1981.

63 Personal interview with Ronald Lewin, East Horsley, 23 October 1981.

64 Peter Oliver, 'Oral History: One Historian's View', *COHA Journal*, 1 (1975–6), p. 14. Quoted in Thompson, op. cit., p. 182.

65 Private information.

66 Keith Middlemas, oral history questionnaire, September 1981.

67 Margaret Morris, oral history questionnaire, November 1981.

68 Thompson, op. cit., p. 180.

Chapter 6   Oral projects: methodology and practice

1 The North West Sound Archive, in conjunction with the Communications Department at the University of Manchester, is also conducting a series of recordings with distinguished members of the university. At the University of Durham, plans are being made to record a considerable number of retired members of staff.

2 Letter, Dr J. A. Edwards to authors, 18 January 1982.

3 Letter, Adrian Allan to authors, 17 September 1981.

4 Letter, Professor W. L. Gage to authors, 29 August 1981.

5 *Economic Journal*, 16, 1906, p. 522. Mentioned in Paul Thompson, *The Voice of the Past*, pp. 38–9.

6 Letter, Sir Peter Parker to authors, 3 November 1981.

7 Information from telephone calls with J. D. Cousin, 19 February 1982, and R. K. Shirley, 15 February 1982, and from a personal interview with Dr W. J. Reader, London, 13 February 1982.

Chapter 7   The evaluation and use of oral evidence

1 Charles Wilson, *The History of Unilever* (London: Cassell, 1954), Preface. Quotation from p. x–xi of the 1970 paperback edition (London: Cassell).

2 Christopher Thorne, 'Talking About Vietnam', BBC Radio 3 broadcast, transmitted 9 January 1979; transcript, pp. 10–11.
3 L. A. Dexter, *Elite and Specialized Interviewing* (Evanston, Ill.: Northwestern University Press, 1970), p. 139.
4 Bernard Crick, oral history questionnaire, December 1981.
5 Philip Williams, 'Interviewing Politicians: The Life of Hugh Gaitskell', *Political Quarterly*, 51, 3 (1980), p. 309.
6 Private information.
7 Charles Raab, oral history questionnaire, October 1981.
8 *The Politics of Education: Edward Boyle and Anthony Crosland in conversation with Maurice Kogan* (Harmondsworth: Penguin, 1971). The questions appear on pp. 119, 161 and 183.
9 Nikolai Tolstoy, oral history questionnaire, 6 October 1981.
10 Personal interview with Martin Gilbert, London, 11 November 1981.
11 Bernard Crick, oral history questionnaire, December 1981.
12 Letter, Lord Dacre of Glanton to authors, 8 April 1982.
13 Ben Pimlott, oral history questionnaire, September 1981.

Chapter 8   Modern and recent history

1 Stephen Koss, oral history questionnaire, September 1981.
2 Stephen Koss, *Nonconformity in Modern British Politics* (London: Batsford, 1975), p. 239.
3 Stephen Koss, *The Rise and Fall of the Political Press in Britain* (London: Hamish Hamilton, 1981).
4 Stephen Koss, oral history questionnaire, September 1981.
5 G. C. Peden, *British Rearmament and the Treasury 1932–39* (Edinburgh: Scottish Academic Press, 1979), p. 210.
6 G. C. Peden, oral history questionnaire, August 1981.
7 Anthony Seldon, *Churchill's Indian Summer* (London: Hodder & Stoughton, 1981).
8 Anthony Seldon, Government Department Seminar Paper on Oral History, LSE, 4 December 1978.
9 David Carlton, 'The Mandarin's Version', *Sunday Times*, 1 November 1981.
10 Enoch Powell, 'Old Men Forget', *The Times*, 5 November 1981, p. 11.
11 Personal interview with Martin Gilbert, London, 5 November 1981.
12 Personal interview with Martin Gilbert, London, 9 December 1981.
13 Martin Gilbert, *Winston S. Churchill* (London: Heinemann, 1977), vol. 5, p. 439.
14 Ibid., pp. 729–30.
15 Ibid., p. 1001.
16 Ibid., vol. 4, p. 936; vol. 5, p. 1141.

17 Bernard Donoughue and G. W. Jones, *Herbert Morrison: Portrait of a Politician* (London: Weidenfeld & Nicolson, 1973), p. xi.

18 Ibid., p. xiv.

19 Quoted in Paul Thompson, *The Voice of the Past* (London: Oxford University Press, 1978), p. 131. Also oral history questionnaires, Bernard Donoughue, September 1981, and G. W. Jones, 28 August 1981.

20 Donoughue and Jones, op. cit., p. 625.

21 Ibid., p. 355.

22 G. W. Jones 'The Value of Recent Biographies, Autobiographies and Diaries', *Parliamentary Affairs*, 34 (1981), p. 342.

23 Philip M. Williams, *Hugh Gaitskell* (London: Cape, 1979), pp. 789–91.

24 Philip Williams, 'Interviewing Politicians: The Life of Hugh Gaitskell', *Political Quarterly*, 51,·3 (1980), pp. 303–16.

25 Williams, *Hugh Gaitskell*, pp. 629 and 934.

26 Williams, 'Interviewing Politicians', p. 306.

27 Personal interview with Philip Williams, Oxford, 16 October 1981.

28 David Marquand, *Ramsay MacDonald* (London: Cape, 1977), pp. xiv–xv.

29 Letter, David Marquand to authors, 9 September 1981.

30 Robert Rhodes James, in D. C. Watt (ed.), *Contemporary History in Europe* (London: Allen & Unwin, 1969), p. 23.

31 Personal interview with Ronald Lewin, East Horsley, 23 October 1981.

32 Sir Peter Gretton, in the *Journal of the Royal United Service Institution* (May 1966), p. 106. Quoted by R. Rhodes James, in D. C. Watt (ed.), op. cit., p. 23.

33 R. Rhodes James, in D. C. Watt (ed.), op. cit., p. 23.

34 Ibid.

35 Nigel Hamilton, oral history questionnaire, September 1981.

36 Ibid.

37 Nigel Hamilton, *Monty: The Making of a General 1887–1942* (London: Hamish Hamilton, 1981), p. xvii.

38 Ibid., p. 731.

39 Letter, Nigel Hamilton to authors, 11 February 1983.

40 Nigel Nicolson, *Alex* (London: Weidenfeld & Nicolson, 1973), pp. 251–2.

41 Nigel Nicolson, oral history questionnaire, August 1981.

42 Ibid.

43 Bond's most recent book is *British Military Policy between the Two World Wars* (London: Oxford University Press, 1981).

44 Brian Bond, oral history questionnaire, August 1981.

45 Ibid.

46 Denis Richards, *Royal Air Force 1939–45*, 3 vols (London: HMSO, 1952–3); *Portal of Hungerford* (London: Heinemann, 1977).

47 Denis Richards, oral history questionnaire, August 1981.

48 Stephen Roskill, oral history questionnaire, August 1981.

49 R. Rhodes James, in D. C. Watt (ed.), op. cit., p. 24.
50 Ronald Lewin, 'One Last Splendid Farewell to History', *The Times*, 3 September 1981.
51 Arthur J. Marder, *Old Friends, New Enemies*, (London: Oxford University Press, 1981).
52 Christopher Thorne, 'On Course for Disaster', *The Times Literary Supplement*, 4 December 1981. With thanks to John Walford.
53 R. N. Rosecrance, *Defense of the Realm* (New York and London: Columbia University Press, 1968); Andrew J. Pierre, *Nuclear Politics* (London: Oxford University Press, 1972); Phillip Darby, *British Defence Policy East of Suez 1947–68* (London: Oxford University Press, 1973). A fourth book covering a similar subject-matter, A. J. R. Groom's *British Thinking About Nuclear Weapons* (London: Francis Pinter, 1974), in contrast does not appear to have been based in part upon interview evidence.
54 Rosecrance, op. cit., p. ix.
55 Pierre, op. cit., p. ix.
56 Darby, op. cit., p. xiii.
57 Personal interview with Geoffrey Warner, Leicester University, 26 October 1981.
58 David Carlton, *Anthony Eden* (London: Allen Lane, 1981).
59 David Carlton, oral history questionnaire, September 1981.
60 David Carlton, *MacDonald versus Henderson: The Foreign Policy of the Second Labour Government* (London: Macmillan, 1970).
61 J. A. Cross, *Sir Samuel Hoare: A Political Biography* (London: Cape, 1977).
62 John Cross, oral history questionnaire, August 1981.
63 Nikolai Tolstoy, oral history questionnaire, 6 October 1981.
64 Avi Shlaim, Peter Jones and Keith Sainsbury, *British Foreign Secretaries Since 1945* (Newton Abbot: David & Charles, 1977), p. 15.
65 Personal interview with Keith Sainsbury, Reading, 10 November 1981.
66 Shlaim *et al.*, op. cit., p. 241.
67 D. J. Morgan, *Official History of Colonial Development*, 5 vols (London: Macmillan, 1979).
68 David Goldsworthy, *Colonial Issues in British Politics 1945–61* (London: Oxford University Press, 1971), p. vii.
69 David Goldsworthy, oral history questionnaire, 7 October 1981.
70 Charles Douglas-Home, oral history questionnaire, September 1981.
71 Charles Douglas-Home, *Evelyn Baring: The Last Proconsul* (London: Collins, 1978), pp. 327–9.
72 Samuel Brittan, *Steering The Economy* (Harmondsworth: Penguin, 1971). First published in 1964 as *The Treasury under the Tories 1951–64*. The second edition (as *Steering The Economy*) was published in 1969.
73 Ibid., pp. 17.
74 Personal interview with Samuel Brittan, London, 18 October 1981.

75 Eric Wigham, *Strikes and the Government 1893–1981* (London: Macmillan, 1982). Interview with Eric Wigham, West Wickham, 30 September 1981.

76 Gerald A. Dorfman, *Government versus Trade Unionism in British Politics since 1968* (London: Macmillan, 1979), pp. 169–170.

77 Ibid, p. 164.

78 Paul Thompson, op. cit., pp. 66–9, 230–2.

79 David J. Mitchell, 'Living Documents: Oral History and Biography', *Biography*, 3 (Winter 1980), p. 288. He is discussing Allan Nevins, *Ford: The Times, the Man, the Company* (New York: Scribner's, 1954).

80 Personal interview with Sir Norman Chester, Oxford, 28 November 1981.

81 T. C. Barker, R. H. Campbell and P. Mathias, *Business History* (London: The Historical Association, 1960), pp. 10–11.

82 Stanley Chapman, *Jesse Boot of Boots the Chemists* (London: Hodder & Stoughton, 1974), pp. 9–10.

83 Ibid., p. 215–6.

84 Charles Wilson, *The History of Unilever*, paperback edn (London: Cassell, 1970), p. x.

85 Ibid.

86 Ibid., vol. 2, pp. 453–5.

87 Ibid., vol. 3, p. vi.

88 Ibid.

89 Leslie Hannah, *Electricity before Nationalization* (London: Macmillan, 1979).

90 Personal interview with Leslie Hannah, LSE, 4 February 1982.

91 T. C. Barker, *The Glassmakers: Pilkington: The Use of an International Company 1826–1976* (London: Weidenfeld & Nicolson, 1977).

92 Personal interview with Professor T. C. Barker, LSE, 14 October 1981.

93 This quotation, and subsequent references, come from a personal interview with Dr W. J. Reader, London, 13 February 1982. See *Imperial Chemical Industries: a history* (London: Oxford University Press, 1970 and 1975).

94 Private interview.

95 Roger Smith, *East Kilbride: The Biography of a Scottish New Town 1947–1973* (London: HMSO, 1979).

96 Roger Smith, oral history questionnaire, October 1981. Personal interview with Roger Smith, London, 28 October 1981.

97 Phoebe Hall, *Reforming The Welfare* (London: Heinemann, 1976), pp. 151–2.

98 Ibid., p. ix.

99 Charles Raab, oral history questionnaire, November 1981.

100 Personal interview with Professor Nicholas Kurti, London, 4 December 1981. The authors are indebted to Margaret Gowing and her research team at the UKAEA for help and advice with this section.

101 Personal interview with Dr Spencer Weart and Jean Warnow, American Institute of Physics, New York, 17 December 1981.

102 R. G. Hewlett and O. E. Anderson, Jr. *A History of the United States Atomic Energy Commission*, vol. 1: *The New World 1939–46* (Pennsylvania State University Press, 1962), p. 662. See also R. G. Hewlett, 'A Pilot Study in Contemporary Scientific History', *Isis*, 53 1962, pp. 31–51.

103 For a survey of the problems and practice of interviews in the history of science and of medicine, see Saul Benison, 'Oral History: A Personal View', in Edwin Clarke (ed.), *Modern Methods in the History of Medicine* (London: Athlone Press, 1971), pp. 286–305. Benison also includes a useful bibliography.

104 Harriet Zuckeman, *Scientific Elite: Nobel Laureates in the United States* (New York and London: Free Press, 1977), pp. 256–81.

105 See M. J. Mulkay, 'Methodology in the Sociology of Science – Reflections on the Study of Radio Astronomy', *Social Science Information*, 13 (1974), pp. 1078–119. G. Nigel Gilbert, 'Being Interviewed: A Role Analysis', *Social Science Information*, 19 (1980), pp. 227–36.

106 David Edge, oral history questionnaire, December 1981. The book concerned is David O. Edge and Michael J. Mulkay, *Astronomy Transformed: The Emergence of Radio Astronomy in Britain* (New York and London: Wiley, 1976).

107 Personal interview with Dr Peter Glasner and David Travis, Polytechnic of North London, 15 October 1981.

108 John Hendry, 'Reminiscence and the Contemporary History of Science', *British Journal for the History of Science*, 13 (1980), pp. 259–60. The essay-review article contains many relevant points of interest.

109 Personal interview with Nicholas Kurti, London, 4 December 1981.

110 Spencer R. Weart and David H. De Vorkin, 'The Voice of Astronomical History', *Sky and Telescope* (February 1982), p. 124.

111 Kenneth Harris, *Conversations* (London: Hodder & Stoughton, 1967); *Kenneth Harris Talking To* (London: Weidenfeld & Nicolson, 1971).

112 Harris, *Conversations*, p. viii. For interview-based works see also pp. 129–30.

113 Ibid., p. v.

114 Ibid., pp. 260 and 270.

115 John Thompson, *On Lips of Living Men* (London: Angus & Robertson, 1962).

116 Robert Stursberg, *Diefenbaker: Leadership Gained 1956–62* and *Diefenbaker: Leadership Lost 1962–67* (Toronto and Buffalo: University of Toronto Press, 1975 and 1976).

117 Stursberg, *Diefenbaker: Leadership Lost*, p. vii and 203–5.

118 Francis Williams, *A Prime Minister Remembers* (London: Heinemann, 1961; Lord Swinton, *Sixty Years of Power: Some Memories of the Men who Wielded it* (London: Hutchinson, 1966).

119 *Felix Frankfurter Reminisces*, 'Recorded in Talks' with Dr Harlan B.

Phillips (London: Secker & Warburg, 1960), p. vii.
120 Merle Miller, *Plain Speaking: An Oral Biography of Harry S. Truman* (New York: Berkley, 1973).
121 Michael Teague, *Mrs L.: Conversations with Alice Roosevelt Longworth* (London: Duckworth, 1981).

Chapter 9 Contemporary history and political science

1 J. A. G. Griffith, *Central Departments and Local Authorities* (London: Allen & Unwin, 1966).
2 Personal interview with J. A. G. Griffith, LSE, 3 November 1981.
3 See Chapter 8. Letter, David Marquand to authors, 9 September 1981.
4 J. G. Kellas, oral history questionnaire, August 1981.
5 R. G. Hewlett and Duncan, *A History of the United States Atomic Energy Commission*, vol. II: *Atomic Shield, 1947–52* (Pennsylvania State University Press, 1969), p. 603.
6 This point is discussed by John Barnes, in D. C. Watt (ed.), *Contemporary History in Europe* (London: Allen & Unwin, 1969), pp. 38–9.
7 Bernard Crick, 'Court History', *New Statesman*, 23 October 1981, p. 21.
8 John Barnes, in Watt (ed.), op. cit., p. 39.
9 W. N. Medlicott, Introduction to Bernard Krikler and Walter Laqueur (eds), *A Reader's Guide to Contemporary History* (London: Weidenfeld and Nicolson, 1972), p. 11. For other interesting contributions to the discussion of contemporary history, see also G. Barraclough, *An Introduction to Contemporary History* (London: Watts, 1964); Llewellyn Woodward, 'The Study of Contemporary History', *The Journal of Contemporary History*, 1, 1 (1966), pp. 1–13; and Watt (ed.), op. cit. R. B. McCallum was a faculty fellow at Nuffield College, Oxford, and co-author with Alison Readman of the first election study to have been sponsored by Nuffield College, *The British General Election of 1945* (London: Oxford University Press, 1947).
10 The criticisms, and merits, of instant history are discussed in David Butler, 'Instant History', *The New Zealand Journal of History* (University of Auckland, October 1968), pp. 107–14. The quotation is from p. 107.
11 James F. Hope, *A History of the 1900 Parliament* (London: Blackwood, 1908); Dean E. McHenry, *The Labour Party in Transition* (London: Routledge, 1938), pp. x–xi.
12 The general election studies are the subject of a forthcoming article by Professor Dennis Kavanagh in the new journal, *Election Studies*. Kavanagh was co-author with David Butler of the studies on the 1974 and 1979 general elections. See also Austin Ranney, 'Thirty Years of "Psephology" ', *British Journal of Political Science*, 6 (1976), pp. 217–30.
13 Butler, op. cit., p. 110.
14 Ibid.
15 Ibid., pp. 111, 111–12 and 108.

16 In the introduction to his book on the 1979 General Election, David Butler
   wrote that he and his co-author 'owe a great deal to the press . . . to writers
   of specialist articles and to pollsters. But we owe even more to the participants . . . who gave us so much of their time.' David Butler and Dennis
   Kavanagh, *The British General Election of 1979* (London: Macmillan, 1980),
   p. viii.
17 Anthony Howard and Richard West, *The Making of the Prime Minister*
   (London: Cape, 1965), p. 7. White's book was published in New York in
   1962.
18 Ibid., p. 8.
19 Anthony Howard, oral history questionnaire, August 1981.
20 Howard R. Penniman (ed.), *Britain at the Polls 1979* (Washington, DC:
   AEI, 1981). See, for example, pp. 87 and 83.
21 Personal interview with Anthony King, London, 21 October 1981.
22 Arthur Conan Doyle, *The British Campaign in France and Flanders* 1914
   (London: Hodder & Stoughton, 1916), pp. vii–viii.
23 G. B. Henderson, 'A Plea for the Study of Contemporary History', *History*
   (June 1941), p. 53. Quoted by W. N. Medlicott, in Krikler and Laqueur
   (eds), op. cit., p. 12.
24 Letter, Lord Dacre of Glanton to authors, 8.4.82. H. R. Trevor-Roper,
   The Last Days of Hitler (London: Macmillan, 1947). Foreword by Lord
   Tedder, pp. xi–xii. Trevor-Roper's 'Note on sources' appears on
   pp. 265–9.
25 Chester Wilmot, *The Struggle for Europe* (London: Collins, 1952),
   pp. 724–5. See also Chester Wilmot, *Tobruk 1941* (London: Angus &
   Robertson, 1944).
26 Robert A. Brady, *Crisis in Britain* (Berkeley, and Los Angeles, Calif.:
   University of California Press, 1950), p. xi.
27 H. H. Wilson, *Pressure Group: The Campaign for Commercial Television*
   (London: Secker & Warburg, 1961).
28 Ibid., pp. 9–10.
29 Paul Johnson, *The Suez War* (London: Macgibbon & Kee, 1957) p. 1.
30 Hugh Thomas, *The Suez Affair* (London: Weidenfeld & Nicolson, 1967)
   p. 2. The later paperback edition identified informants who had died.
31 Compare with the rigidly anonymous references to interviews in a more
   recent work on the subject: Roy Fullick and Geoffrey Powell, *Suez: The
   Double War* (London: Hamish Hamilton, 1979).
32 David Nunnerley, *President Kennedy and Britain* (London: Bodley Head,
   1972), pp. vii–xii. The author does not, however, provide source notes
   for interview evidence: as he writes, some people he talked to preferred
   not to be attributed and he therefore thought it best to dispense with notes
   altogether.
33 Clive Irving, Ron Hall and Jeremy Wallington, *Scandal '63* (London:
   Heinemann, 1963). The official inquiry endorsed many of its findings.

34 Anthony Shrimsley, *The First Hundred Days of Harold Wilson* (London: Weidenfeld & Nicolson, 1965), p. ix.
35 Stephen Haseler, *The Death of British Democracy* (London: Paul Elek, 1976), p. 15; *The Gaitskellites* (London: Macmillan, 1969), p. 269.
36 Personal interview with Ian Bradley, London, 29 October 1981.
37 David Butler, op. cit., p. 109.
38 Beatrice Webb, *My Apprenticeship* (London: Longman, 1926), p. 423; L. A. Dexter, *Elite and Specialised Interviewing* (Evanston, Ill.: Northwestern University Press, 1970), p. 12.
39 G. R. Elton, *Modern Historians on British History 1485–1945* (London: Methuen, 1970), p. 151.
40 R. T. McKenzie, *British Political Parties* (London: Heinemann, 1955), p. viii.
41 Ibid.
42 John P. Mackintosh, *The British Cabinet* (London: Stevens, 1962), p. ix.
43 Ibid., 2nd rev. edn (London: Stevens, 1968), p. xi.
44 Anthony Sampson, *Anatomy of Britain* (London: Hodder & Stoughton, 1962), p. xi.
45 Peter Kellner and Lord Crowther-Hunt, *The Civil Servants* (London: Raven Books, 1980).
46 Peter Kellner, oral history questionnaire, 11 September 1981.
47 Hugh Heclo and Aaron Wildavsky, *The Private Government of Public Money* (London: Macmillan, 1974), p. xix.
48 Hugo Young 'The Legal Eagles', *Sunday Times*, 15.8.82. The book he is discussing is Alan Paterson, *The Law Lords*, (London: Macmillan, 1982).
49 John Maud, *Local Government in Modern England* (London: Thornton Butterworth, 1932), p. 7.
50 Herman Finer, *English Local Government* (London: Methuen, 1933), p. xi.
51 Personal interview with Alan Alexander, Reading University, 10 November 1981.
52 George W. Jones, oral history questionnaire, 28 August 1981.

Chapter 10 Cultural history

1 *Writers at Work: The 'Paris Review' Interviews*, 3rd series (London: Secker & Warburg, 1968), p. vii.
2 Robert Gittings, *The Nature of Biography* (London: Heinemann, 1978), p. 19.
3 Ibid., p. 35.
4 Peter Stansky and William Abrahams, *The Unknown Orwell* (London: Constable, 1972), pp. 183–90.
5 Bernard Crick, *George Orwell: A Life* (London: Secker & Warburg, 1980), p. 425 (Rev. ed. published in 1982). Footnote reference to the author's interview with Ruth Pitter, an early friend of Orwell.

6 Quoted in Humphrey Carpenter, *W. H. Auden: A Biography* (London: Allen & Unwin, 1981), Preface, p. xv.

7 Quoted in Michael Holroyd, *Lytton Strachey: A Biography*, rev. edn (London: Heinemann, 1973), p. 17.

8 Wilfrid Sheed, Introduction to *Writers at Work*, 4th series (1977), ed. George Plimpton, p. ix.

9 Personal interview with Michael Holroyd, London, 11 September 1981.

10 Gittings, op. cit., p. 69.

11 Roger Berthoud, *Graham Sutherland: A Biography* (London: Faber, 1982).

12 Personal interview with Roger Berthoud, London, 17 September 1981.

13 This principle operates in another way: *ad hoc* interviews conducted at an earlier point in an author's career may prove useful in a subsequent book. This was the case with Paul Ferris, who interviewed Dylan Thomas's mother in 1955 for an article, and found, twenty years later, that he was able to incorporate the notes he had preserved in his biography of the poet: *Dylan Thomas* (London: Hodder & Stoughton, 1977).

14 Interview with Michael Holroyd, London, 11 September 1981.

15 Personal interview with Roger Berthoud, London, 17 September 1981.

16 Gittings, op. cit., p. 78.

17 Holroyd, op. cit., p. 20.

18 Private information, oral history questionnaire.

19 Interview with Michael Holroyd, London, 11 September 1981; Holroyd, op. cit., p. 20.

20 Roger Berthoud, oral history questionnaire, 26 August 1981.

21 Quentin Bell, oral history questionnaire, 23 August 1981.

22 Jeffrey Meyers, *Katherine Mansfield: A Biography* (London: Hamish Hamilton, 1978); *The Enemy: A Biography of Wyndham Lewis* (London: Routledge & Kegan Paul, 1980).

23 This is the case in the books of Bernard Crick, Quentin Bell and Michael Holroyd, in Victoria Glendinning's two biographies, *Elizabeth Bowen: Portrait of a Writer* (London: Weidenfeld & Nicolson, 1977) and *Edith Sitwell: A Unicorn among Lions* (London: Weidenfeld & Nicolson, 1981), in Humphrey Carpenter's *W. H. Auden: A Biography*, and Paul Ferris, *Dylan Thomas*.

24 Ted Morgan, *Somerset Maugham* (London: Cape, 1980), p. 622.

25 Meyers, *Mansfield*, p. 263.

26 Ferris, op. cit., p. 317.

27 Quentin Bell, *Virginia Woolf* vol. 2, (London: Hogarth Press, 1972) p. 261.

28 Michael Holroyd, oral history questionnaire and letter to authors, 2 June 1982.

29 Ferris, op. cit., p. 318.

30 Interview with Dorothy Brett. Meyers, *Mansfield*, p. 37.

31 Ibid., p. 277, n. 16. Another important witness in this biography was

Colin Murry (John Middleton Murry's son), who talked to the author for twelve hours (Acknowledgements, p. xi).

32 Ferris, op. cit., p. 50.

33 Crick, op. cit., p. 59.

34 Ibid., p. 73.

35 Letter, Bernard Crick to authors, 4 June 1982. Perhaps this stirring of old emotions explains the behaviour of Harold Nicolson, one of the people who had 'disliked' Lytton Strachey, and whom Michael Holroyd therefore made a point of interviewing for his biography. When he visited him in his rooms at the Albany, Nicolson kept offering his interviewer a drink and then neglecting to pour it out. See Holroyd, op. cit., p. 19.

36 Crick, op. cit., p. 106. Similarly, Paul Ferris's interview with Eric Hughes, who subedited Dylan Thomas's work for the *South Wales Daily Post* (the poet's first job was as a reporter), yielded the information that Thomas's copy was 'appalling, with many lacunae'. Ferris, op. cit., p. 74.

37 Crick, op. cit., p. 439, n. 63.

38 Ibid., p. 216 and p. 436, n. 24. Similarly, Lord (formerly Fenner) Brockway's explanation in interview of why he turned down, 'to my ever-lasting regret', Orwell's offer to write regularly for *New Leader* has the ring of a spacious rationalization: hence Crick's suggestion of an alternative reason. Ibid., p. 233.

39 Ibid., p. 139.

40 Ibid., p. 357.

41 Meyers, *The Enemy*, p. 67. Meyers's chief 'family' witness was the artist's wife Froanna, with whom he conducted a six-hour interview in Torquay, in August 1977. Ibid., p. 353, n. 27.

42 Ibid., p. 48.

43 Ibid., pp. 48–9.

44 Quentin Bell, oral history questionnaire.

45 Ferris, op. cit., p. 128.

46 Ibid., p. 188.

47 Ibid., pp. 234–5. A similar occasion was recalled in interview by Mrs Gardner Cox, with reference to Thomas's 1953 trip to Harvard: there, she reported, the critic I. A. Richards's allusions to T. S. Eliot left the poet quite tongue-tied: 'Dylan Thomas shuffled his feet and said, "I s'pose so." And then the silence descended for ever.' Ibid., p. 288.

48 Michael Holroyd, *Shaw and his Biographers*, Lecture delivered to English Centre of PEN, 1982.

49 Francis King, *A bit of Koestler*, Sunday Telegraph, 18 April 1982. See Iain Hamilton, *Koestler: A Biography* (London: Secker, 1982).

50 Richard Ellmann, *James Joyce* (London: Oxford University Press, 1959; New and Revised Edition, 1982). With especial thanks to Boyd Tonkin for this section.

51 Michael Davie, *A James Joyce odyssey*, The Observer, 2 January 1983, p. 16;

Hugh Kenner, *The impertinence of being definitive*, TLS, 17 December 1982, pp. 1383–4.

52 Robin Daniels, *Conversations with Menuhin* (London: Macdonald, 1979).

53 Ibid., p. 13. All other information is from personal interview with Robin Daniels, London, 9 October 1981.

54 David Sylvester, *Interviews with Francis Bacon* (London: Thames & Hudson, 1975).

55 Ibid., p. 7.

56 Ibid., p. 26.

57 Ibid., p. 72.

58 Ibid., p. 50.

59 The first volume of *Writers at Work*, edited by Malcolm Cowley and published in 1958, included interviews with E. M. Forster, François Mauriac, Dorothy Parker and William Faulkner.

60 *Writers at Work*, 3rd series (1968), p. 105.

61 Ibid., 4th series (1977), p. 48.

62 Ibid., 3rd series (1968), p. 282.

63 Ibid., p. 179.

Chapter 11   Oral archives in Britain (non-media)

1 The BIRS (now the National Sound Archive) is, at the time of going to press, undergoing reorganization, so it is impossible to discuss it in this book.

2 *British Archives*, edited by Janet Foster and Julia Sheppard (London: Macmillan, 1982) also includes information on oral archives. The oral archives described in Chapter 11 reflect those archives that came to our attention through appeals in the press or from some 150 letters the authors wrote to institutions they felt might possess such records.

3 At the Central Library, Drake Circus, Plymouth; Area Librarian, J. R. Elliott.

4 See Appendix A.

5 Letter, J. R. Elliott to authors, 1 October 1981.

6 County Library, Angel Row, Nottingham; Director of Leisure Services, Wyndham Heycock.

7 Old Steward's Office, Castle Grounds, Clitheroe Castle, Lancashire.

8 Pamphlet issued by the North West Sound Archive. Other information from an undated letter, Ken Howarth to authors.

9 There is also a taped interview with Sir Harold Wilson at the central library of his constituency in Derby Road, Huyton, Liverpool. The interview, conducted in Huyton by the librarian, T. W. Scragg, in 1977, lasts 1 hour 20 minutes, and covers Sir Harold's career in relation to Merseyside.

10 Based at Uplands, Braid Mount Crest, Edinburgh.

11 Tape recording made by John Dundas for the authors, September 1981.

12 Gillian Peele, 'The Bad, the Good and the Great', *The Times Educational Supplement*, 6 November 1981, p. 25.
13 Letter, John Palmer to authors, 4 September 1981. Personal interview, Jonathan Morgan, Parliamentary Sound Archives, 4 February 1982.
14 Letter, Edmund Ions to authors, 16 December 1981.
15 Personal interview with David Butler, Taston, 12 September 1981.
16 The archive was based at the British Library of Political and Economic Science, 10 Portugal Street, London WC2.
17 BOAPAH's pilot project was written up in *The Times*, 26 November 1980; *The Guardian*, 6 December 1980; *New Society*, 8 December 1981, pp. 40–1; and the *LSE Magazine*, 61 (June 1981), pp. 7–8.
18 Letter, Secretary of Political Science and International Relations Committee to D. A. Clarke, 18 December 1981.
19 Part of the Foreign and Commonwealth Office, 197 Blackfriars Road, London SE1.
20 Laundress Lane, Cambridge; archivist, Miss T. M. Thatcher.
21 Queen Elizabeth House, 21 St Giles, Oxford; director, Anthony Kirk-Greene.
22 The Oxford Colonial Records Project and the Oxford Development Records Project. *Journal of the Society of Archivists*, 6 (October 1978), p. 80.
23 Personal interview with Anthony Kirk-Greene and Ingrid Thomas, Oxford, 15 October 1981.
24 Lambeth Road, London SE1.
25 Letter, Margaret Brooks to authors, 19 October 1981. See also David Lance, 'Oral History in Britain', *Oral History Review* (1974), pp. 66–70.
26 Lacon House, Theobalds Road, London WC1. The work was the initiative of Group Captain Haslam, then head of the branch, one of whose particular interests was to write a history of the RAF College, Cranwell.
27 Personal interview with Air Commodore H. A. Probert, London, 16 October 1981.
28 Personal interview with J. P. McDonald, London, 16 October 1981.
29 Letter, Group Captain R. A. Mason to authors, 26 October 1981.
30 HMS *Dolphin*, Gosport, Hampshire.
31 Letter, Commander P. R. Compton-Hall to authors, 19 October 1981.
32 Ibid.
33 Letter, Major A. J. Donald to authors, 19 October 1981.
34 Letter, Campbell McMurray to authors, 4 February 1982.
35 Letter, David Gerard to authors, 2 September 1981. David Gerard's series of interviews with contemporary writers includes John Braine, Iris Murdoch and Angus Wilson. Available on cassette from Drake Educational Associates, Cardiff, the series is entitled *My Work as a Novelist*.
36 Information supplied by Sarah Fox-Pitt, head of archives department, letter to authors, 8 March 1982.
37 British Medical Association, Tavistock Square, London WC1.

38 BMA Film Library catalogue.
39 Ibid.
40 11 St Andrews Place, Regent's Park, London NW1. The interviews in 1969–77 were conducted by former Harveian Librarian, Dr C. E. Newman.
41 Letter, Sir Gordon Wolstenholme (the Harveian Librarian) to authors, 18 September 1981.
42 Gosta Green, Birmingham.
43 The interviews will be combined with written sources to provide an extensive history of solid state physics.
44 Sherfield Building, Kensington, London SW7.
45 Letter, Jean Pingree to authors, 22 January 1982.
46 David Lance, *An Archive Approach to Oral History* (London: Imperial War Museum, 1978).
47 Brian Harrison, 'Introduction to the Tapes' (July 1981), p. 7. This paper was Dr Brian Harrison's report on his research project on the women's movement in Britain.
48 Personal interview with Professor Donald C. Watt, LSE, 14 October 1981.
49 Nigel Nicolson, oral history questionnaire, August 1981.
50 This point is taken from David J. Mitchell, 'Living Documents: Oral History and Biography', *Biography*, 3 (Winter 1980), p. 284.
51 Milton Meltzer, 'Using Oral History: A Biographer's Point of View', *Oral History Review* (1979), p. 44.
52 Mitchell, op. cit., pp. 291–2.
53 Lord Blake, oral history questionnaire, August 1981.
54 Letter, Sir Stanley Hooker to authors, 20 January 1982.
55 Louis M. Starr, 'Oral History', *Encyclopedia of Library and Information Science*, 20 (New York, 1977), p. 444.
56 Letter, Elizabeth B. Mason to authors, 9 October 1981.
57 Personal interview with Spencer R. Weart, American Institute of Physics, New York, 17 December 1981.
58 Cullom Davis, Kathryn Back, Kay MacLean, *Oral History: From Tape to Type* (Chicago, Ill.: American Library Association, 1977). Strongly recommended too for oral archives primarily orientated towards transcripts are two other US publications: William W. Moss, *An Oral History Program Manual* (New York: Praeger, 1974), and Willa K. Baum, *Oral History for the Local Historical Society*, 4th, rev. edn (Nashville, Tenn.: American Association for State and Local History, 1974). For oral archives orientated primarily towards sound, see also David Lance, *An Archive Approach to Oral History*.
59 Louis M. Starr, 'Oral History: Problems and Prospects', in *Advances in Librarianship*, vol. 11 (New York: Seminar Press, 1971), p. 288.
60 See Paul Thompson, *The Voice of the Past* (London: Oxford University Press, 1978), pp. 59–60, and T. C. Barker, 'Oral History in Britain', 15th

International Congress of the Historical Sciences, Bucharest, 10–17 August 1980, Report, vol. 1, pp. 560–2, for a discussion of funding of oral history.

Chapter 12   Oral archives in Britain (media)

1 C. L. Mowat, *Great Britain since 1914* (London: Sources of History, 1971), p. 172.
2 *Parliamentary Debates (House of Commons)*, vol. 945 (1977–8), 28 February 1977, column 423. The Whitford Committee on copyright law in 1977 had expressed itself in favour of national sound and film archives.
3 Ibid., cols 429–30; reply from the Minister of State at the Home Office, Brynmor John, MP.
4 Ibid., cols 426–7.
5 *Report of the Advisory Committee on Archives* (British Broadcasting Corporation, April 1979), p. 7.
6 Ibid., p. 48.
7 Personal interview with Lord Briggs, Oxford.
8 Personal interview with Mark Jones, Broadcasting House, 26 August 1981. See also Paul Thompson's now rather dated article on 'The BBC Archives', *Oral History* [1], 2. (1972).
9 See below. The British Institute of Recorded Sound (BIRS) is permitted to record off the air from the BBC, which also sends it a selection of discs.
10 All information on the Written Archives is from personal interview with Gwyniver Jones, Caversham Park, 30 October 1981.
11 Interestingly, there were before the last war more discussion programmes on regional radio, which tended to be more pioneering than the central BBC.
12 For the addresses of the various television authorities, both BBC and independent, readers are referred to the excellent *Researcher's Guide to British Film and Television Collections*, edited by Elizabeth Oliver (London: British Universities Film Council, 1981), which supplies brief details on collections throughout the country, and indicates whether or not they are inclined to grant access to outsiders. Also of interest to the historian are the listenings of newsreel libraries such as that of EMI Pathe, and the descriptions of the film libraries at Visnews, the international television news agency, and Independent Television News. In a letter to *The Times*, 23 February 1982, Elizabeth Oliver (who is director of the British Universities Film Council) suggested that a video equivalent to the newspaper library at Colindale would provide a useful complement to the existing work of the National Film Archive and the television companies, which preserve only selections: 'Historians in the future will certainly find it hard to understand why a medium so influential and all-pervasive was allowed to disappear into the ether leaving only a patchy and unrepresentative record behind.'
13 At the time of the 1978 parliamentary debate on the preservation of broad-

casting material, the National Film Archive received 45 per cent of its
television material from the independent television companies, and only
12–15 per cent from the BBC: *Parliamentary Debates*, op. cit., col. 424. On
the television work of the National Film Archive *see* Paul Madden (ed.)
Keeping Television Alive. (London: British Film Institute, 1981).

14 See Oliver (ed.), op. cit., p. 38.
15 Personal interview with Lord Briggs, Oxford.
16 *The Times*, 29 November 1960, p. 16.
17 Telephone call with Barrie Heads, 3 December 1981.
18 For example, three more interviews were conducted in the 1970s on sound
tape with some film inserts. Letter, Barrie Heads to authors, 7 January 1982.
19 Editor, *News Chronicle* (1936–47); Director-General, Festival of Britain
(1948–51).
20 Personal interview with Lord Briggs, Oxford.

Appendix A   Legal considerations

1 E. P. Skone James *et al.*, *Copinger and Skone James on Copyright*, 12th edn
(London: Sweet and Maxwell, 1980), p. 60, paragraph 153.
2 David Lance, *An Archive Approach to Oral History* (London: Imperial War
Museum, 1978), p. 36.
3 Ibid., pp. 36–7. David Lance's chapter on 'Deposit and access' (from which
this extract is taken) provides an invaluable guide to the legal aspects of establishing an oral history archive.

Appendix B   Video and oral history

1 W. Richard Whitaker's article 'Why not try videotaping oral history?' *Oral
History Review* (1981), pp. 115–24, raises some of the issues, and discusses
equipment and filming techniques. Peter Turner discusses the potential of
video recorders in teaching in 'Independent means', *The Times Educational
Supplement*, 7 May 1982, p. 45. The Oral History Society held a one-day
conference and workshop on videotaping oral history on 8 May 1982, during
which many of these issues were raised.
2 W. Richard Whitaker, op. cit., p. 123.
3 This point was raised by Paul Thompson at the plenary session of the Oral
History Society's conference on 8 May 1982.